The Marvellous and the Miraculous in María de Zayas

LEGENDA

LEGENDA is the Modern Humanities Research Association's book imprint for new research in the Humanities. Founded in 1995 by Malcolm Bowie and others within the University of Oxford, Legenda has always been a collaborative publishing enterprise, directly governed by scholars. The Modern Humanities Research Association (MHRA) joined this collaboration in 1998, became half-owner in 2004, in partnership with Maney Publishing and then Routledge, and has since 2016 been sole owner. Titles range from medieval texts to contemporary cinema and form a widely comparative view of the modern humanities, including works on Arabic, Catalan, English, French, German, Greek, Italian, Portuguese, Russian, Spanish, and Yiddish literature. Editorial boards and committees of more than 60 leading academic specialists work in collaboration with bodies such as the Society for French Studies, the British Comparative Literature Association and the Association of Hispanists of Great Britain & Ireland.

The MHRA encourages and promotes advanced study and research in the field of the modern humanities, especially modern European languages and literature, including English, and also cinema. It aims to break down the barriers between scholars working in different disciplines and to maintain the unity of humanistic scholarship. The Association fulfils this purpose through the publication of journals, bibliographies, monographs, critical editions, and the MHRA Style Guide, and by making grants in support of research. Membership is open to all who work in the Humanities, whether independent or in a University post, and the participation of younger colleagues entering the field is especially welcomed.

ALSO PUBLISHED BY THE ASSOCIATION

Critical Texts
Tudor and Stuart Translations • New Translations • European Translations
MHRA Library of Medieval Welsh Literature

MHRA Bibliographies
Publications of the Modern Humanities Research Association

The Annual Bibliography of English Language & Literature
Austrian Studies
Modern Language Review
Portuguese Studies
The Slavonic and East European Review
Working Papers in the Humanities
The Yearbook of English Studies

www.mhra.org.uk
www.legendabooks.com

STUDIES IN HISPANIC AND LUSOPHONE CULTURES

Studies in Hispanic and Lusophone Cultures are selected and edited by the Association of Hispanists of Great Britain & Ireland. The series seeks to publish the best new research in all areas of the literature, thought, history, culture, film, and languages of Spain, Spanish America, and the Portuguese-speaking world.

The Association of Hispanists of Great Britain & Ireland is a professional association which represents a very diverse discipline, in terms of both geographical coverage and objects of study. Its website showcases new work by members, and publicises jobs, conferences and grants in the field.

Editorial Committee
Chair: Professor Trevor Dadson (Queen Mary University of London)
Professor Catherine Davies (University of Nottingham)
Professor Sally Faulkner (University of Exeter)
Professor Andrew Ginger (University of Bristol)
Professor James Mandrell (Brandeis University, USA)
Professor Hilary Owen (University of Manchester)
Professor Christopher Perriam (University of Manchester)
Professor Philip Swanson (University of Sheffield)

Managing Editor
Dr Graham Nelson
41 Wellington Square, Oxford OX1 2JF, UK

www.legendabooks.com/series/shlc

STUDIES IN HISPANIC AND LUSOPHONE CULTURES

1. *Unamuno's Theory of the Novel*, by C. A. Longhurst
2. *Pessoa's Geometry of the Abyss: Modernity and the* Book of Disquiet, by Paulo de Medeiros
3. *Artifice and Invention in the Spanish Golden Age*, edited by Stephen Boyd and Terence O'Reilly
4. *The Latin American Short Story at its Limits: Fragmentation, Hybridity and Intermediality*, by Lucy Bell
5. *Spanish New York Narratives 1898–1936: Modernisation, Otherness and Nation*, by David Miranda-Barreiro
6. *The Art of Ana Clavel: Ghosts, Urinals, Dolls, Shadows and Outlaw Desires*, by Jane Elizabeth Lavery
7. *Alejo Carpentier and the Musical Text*, by Katia Chornik
8. *Britain, Spain and the Treaty of Utrecht 1713-2013*, edited by Trevor J. Dadson and J. H. Elliott
9. *Books and Periodicals in Brazil 1768-1930: A Transatlantic Perspective*, edited by Ana Cláudia Suriani da Silva and Sandra Guardini Vasconcelos
10. *Lisbon Revisited: Urban Masculinities in Twentieth-Century Portuguese Fiction*, by Rhian Atkin
11. *Urban Space, Identity and Postmodernity in 1980s Spain: Rethinking the Movida*, by Maite Usoz de la Fuente
12. *Santería, Vodou and Resistance in Caribbean Literature: Daughters of the Spirits*, by Paul Humphrey
13. *Reprojecting the City: Urban Space and Dissident Sexualities in Recent Latin American Cinema*, by Benedict Hoff
14. *Rethinking Juan Rulfo's Creative World: Prose, Photography, Film*, edited by Dylan Brennan and Nuala Finnegan
15. *The Last Days of Humanism: A Reappraisal of Quevedo's Thought*, by Alfonso Rey
16. *Catalan Narrative 1875-2015*, edited by Jordi Larios and Montserrat Lunati
17. *Islamic Culture in Spain to 1614: Essays and Studies*, by L. P. Harvey
18. *Film Festivals: Cinema and Cultural Exchange*, by Mar Diestro-Dópido
19. *St Teresa of Avila: Her Writings and Life*, edited by Terence O'Reilly, Colin Thompson and Lesley Twomey
20. *(Un)veiling Bodies: A Trajectory of Chilean Post-Dictatorship Documentary*, by Elizabeth Ramírez-Soto

The Marvellous and the Miraculous in María de Zayas

Sander Berg

LEGENDA

Studies in Hispanic and Lusophone Cultures 40
Modern Humanities Research Association
2019

*Published by Legenda
an imprint of the Modern Humanities Research Association
Salisbury House, Station Road, Cambridge CB1 2LA*

*ISBN 978-1-78188-827-8 (HB)
ISBN 978-1-78188-828-5 (PB)*

*First published 2019
Paperback edition 2021*

All rights reserved. No part of this publication may be reproduced or disseminated or transmitted in any form or by any means, electronic, mechanical, photocopying, recording or otherwise, or stored in any retrieval system, or otherwise used in any manner whatsoever without written permission of the copyright owner, except in accordance with the provisions of the Copyright, Designs and Patents Act 1988, or under the terms of a licence permitting restricted copying issued in the UK by the Copyright Licensing Agency Ltd, Saffron House, 6–10 Kirby Street, London EC1N 8TS, England, or in the USA by the Copyright Clearance Center, 222 Rosewood Drive, Danvers MA 01923. Application for the written permission of the copyright owner to reproduce any part of this publication must be made by email to legenda@mhra.org.uk.

Disclaimer: Statements of fact and opinion contained in this book are those of the author and not of the editors or the Modern Humanities Research Association. The publisher makes no representation, express or implied, in respect of the accuracy of the material in this book and cannot accept any legal responsibility or liability for any errors or omissions that may be made.

Trademark notice: Product or corporate names may be trademarks or registered trademarks, and are used only for identification and explanation without intent to infringe.

© Modern Humanities Research Association 2019

Copy-Editor: Richard Correll

CONTENTS

	Introduction	1
1	The Ghostly Sybil from Madrid	11
1.1	'Me conocéis por lo escrito': Hidden behind a Screen of Fiction	11
1.2	A Feminist Phoenix: Fame, Oblivion and Recognition	27
1.3	Magic in Zayas: A Brief Overview of the Literature	31
2	Witches and Watermelons: The Supernatural in Early Modern Spain	41
2.1	The Natural, Preternatural and Supernatural Orders	42
2.2	Magic: A Bird's-eye View	45
2.3	Magic and Sorcery in Golden Age Literature	49
2.4	*Hechiceras* (Sorceresses) versus *brujas* (Witches)	52
2.5	Inquisitorial Responses to Witchcraft and Magic	55
2.6	The Seventeenth-Century Epistemological Shift	58
2.7	'Betwixt Charybdis and Scylla': The Indeterminacy of Magic	61
3	Slippery Sorcery	70
3.1	Fraudulent Magic in 'El castigo de la miseria'	71
3.2	A Wily Sorceress and a Haunted Roadside Chapel in 'La fuerza del amor'	73
3.3	A Funny Spell in 'El desengaño amando'	77
3.4	Voodoo Rape in 'La inocencia castigada'	81
3.5	Verisimilitude and Magic	85
3.6	Seeds of Doubt: The Indeterminacy of the Preternatural	87
4	Baroque Games with the Devil	92
4.1	Ugly Devils	93
4.2	Evil Inspirations	94
4.3	The Devil Vanishes in 'El castigo de la miseria'	97
4.4	The Devil Bites the Dust in 'La perseguida triunfante'	99
4.5	The Devil's Purported Magnanimity in 'El jardín engañoso'	103
5	The Miraculous, the Fantastic and the Fatalistic	111
5.1	Zayas, Miracles and Hagiography: Between Tradition and Innovation	114
5.2	The Fantastic in Zayas	123
5.3	Written in the Stars: Astrology and the Subordination of Free Will	134
	Conclusion	141
	Appendix	148
	Bibliography	153
	Index	174

INTRODUCTION

> María de Zayas — the most unabashed, militant
> Hispanic feminist of her age.[1]

In the last thirty years or so María de Zayas y Sotomayor has made a remarkable come-back. Although she was very popular and well-known in Spain in the 1630s and 1640s, her fame gradually waned. By the end of the nineteenth and beginning of the twentieth century she was barely known outside of a small circle of erudites like Menéndez Pelayo and pioneers of Hispanic studies like George Ticknor and Ludwig Pfandl. Her journey back to renown and recognition started in 1948, when Agustín Amezúa rescued her from oblivion by publishing the first complete edition of her work since 1847. Success was not immediate, although in the decades that followed this publication there were the first flickers of academic interest. It was Juan Goytisolo who put her on the map by devoting a chapter to her in his *Disidencias* (1977), called 'El mundo erótico de María de Zayas'. He praised her description of women as desiring subjects and put the nail in the coffin of the idea that Zayas was a *costumbrista* writer faithfully transcribing the treatment of women in the seventeenth century. The tide of interest gradually swelled as more and more scholars turned their attention to the sensationalist tales and in the last two decades numerous articles and monographs have been devoted to her and her oeuvre. From being a virtually unknown author she has now become part of the canon: her novellas are published by Cátedra and have been translated into English (three times), as well as Italian, French, and German.[2]

Zayas has been often hailed as a militant feminist *avant la lettre* and celebrated as a subversive writer who offers a savage critique of her society, especially the impossible position of women within it. In the prologue to her first collection she defies men and claims that women are just as able and could rival them if only they were given a proper education, thus suggesting an awareness that gender is a social construct. Her novellas abound in violence perpetrated on women, in particular within the confines of marriage; her heroines are raped, tortured and killed, and the ones who survive usually end up seeking refuge in a convent. Understandably, therefore, there has been no shortage of critical attention to Zayas's description of the plight of women under patriarchy and her transgressive prose. Much of the research on Zayas since the 1980s has been done from a feminist perspective, reaching a high-water mark around the turn of the millennium with three monographs and a chapter devoted to her work in an important study on Golden Age women writers. However, there is a danger in interpreting everything she has written as subversive, 'retrofitting' her, as it were, with a modern feminist agenda, or considering her sometimes imperfect syntax as typifying *écriture féminine* intended to *bouleverser la syntaxe*, as Paul Julian Smith suggests when he remarks that 'woman's experience cannot be spoken in a man-made language without gaps and discontinuities; and that the utopia of a purely female space must be a break or threshold in a dominant male order'.[3] Nevertheless, if we apply Gerda Lerner's definition of feminist consciousness, Zayas undoubtedly fits most of the criteria:

> I define feminist consciousness as the awareness of women that they belong to a subordinate group; that they have suffered wrongs as a group; that their condition of subordination is not natural, but societally determined; that they must join with other women to remedy these wrongs; and finally that they must and can provide an alternative vision of societal organization in which women as well as men will enjoy autonomy and self-determination.[4]

It is obvious that Zayas sees women as subordinate victims of irrational male cruelty and she denounces women's lack of education. In one of the novellas a female character exclaims in despair: '¿Por qué, vanos legisladores del mundo [...] nos negáis letras y armas?' [Why, vain legislators of the world [...] do you deny us learning and arms?] (*Novelas*, p. 364). Scholars like O'Brien have also convincingly argued that Zayas seeks to highlight the need for female solidarity or gyn/affection.[5]

As for her alternative vision of a society in which men and women enjoy autonomy and self-determination, things get more complicated. At the very end of her collection, she paints a nostalgic picture of a golden age of gender relations under Ferdinand the Catholic, when men were real men and treated their women with respect, rather than being long-haired fops cavorting on the banks of the Manzanares, refusing to fight for King and Country and abusing their women at home. Apart from being pro-woman, Zayas is a reactionary who sees the decline of gender relations as symptomatic of Spain's political crisis and who yearns for a bygone age of imagined political dominance and a more harmonious rapport between the sexes. Like so many writers before her, she looks to the past for the ideal society, not the future; she laments a loss rather than envisaging a bright new dawn of gender equality. This should not surprise us in an early modern Spanish author; indeed, it is the reverse that would be unheard of. Zayas is also a xenophobic classist, criticizing servants as inherently untrustworthy, comparing them to domestic animals at one point and blaming much of Spain's travails on the nefarious influence of foreigners. We could say that she is an ideologically conflicted writer, although she undoubtedly did not see herself that way. In his study on Cervantes and Quevedo, George Mariscal posits that 'the idea of the subject in Spain in the 1600s, as it was constructed through a variety of discourses including literature, was in no way fixed and was something quite different from those forms that dominate literary criticism and the humanities in the West today'.[6] Instead, each individual 'stands for a complex intersection of competing ideologies and practices' (Mariscal, p. 9). And what is true for Cervantes and Quevedo equally applies to Zayas. If we want to gain a fuller understanding of Zayas, then, we ought to study her work from a cultural-historical point of view as well as through what O'Brien has called a 'gynocentric lens'.

Although much less has been written about Zayas as a baroque author as opposed to an early modern feminist, this is changing. The application of the notion of 'baroque' to literature started in the interbellum and was soon applied to authors like Góngora and Calderón de la Barca.[7] In his seminal study of the baroque from 1975, José Antonio Maravall mentions Zayas a number of times, even if he does not analyse her novellas.[8] In his early monograph on Zayas Salvador Montesa Peydro builds on Maravall's work and focuses his analysis of her oeuvre on her cultural and literary context.[9] Not much later Susan Griswold opened the firing shot of a long debate about whether Zayas's feminism is merely a baroque literary device that slots into the *querelle des femmes* or more than that.[10] More recently, one of the studies that has done the most to counterbalance the feminist emphasis, without discarding any of its merits, is a collection of essays edited by Irene Albers and Uta Felten.[11] Marina Brownlee too treats Zayas as a writer of her time without relinquishing the insights provided by feminist scholarship.

This study strives to contribute to this broadening field of Zayan studies by looking at her as a woman writer within the literary and cultural context of her age, which was not only a period of political crisis and societal chaos — especially the 1640s during which she wrote her second, darker collection of novellas — but also a time when the thaumaturgical order was revised as a result of a shift in epistemology, which affected amongst other things the way the supernatural was seen and experienced.

Early modern Europe saw the execution of tens of thousands of innocent women (and some men) who had been accused of being witches. Although Spain was spared the worst of the excesses, a large-scale and widely publicized witchcraft trial took place in Logroño in 1610. In the end, however, only a small number of the accused were burnt at the stake as the result of the clear-headed intervention of one inquisitor who refused to take either the witches or their detractors at their word and demanded independent, verifiable proof. In the same period, the finest minds of the country could not agree on whether witches could actually fly through the night to meet their Satanic overlord at their sabbaths or whether it all happened in their imagination. If Devil-worshipping witches were relatively rare in Spain, villages and cities were teeming with *saludadores*, *santiguadores*, and *hechiceras*, cunning-folk and love-sorceresses. The Inquisition treated most of them as charlatans and their victims (clients) as deluded fools; they saw their claims of wielding supernatural power as fraudulent and were especially harsh with regards to recidivists. Magic, though possible in theory, was suspect. Miracles too were subject to scrutiny and brought under the control of the Church. *Beatas* who claimed to be able to work wonders ran the risk of being accused of fraud.[12] The boundaries of belief in the supernatural shifted and its borders were more strictly policed.[13] What seemed plausible at the start of the period was seen as inherently ridiculous a century or two later.[14] This change in attitude, at least within the educated segment of society, is described by Foucault as one episteme superseding the other. Whereas in the Middle Ages and Renaissance learned men espoused a belief in alchemy, magic, occult forces and an elusive network of sympathies and correspondences, the following system of thought was marked by an interest in taxation and tabulation and sceptical about what by then had come to be seen as superstition and mumbo jumbo.[15] In the first half of the seventeenth century the elite belief in magic was in retreat, although still much in evidence in less-educated segments of the population, as can be surmised from inquisitorial records.[16]

The supernatural is an important but under-studied aspect of Zayas's novelistic output; in twelve out of her twenty novellas something occurs that could be categorized as marvellous, miraculous or fantastic. Despite this preponderance, there is a marked paucity of research into this aspect, and, as far as I am aware, there has been no attempt to give a complete overview of the supernatural in Zayas's oeuvre or connect it to the seventeenth-century shift in epistemology. That is not to say we are in terra incognita: a number of outstanding critics have analysed magic in Zayas's work and devoted chapters or articles to it. Both Margaret Greer and Marina Brownlee devote a chapter to the supernatural and magic in their studies of Zayas.[17] Susan Paun de García, Yvette Cardaillac Hermosilla and Judith Whitenack have all published articles on magic and enchantment in a number of novellas by Zayas.[18]

The aim of this study, in addition to giving a more complete overview of all aspects of the supernatural in Zayas's novellas, is to assess these approaches critically in the context of the seventeenth-century belief in the supernatural, building on some, rejecting or nuancing others. I will also address areas that have received less attention, such as the miraculous, the fantastic and the author's fatalism. Given the fact that more than half of Zayas's novellas contain at least one supernatural event, and taking into consideration the scope of these occurrences — which range from Marian miracles to voodoo rape, from sorcery to disembodied voices — our main question must be to ask *why* Zayas had a predilection for the supernatural. What does this tell us about her oeuvre? What does she achieve by her frequent recourse to magic and the fantastic? Where do her tales dealing with sorcery, the Devil and the miraculous stand with regards to the ideology and epistemology of her period? How might the authorities have reacted to these episodes? And her public? How unusual are her descriptions of the supernatural? Is she unique in this respect?

We can only begin to answer these questions once we have a good idea about what the supernatural meant to her and her readers. Strictly speaking there was a divide between the marvellous and the miraculous; the two pertained to different orders and were the theatre of operations of preternatural and divine agents respectively. Of the two, the marvellous order is the most salient in Zayas's novellas — there are more episodes featuring magic or the Devil than miraculous ones, and they are less straightforward. If we look at the magical episodes it becomes clear that there is a notable variety in attitude and tone — the belief in magic is problematized. When we examine the stories featuring the Devil under a loupe, it becomes apparent that things are not always what they seem and that a clever game is being played with the reader. Both aspects are testament to Zayas's baroque style and sensibilities. If the seventeenth century saw the belief in magic wane, the belief in miracles was shored up by the Church, prompting the question of how this is articulated in Zayas. Most miracles in her novellas appear to follow well-established patterns and would not be out of place in a classic hagiography, but in some instances the miraculous becomes imbued with the fantastic, which introduces a hesitation in the reader: we are not sure if what we read is real — whether of divine or diabolical origin — or merely imagined. This is also true for supernatural episodes that are not overtly miraculous or magical such as premonitory dreams, dead bodies mysteriously lit up, disembodied voices and so on.

It is only when we take into account Zayas's treatment of the supernatural in all its forms and variations, and see these episodes as an integral part of her sensationalist approach that cleverly plays — subconsciously, no doubt — on the epistemological uncertainty and indeterminacy of her period, that we can get a better understanding of the writer that Zayas was.

★ ★ ★ ★ ★

The first two chapters of this book will provide the necessary background needed to begin a discussion of the novellas proper. In the first chapter an overview will be given of the little we know about Zayas's life. This lack of biographical knowledge has led scholars to speculate about her beauty, her marital status, her sexuality and her possible entry into a convent at the end of her life. I will discuss and assess these conjectures and will add some more evidence for her stay in Italy. The first chapter will also discuss the reception of her work in the seventeenth century and the claim of her being the most popular author after Cervantes and Mateo Alemán. We shall see that this claim needs to be weakened, although that is not to say that Zayas was not a popular and successful author — her work survived in an edited version and was probably read largely as pulp fiction. Furthermore, I shall trace the history of her critical rediscovery, from the scant attention her work received in the nineteenth and early twentieth century to her rediscovery as a proto-feminist in the late twentieth century and her present status as a canonical writer. This will be followed by a brief overview of the literature that deals with the supernatural (mainly magic) in Zayas.

The second chapter will discuss the epistemology of the supernatural in the seventeenth century and look at attitudes to magic and witchcraft in Spain and the way they were treated by the Inquisition and portrayed in Golden Age literature. The discussion will start with an investigation into the various subcategories of the supernatural followed by the briefest of overviews of the ideas behind magic, with some telling examples of magical practices in early modern Spain. The difference between Satan-worshipping witches (*brujas*) and cauldron-stirring love-sorceresses (*hechiceras*) will also be addressed. We shall see just how lenient the Holy Office was with regards to 'magical crimes'. Even when it came to diabolical forms of witchcraft, the Inquisition acted as a brake on widespread persecution rather than being its instigator. In the literature of the period diabolical witches make an occasional appearance, in Cervantes's 'El coloquio de los perros' for example, but they are eclipsed in popularity by the literary descendants of the archetypical love-sorceress Celestina. Her kind of amatory magic was hardly ever taken seriously in plays and novellas and more often than not a source of amusement, which is a far cry from the harrowing treatment it gets in some (but not all) of Zayas's stories. Lastly, we shall turn to the epistemological shift of the seventeenth century and look at the resulting indeterminacy to see how this is reflected in the writings of humanists like Pedro de Valencia, churchmen like Del Río, Salazar, Castañega and Ciruelo, lexicographers such as Covarrubias, and writers like Cervantes and Calderón de la Barca.

Having thus set the scene, the next three chapters are devoted to a close reading of the novellas that feature the marvellous, the Devil, the miraculous and the fantastic. Chapter 3 offers a reading of four novellas containing sorcery, which will reveal the multivalent ways in which Zayas uses magic and the extent to which the discourse surrounding magic becomes infused with doubt. As we shall see, sometimes Zayas treats magic as real, sometimes as fraudulent, now as something comical, then as something with tragic consequences. We shall also look at studies on the early modern popular belief in magic which cite actual cases that are echoed in the novellas. At the end of the chapter I shall address the indeterminacy that permeates Zayas's work, and not merely with regards to magical episodes. Often in her prose the reader is offered various causes why something pertains, thus planting seeds of doubt.

In Chapter 4 the role of the Devil will be analysed and it will become apparent that the author is playing a baroque game with the reader, partly because she uses the Devil as a correlate of evil and blackness to be contrasted, in a Caravaggesque manner, with innocence, purity and whiteness, but more importantly because we are led — wrongly, I contend — to believe that the Devil is capable of doing good. In one story the Devil hands back a contract saying he will not be outdone in generosity. This assertion is believed by the protagonists in the story as well as the characters in the frame narrative. What is more, it has also been taken at face value by many a modern critic. But because we do not know anything about the death of the protagonist or his eventual salvation or damnation, we cannot be sure the Arch-Deceiver does not have the last laugh.

Chapter 5 deals with the remaining supernatural events in Zayas. We shall begin by discussing the miraculous, describing the conventional miracles that occur in her novellas. The miraculous order, like the belief in magic, was being redefined and its domain shrinking. That is not to say that miracles were treated with disbelief. In the *Avisos* by Pellicer and Barrionuevo miracles are often reported in a straightforward fashion, whereas other supernatural claims and events receive a more sceptical treatment. This is also true in Zayas, although the miraculous is not always described straightforwardly. In some cases she infuses her miraculous stories with an eerie atmosphere that seems to foreshadow the eighteenth-century Gothic, even if it is impossible to claim her work as actually belonging to that genre. There are other episodes, too, that can be described as fantastic, such as the scene in which a lover chances upon his beloved who has been murdered by her brother and whose bleeding corpse is inexplicably illuminated and whose disembodied voice tells him she has been dead for nine hours and urges him to leave. We shall also briefly touch upon the fact that in Zayas not all males are evil and that alongside perfidious women we have a few good men. Lastly, we shall turn to Zayas's fatalistic conviction that our lives and destinies are determined by the stars with some of her characters making the daring suggestion that astrology trumps free will. This is a subversive and yet hardly ever commented-on aspect of Zayas's oeuvre.

A note on the titles and quotations

Zayas's publisher called her first collection, published in 1637, *Novelas amorosas y ejemplares*, although in the text the author always refers to her work as *Honesto y entretenimiento sarao*, or simply *Sarao*, and to the tales of her first collection as *maravillas*.[19] Her second collection, published in 1647, received the title *Desengaños amorosos*. The term 'desengaño' is often rendered as 'disappointment' or 'disillusion' but in this context neither translation is entirely satisfactory. The word designates the opposite of 'engaño', which is a deception, a trick, the act of being fooled. The opposite, then, is to be un-deceived, to have the scales fall from your eyes, to be disabused of a notion, to see through deceit, to realize what is going on — to wise up, so to speak. That is the significance of the title of the second collection of Zayas's novellas: they are tales that make women understand the deceitful nature of men and the fact that love and marriage are not what they are cracked up to be. That is why the tales are called *desengaños* and the women who tell them *desengañadoras*.

The *Novelas* were published with individual titles for each story. In the second collection only the first tale was published with a title, the other stories merely having an ordinal number: *segundo desengaño*, and so forth. But in the edition by Pablo Campins, from 1734, all the *desengaños* were given a (melodramatic) title, and that is how they have been known ever since.[20] In the table below, I have given the original title, a more or less literal translation, and the titles given by Patsy Boyer, Margaret Greer and Elizabeth Rhodes, and John Sturrock in their translations.

Except where indicated otherwise, I have translated all the quotations from Zayas and all other texts myself. In order to avoid tedious repetition, I have refrained from translating every occurrence of a title of a novella.

Original title	Literal translation	Boyer	Greer and Rhodes	Sturrock
Novelas amorosas y ejemplares (1637)	Amorous and exemplary novellas	The Enchantments of Love	Exemplary Tales of Love and Tales of Disillusion	A shameful revenge and other stories
1. Aventurarse perdiendo	To venture (while) losing (everything)	Everything Ventured	Taking a Chance on Losing	-
2. La burlada Aminta y venganza de honor	The duped Aminta and (her) honour avenged	Aminta Deceived and Honor's Revenge	-	-
3. El castigo de la miseria	The punishment of miserliness	The Miser's Reward	-	-
4. El prevenido engañado	The (one who has been) forewarned (is) deceived	Forewarned but not Forearmed	Forewarned but Fooled	forewarned but forestalled

5. La fuerza del amor	The power of love	The Power of Love	–	–
6. El desengañado amando y premio de la virtud	The (one who has been) un-deceived (by) loving and virtue's reward	Disillusionment in Love and Virtue Rewarded	–	–
7. Al fin se paga todo	At the end everything is paid for	Just Desserts [sic]	–	there always comes the reckoning
8. El imposible vencido	The impossible overcome	Triumph over the Impossible	–	–
9. Juez de su causa	The judge of her (own) case (at her own trial)	Judge Thyself	The Judge of Her Own Case	–
10. El jardín engañoso	The deceptive garden	The Magic Garden	The Deceitful Garden	–
Desengaños amorosos (1647)	(Tales of) disillusion (un-deception) of love	The Disenchantments of Love	–	–
1. La esclava de su amante	The slave of her lover	Slave to Her Own Lover	Her Lover's Slave	–
2. La más infame venganza	The most despicable revenge	Most Infamous Revenge	–	a shameful revenge
3. El verdugo de su esposa	The executioner of his wife	His Wife's Executioner	–	–
4. Tarde llega el desengaño	The realization of deceit comes (too) late	Too Late Undeceived	–	–
5. La inocencia castigada	Innocence punished	Innocence Punished	–	an innocent punished
6. Amar sólo por vencer	To love only for the sake of conquering	Love for the Sake of Conquest	–	–
7. Mal presagio casar lejos	(It is a) bad omen to marry far away	Marriage Abroad: Portent of Doom	–	–
8. El traidor contra su sangre	The traitor to his blood	Traitor to His Own Blood	–	a traitor to his own flesh and blood
9. La perseguida triunfante	The triumph of she who is persecuted	Triumph over Persecution	–	–
10. Estragos que causa el vicio	The ravages that vice causes	The Ravages of Vice	–	the ravages of vice

Notes to the Introduction

1. Stephanie Merrim, *Early Modern Women's Writing and Sor Inés de la Cruz* (Nashville, TN: Vanderbilt University Press, 1999), p. xxxvi.
2. The Spanish editions by Cátedra to which I shall refer throughout this study are: María de Zayas y Sotomayor, *Novelas amorosas y ejemplares*, ed. by Julián Olivares (Madrid: Cátedra, 2000) and *Desengaños amorosos*, ed. by Alicia Yllera (Madrid: Cátedra, 1983) — in short, *Novelas* and *Desengaños*. More recently an excellent edition was published in Zaragoza under the original name: *Honesto y entretenido sarao (primera y segunda parte)*, ed. by Julián Olivares, 2 vols (Zaragoza: Universidad de Zaragoza, 2017). English translations are: *A Shameful Revenge and Other Stories*, trans. by John Sturrock (London: The Folio Society, 1963); *The Enchantments of Love*, trans. by Patsy Boyer (Berkeley: University of California Press, 1990); *The Disenchantments of Love*, trans. by Patsy Boyer (Albany: State University of New York Press, 1997); *Exemplary Tales of Love and Tales of Disillusion*, trans. by Margaret Greer and Elizabeth Rhodes (Chicago, IL: University of Chicago Press, 2009). Translation into other languages include *Novelle amorose ed esemplari* (Turin: Einaudi, 1995); *Nouvelles amoureuses et exemplaires* (Belval: Circé, 2013); and *Erotische Novellen: exemplarische Liebesnovellen* (Frankfurt: Insel Verlag, 1991).
3. Paul Julian Smith, *The Body Hispanic: Gender and Sexuality in Spanish and Spanish American Literature* (Oxford: Clarendon Press, 1989), p. 38.
4. Gerda Lerner, *The Creation of Feminist Consciousness from the Middle Ages to Eighteen-seventy* (Oxford: Oxford University Press, 1993), p. 14.
5. Eavan O'Brien, *Women in the Prose of María de Zayas* (Woodbridge: Tamesis, 2010).
6. George Mariscal, *Contradictory Subjects: Quevedo, Cervantes and Seventeenth-Century Spanish Culture* (Ithaca, NY: Cornell University Press, 1991), p. 3. One wonders, though, to what extent the modern subject is as monolithic as Mariscal appears to suggest. The notion of a more fluid and fragmented subjectivity certainly seems to be making a come-back. See for example Amin Maalouf, *On Identity* (London: Harvill Press, 2000).
7. See René Wellek, 'The Concept of Baroque in Literary Scholarship', *Journal of Aesthetics and Art Criticism*, 5.2 (1946), 77–109. For an elaborate study of French baroque literature (much of which can be transposed to other literatures), see Jean Rousset, *La Littérature de l'âge baroque en France: Circé et le paon* (Paris: Librairie José Conti, 1983).
8. José Antonio Maravall, *La cultura del Barroco* (Barcelona: Ariel, 1975).
9. Salvador Montesa Peydro, *Texto y contexto en la narrativa de María de Zayas* (Madrid: Dirección General de la Juventud y Promoción Sociocultural, 1979).
10. Susan Griswold, 'Topoi and Rhetorical Distance: The "Feminism" of María de Zayas', *Revista de Estudios Hispánicos*, 14.2 (1980), 97–116.
11. Irene Albers and Uta Felten (eds), *Escenas de transgresión: María de Zayas en su contexto literario-cultural* (Madrid: Iberoamericana, 2009).
12. See Andrew Keitt, *Inventing the Sacred: Imposture, Inquisition, and the Boundaries of the Supernatural in Golden Age Spain* (Leiden: Brill, 2005).
13. See Fabián Alejandro Campagne, 'Witchcraft and the Sense-of-the-Impossible in Early Modern Spain: Some Reflections Based on the Literature of Superstition (ca. 1500–1800)', *Harvard Theological Review*, 96.1 (2003), 25–62.
14. See Keith Thomas, *Religion and the Decline of Magic* (London: Penguin, 1971).
15. See Michel Foucault, *The Order of Things* (London: Routledge, 1989; first pub. in English by Tavistock, 1970).
16. See, for example, Henry Kamen, *The Spanish Inquisition: An Historical Revision* (London: Phoenix, 1997); María Tausiet, *Urban Magic in Early Modern Spain: Abracadabra Omnipotens* (Basingstoke: Palgrave Macmillan, 2014); and María Helena Sánchez Ortega, 'Sorcery and Eroticism in Love Magic', in *Cultural Encounters: The Impact of the Inquisition in Spain and the New World*, ed. by Mary Elizabeth Perry and Anne Cruz (Berkeley: University of California Press, 1991).
17. Marina Brownlee, *The Cultural Labyrinth of María de Zayas* (Philadelphia: University of Pennsylvania Press, 2000) and Margaret Greer, *María de Zayas Tells Baroque Tales of Love and the Cruelty of Men* (University Park: Pennsylvania State University Press, 2000).

18. Susan Paun de García, 'Magia y poder en María de Zayas', *Cuadernos de ALDEUU*, 8 (1992), 43–54; Yvette Cardaillac Hermosilla, 'La magia en las novelas de María de Zayas', in *La creatividad femenina en el mundo barroco hispánico: María de Zayas — Isabel Rebeca Correa — Sor Juana Inés de la Cruz*, ed. by Monika Bosse, Barbara Potthast and André Stoll, 2 vols (Kassel: Reichenberger, 1999), I, 351–77 and Judith Whitenack, '"Lo que ha menester": Erotic Enchantment in "La inocencia castigada"', in *María de Zayas: The Dynamics of Discourse*, ed. by Amy Williamsen and Judith Whitenack (London: Associated University Presses, 1995), pp. 170–91.
19. This is the title Julián Olivares gives to his recent edition of her novellas: *Honesto y entretenido sarao (primera y segunda parte)*, ed. by Julián Olivares, 2 vols (Zaragoza: Universidad de Zaragoza, 2017).
20. See Yllera's introduction to her edition of the *Desengaños amorosos* (Madrid: Cátedra, 1983) and Julián Olivares's introduction to *Honesto y entretenido sarao* (Zaragoza: Universidad de Zaragoza, 2017).

CHAPTER 1

The Ghostly Sybil from Madrid

María de Zayas y Sotomayor, que con justo título ha merecido el nombre de Sibila de Madrid, adquirido por sus admirables versos, por su felice ingenio y gran prudencia. (Castillo Solórzano)[1]

[María de Zayas y Sotomayor, who has rightly deserved the name of Sybil of Madrid, earned on account of her admirable verse, her felicitous genius and her great prudence.]

It is commonplace to start a discussion of María de Zayas's life by stating that we do not know much about it. All we know is that she was active in literary circles in Madrid during the first part of Philip IV's reign and left one play and two collections of novellas. Faced with such a dearth of information there have been a fair few speculations about various aspects of her life, including her sexuality. Much of what scholars have assumed is based on a biographical reading of her novellas and a few purported personal interpolations. Conjectures about her life have also been made on the basis of the history of her publications. We find ourselves on much firmer ground when we consider the scholarly attention that she has attracted. Her novellas went from being 'instant best-sellers' (Boyer, *Enchantments*, p. xii) in the 1600s and 1700s to being all but forgotten, or else deemed lascivious and repulsive by the few Hispanists who read her in the nineteenth and early twentieth century. A slow re-evaluation began in the second half of the last century and gathered speed in the 1990s. Nancy Lagreca estimates that in the last two decades scholarly interest has quadrupled and adds that the analyses have matured.[2] Today her novellas have become part of the canon and her work is studied at universities around the world, with scholars directing their attention to a wide variety of themes in her work, including magic.

1.1 'Me conocéis por lo escrito': Hidden behind a Screen of Fiction

Despite the fact that Zayas may have been one of the best-selling authors of the Spanish Golden Age — more on that assertion below — not much is known about her life. These two facts imply less of a contradiction than might appear at a first glance. Parts of Cervantes's life are shrouded in mystery and there are a great many gaps in Shakespeare's biography that generations of determined scholars have failed to fill, to give but two examples. In María de Zayas's case the scarcity of biographical information is compounded by her gender, since she would not have been required to sign contracts and other legal documents.[3] Nevertheless, there is one instance in which we do appear to have her signature, namely in the register of the *Hermandad de defensores de la Purísima Concepción* [Brotherhood of the Defenders of the Most Pure Conception] of the Hieronymite convent of the Immaculate Conception in Madrid. Furthermore, in one of the early editions of her novellas someone has penned the words: 'alabado sea el Santísimo Sacramento y la limpia y pura Concepción de la Virgen sin mancilla, concebida sin la mancha de pecado original' [praised be the Holy Sacrament and the unsullied and pure Conception of the Immaculate Virgin, conceived without the stain of original sin], which has sometimes been viewed as an autograph by the author.[4]

It is quite possible that Zayas had a special devotion to the Virgin of the Immaculate Conception. One of the narrators of the novellas' frame story, Estefanía, is a nun of that order and a number of heroines enter Conceptionist convents — Laura in 'La fuerza del amor', Juana in 'El desengaño amando', and Ana's sisters in 'El traidor contra su sangre'.[5] Furthermore, in a list of erudite women the author makes mention of 'doña María Barahona, religiosa en el convento de la Concepción Jerónima' [doña María Barahona, nun of the Hieronymite convent of the Immaculate Conception] (*Desengaños*, p. 230).

However, apart from circumstantial evidence, the reality is that, apart from her novellas, we have virtually no written documents that tell us anything about her life; the real María de Zayas remains hidden behind a screen of fiction. As if she were aware of the way posterity would see her, she writes at the end of her collection, in a literary trompe l'oeil that collapses the distance between the real-life author and the protagonist of the frame narrative: 'me conocéis por lo escrito, mas no por la vista' [you know me by my writings but not by sight] (*Desengaños*, p. 507). The flesh-and-blood María de Zayas has remained invisible and has hardly left a trace, except for her oeuvre, which is why Ximénez de Sandoval refers to her as 'una escritora fantasma' [a ghostly writer].[6] Despite this documentary void, however, it is possible to reconstruct some parts of her life, although much of it is perforce conjecture and in general one would do well to heed Griswold's injunction against indulging in 'psychoanalytical flights of deductive biography' (Griswold, p. 108).

Family and Birth

We know that María de Zayas y Sotomayor was born on 12 September 1590 in the parish of San Sebastián in Madrid. She was the daughter of Fernando de Zayas and María de Barasa. Her birth certificate (*partida de bautismo*) reads:

> María de Çayas — En doce días del mes de Septiembre de mil y quinientos nobenta años, yo el bachiller Altamirano, theniente de cura, bapticé á María, hija de Don Fernando de Çayas y de Doña María de Barasa su muger.[7]

> [María de Çayas — On the twelfth day of September in the year fifteen hundred and ninety, I, bachelor Altamirano, assistant priest, baptized María, the daughter of Don Fernando de Çayas and Doña María de Barasa, his wife.]

In his *Apuntes para una biblioteca de escritoras españolas* Serrano y Sanz discusses María de Zayas's genealogy and mentions that her father's paternal grandparents were Alonso de Zayas and Inés Sánchez originally from Zafra in Extremadura; his maternal grandparents were Antonio de Sotomayor and Catalina de Zayas, both from Madrid. So it would appear that both María's paternal grandfather and grandmother were called Zayas.

Yolanda Gamboa claims that the author of the *Sarao* might have been of Converso origin, basing her hypothesis on the supposed Jewish origin of the name Zayas as well as her assumption that Zayas's publisher was Jewish.[8] This seems unlikely given the fact that Zayas's father was made a Knight of the Order of Santiago in 1628, which required rigorous genealogical checks. It is also a mistake to call Escuer or Esquer (the Aragonese bookseller and printer used both names) Jewish, since Jews had been exiled in 1492, although he might have been from a Converso family. By contrast, in an article about three Spanish women writers, Redondo Goicoechea explicitly states that Zayas was *not* of Converso origin, whereas her other two subjects, Teresa de Cartagena and Teresa de Jesús, were.[9] This seems a more likely state of affairs.

Amezúa has suggested that Zayas's father took his family to Valladolid when Philip III decided to move his court there between 1601 and 1606; if true, this means that María spent her early teenage years there.[10] Olivares mentions this purported stay in Valladolid too, but disregards it as less convincing than the suggestion she might have lived in Italy, even though the two possibilities are not mutually exclusive.[11]

In Italy

Fernando de Zayas y Sotomayor was the *mayordomo* of Don Pedro Fernández de Castro y Andrade, the 7th Count of Lemos, and accompanied him to Naples, where the Count served as the Viceroy from 1610 to 1616. The Count was a 'refined mind and enlightened protector of *belles-lettres*',[12] and when he was appointed to the Viceroyalty he ordered his secretary Lupercio Leonardo de Argensola to select a group of literati to be incorporated into his literary court. Both Cervantes and Góngora aspired to be in his retinue, but Argensola — a mediocre literary talent loath to be outshone, according to Cervantes's biographer Canavaggio — denied both of them the opportunity. Had it been otherwise, María de Zayas might have spent her formative years in the company of two of the greatest Spanish writers of all time; that is, if we assume that she followed her father to Naples. This is an important assumption, since if she did, it would stand to reason that she was not married when her father was appointed or she would have stayed in Spain with her husband.

There are a number of reasons to think this assumption is correct. The author sets her novellas in a wide range of cities — Madrid, Toledo, Salamanca, Seville, Granada, Zaragoza, Valladolid, Palermo, Lisbon, Brussels and Naples: all important imperial centres — but she rarely gives detailed descriptions, except for the viceregal seat. This is especially clear in 'La fuerza del amor', where the narrator Nise offers precise geographical information on a number of occasions:

> Hay en Nápoles, como una milla apartada de la ciudad, camino de Nuestra Señora del Arca, imagen muy devota de aquel reino, y el mismo por donde se va a Piedra Blanca, como un tiro de piedra del camino real, a un lado de él, un humilladero de cincuenta pies de largo y otros tantos de ancho, la puerta del cual está hacia el camino, y enfrente de ella un altar con una imagen pintada en la misma pared. (*Novelas*, p. 365)
>
> [In Naples, about a mile out of town, on the way to the Madonna dell'Arco, a very popular shrine in that kingdom, which is the same road that leads to Pietra Bianca, at about a stone's throw from the highway to one side, there stands a roadside chapel fifty feet in length and of the same width, whose door faces the road and which has an altar in front of it and an image painted directly onto the wall.]

She also gives details about a local custom: 'Úsase en Nápoles llevar a los festines un maestro de ceremonias, el cual saca a danzar a las damas y las da al caballero que le parece' [In Naples they usually bring a master of ceremonies to their balls, who invites the ladies to join the dance and hands them over to a gentleman of his choosing] (*Novelas*, p. 347). This tradition is again referred to in 'La más infame venganza', set in Milan and told by Lisarda:

> Ya he dicho el uso y costumbre de aquellos reinos, que son los festines, que un día se celebran en unas casas y otros en otras, y que es permitido a las damas casadas y doncellas, y aun a las viudas, a ir a ellos, y a los caballeros, con máscaras y sin ellas, entrar y sacar a danzar la dama que les parece. (*Desengaños*, pp. 190–91)
>
> [I have already said that in those kingdoms it is customary to hold balls, which are celebrated in one house one day and in another the next, and which ladies, married and unmarried alike — and even widows — are allowed to attend, and where gentlemen, with or without masks, can enter the dance and ask any lady they like to dance with them.]

Zayas's voice comes through when she puts the words 'ya he dicho' [I have already said] in the mouth of Lisarda, when in reality it was Nise who mentioned this costume in a previous tale. It is one of the instances in the collection where the distance between Zayas and one of her characters collapses.

Furthermore, the novella 'El traidor de su sangre' includes a description of the viceregal fleet led by the Marquis of Santa Cruz on its way back to Spain in 1616. The event is probably the return to Spain of the Viceroy Pedro Fernández de Castro y Andrade. Later that year the Duke of Osuna — Quevedo's patron — would replace the Count of Lemos as Viceroy in Naples. In the same novella, Alonso strikes up a friendship with a dubious character who is described as one of the 'prevetes salvajes' [wild priests]. The word 'prevete' is not standard Italian and appears to be Neapolitan dialect.[13] In the story Zayas explains who these people are: 'hay en Italia unos hombres que, sin letras ni órdenes, tienen renta por la Iglesia, sólo con andar vestidos de clérigos y llámanlos "prevetes salvajes"' [in Italy there are men who, without having studied or taken orders, receive a stipend from the Church, only by dressing as priests, and they are called 'wild priests'] (*Desengaños*, p. 386). This detailed knowledge, absent from stories set elsewhere, make her stay in Naples between 1610 and 1616 more than likely. Olivares (*Honesto sarao*) suggests that Zayas could have picked up such details from reading. However, not only is she is very specific in her geographical identification of the chapel and use of dialect, but she only makes comments like this when she writes about Italy, and specifically about Naples. If she were interested in *couleur locale*, she could have found out specifics for other towns as well — but she doesn't.

A further argument for her stay in Italy, referred to by many scholars, is a passage from the novella 'La perseguida triunfante', which is usually taken to be an autobiographical interpolation.[14] That story ends by saying that the protagonist of the hagiographical tale, Beatriz, 'en toda Italia es tenida por santa, donde vi su vida manuscrita, *estando allí con mis padres*' [is considered a saint in all of Italy, where I saw a manuscript of her life story *when I was there with my parents*] (*Desengaños*, p. 467 — emphasis added). Supposing this is in effect a biographical interpolation, it is another instance of the collapse of the distance between the author and a character of the frame narrative.

Knowledge of Italian and French

If Zayas lived in Italy between the age of twenty and twenty-six she might have learnt enough Italian to read Boccaccio and other *novellieri* like Bandello and Masuccio in the original. Zayas uses at least one of Boccaccio's stories as the basis of a novella ('El jardín engañoso' and possibly also 'El imposible vencido'), although it is by no means certain that she took the story directly from the *Decameron* since there were Spanish adaptations of these Italian tales too, such as Juan de Timoneda's *Patrañuelo*. There are at least three novellas that are probably based on Bandello ('Tarde llega el desengaño', 'El imposible vencido' and 'La burlada Aminta') and another three that have elements in common with Masuccio ('El prevenido engañado' and some aspects of 'El castigo de la miseria'). Given the proximity between Spanish and Italian, it is not unreasonable to assume that she had at least a working knowledge of Dante's language.

The same cannot be said for her knowledge of French, contrary to what has been suggested by Barbeito Carneiro amongst others. The assumption is that since some sections of her novellas appear to be reworkings of tales from Marguerite de Navarre's *Heptaméron*, which was not available in Spanish at the time, Zayas must therefore have read that work in French.[15] Barbeito Carneiro goes on to suggest that the Conde de Lemos might have had a copy of this collection of tales in his library:

> Por otra parte, tampoco podemos descartar que existiera dentro de la copiosísima biblioteca del Conde de Lemos, en Nápoles, alguna versión del *Heptamerón* de Margarita de Navarra, en cuyo caso, ese libro de autoría femenina supondría un acicate determinante como fuente de inspiración digna de ser emulada. (Barbeito Carneiro, *Mujeres y literatura*, p. 165)

> [On the other hand, we cannot exclude the possibility that the vast library of the Count of Lemos in Naples contained a copy of the *Heptaméron* by Marguerite

de Navarre, in which case, this female-authored book would have been an important stimulus and a source of inspiration worthy of being emulated.]

There is no need to assume that Zayas could read French, since the story referred to — 'Tarde llega el desengaño', about a man who punishes his adulterous wife by locking her up with the corpse of her lover — is also told by Bandello (novella XII of the *Seconda Parte*). Donovan too assumes that 'Tarde llega el desengaño' derives from Marguerite de Navarre and adds 'El prevenido engañado' and 'El imposible vencido' as adaptations of tales from the *Heptaméron*, even though for the first Masuccio's novella XXIV is a more likely candidate (see 4.1), whereas the plot of the second is the same as Lope de Vega's *La difunta pleiteada*, Bandello's novella XLI and the fourth story of the tenth day of Boccaccio's *Decameron* (see 5.1).[16] The suggestion that Zayas must have known the *Heptaméron* seems to go back to an early study by Edwin Place (1923) and has been uncritically accepted by many scholars since.[17] However, it is much more likely that Zayas adapted her stories from Spanish and Italian sources and that she did not speak or read French. Nor had she probably heard of Marguerite de Navarre. At the start of Zayas's 'Tarde llega el desengaño', the narrator mentions a string of famous learned noblewomen and women writers: Charles V's sisters, Isabel Clara Eugenia, the Countess of Lemos, Margaret of Parma, three nuns known for their erudition or verse and her friend Ana Caro Mallén de Soto. In this list Marguerite de Navarre, as a noblewoman and novella writer whose story Zayas is supposedly about to integrate into her own, is conspicuous by her absence. Had Zayas known about Marguerite de Navarre and read her *Heptaméron*, this would have been an inexplicable omission.

Relations with the Condes de Lemos

Whether or not she spent six years at the viceregal court in Naples, Zayas speaks highly of the Counts and Countesses of Lemos throughout her oeuvre, mentioning them in at least five novellas. In 'La fuerza del amor', Laura refuses to return to her abusive husband and her case is brought before the Viceroy 'don Pedro Fernández de Castro, Conde de Lemos, nobilísimo, sabio y piadoso príncipe, cuyas raras virtudes y excelencias no son para escritas en papeles, sino en láminas de bronce y en las lenguas de fama' [Don Pedro Fernández de Castro, Count of Lemos, that most noble, wise and pious prince, whose rare virtues and qualities ought not to be written on paper but engraved on bronze plates and spread by the tongues of fame] (*Novelas*, p. 368). He decides in her favour and allows her to enter a convent. This is a clear reference to her father's employer, who died in 1622. At the beginning of the second night of the *Desengaños amorosos* one of the guests sings a ballad said to be composed 'estando ausente el excelentísimo señor conde de Lemos, que hoy vive y viva muchos años, de mi señora la condesa, su esposa' [in the absence of the most excellent Count of Lemos, who is still alive today — and may he live for many more years — by my mistress the Countess, his wife] (*Desengaños*, p. 259).[18] Since the novella was published in 1647, the question arises which Count of Lemos she refers to here. The most likely candidate is Don Francisco Fernández de Castro y

Andrade (1613–1662), the 9th Count of Lemos and Viceroy of Aragón (1649–1652).[19] One of the illustrious women listed at the start of 'Tarde llega el desengaño' (see above) is the Countess, the 9th Count's grandmother:

> Pues la excelentísima condesa de Lemos, camarera mayor de la serenísima reina Margarita, y aya de la emperatriz de Alemania, abuela del excelentísimo conde de Lemos, que hoy vive y viva muchos años, y que fue de tan excelentísimo entendimiento, de más haber estudiado la lengua latina, que no había letrado que la igualase. (*Desengaños*, p. 229)

> [Then we have the Countess of Lemos, who was lady-in-waiting to Her Majesty Queen Margaret of Austria, governess to the Empress of Germany and the grandmother of the most excellent Count of Lemos, who is still alive today — and may he live for many more years — whose intelligence was such that, not only had she studied Latin, there was no scholar who could claim to be her equal.]

These references suggest a rather close relationship between the author and the Count and Countess of Lemos. Barbeito Carneiro (*Mujeres y literatura*) has proposed that Zayas may have been in the employment of the Countess after her return from Naples, although she produces no evidence for this claim.

Literary activities in Madrid

Whether or not Zayas lived in Italy, it is certain that by 18 October 1618 she resided in Madrid, because that is when she signed the register of the *Hermandad de defensores de la Purísima Concepción* mentioned earlier. In the years that followed it seems she formed part of a literary circle that included Castillo Solórzano, Pérez de Montalbán, whom Amezúa calls 'su gran amigo' [her great friend],[20] as well as Lope de Vega. Zayas mentions Lope de Vega in two of her novellas, 'El castigo de la miseria' and 'El traidor contra su sangre' and does so eulogistically, calling him 'aquel príncipe del Parnaso, Lope de Vega Carpio, cuya memoria no morirá mientras el mundo no tuviere fin' [that Parnassian Prince, Lope de Vega Carpio, whose memory will not die as long as this world lasts] (*Desengaños*, p. 369). She competed in poetic competitions (*justas poéticas*) at Francisco de Mendoza's *academia* between 1621 and 1639 and before that probably at Sebastián Francisco de Medrano's (1617–22).[21]

One of her sonnets appears in the prologue of Miguel Botello's *La fábula de Píramo y Tisbe* (1621) and other poems by her hand were printed in works published in the 1620s and 1630s. Four more of her compositions appear in works written by others, namely the *Prosas y versos del Pastor de Cleonarda* (1622), also by Miguel Botello, the *Orfeo en lengua castellana* (1624) by Pérez de Montalbán, Francisco de la Cuevas's *Experiencias de Amor y Fortuna* (1625) and *El Adonis* (c. 1632) by Castillo de Larzaval. Furthermore she contributed a romance to *Las lágrimas panegíricas a la temprana muerte del gran poeta Pérez de Montalbán* (1639).[22] She also wrote an epigram on the death of Lope de Vega (1635).[23]

The paratext of her *Novelas ejemplares y amorosas* (1637) includes two laudatory poems by Castillo Solórzano, sonnets by Pérez de Montalbán and Francisco de Aguirre Vaca, and décimas by Ana Caro Mallén de Soto. The anonymous *Prólogo de un desapasionado* is sometimes attributed to Castillo Solórzano.[24] In the *edición príncipe* (1637) four more poems were printed. One by Don Alonso Bernardo de Quirós, who describes Zayas as neither male nor female: 'no eres mujer ni eres hombre' [you are neither a woman nor a man]. There was also a poem in Portuguese by Diego Pereira, one by Doña Ana Inés Victoria de Mires y Arguillur, and a sonnet by Don Victorián Josef de Esmir y Casanate.[25] She is also mentioned by Lope de Vega in his *Laurel de Apolo* (1630) and in Pérez de Montalbán's *Para todos* (1632).

Zayas and Ana Caro Mallén de Soto

Zayas is thought to have been very close to Ana Caro Mallén de Soto, the Sevillian poetess and playwright, who might well have stayed with Zayas when she was in Madrid, where she wrote her *Contexto de las Reales Fiestas que se hizieron en el Palacio del Buen Retiro* in 1637. Like the Countess of Lemos, she makes an appearance in Zayas's list of illustrious women:

> la señora doña Ana Caro, natural de Sevilla: ya Madrid ha visto y hecho experiencia de su entendimiento y excelentísimos versos, pues los teatros la han hecho estimada y los grandes entendimientos le han dado laureles y vítores, rotulando su nombre por las calles. (*Desengaños*, p. 230)

> [Doña Ana Caro, native of Seville: Madrid has already seen and experienced her intelligence and most excellent poetry, since she earned respect in the theatres, and learned men have bestowed laurels on her and applauded her, so that her name is known on all the streets.]

In *La Garduña de Sevilla* (1642) Castillo Solórzano praises both women in the same paragraph, adding that they were in each other's company:

> en estos tiempos luce y campea con felices lauros el ingenio de doña María de Zayas y Sotomayor, que con justo título ha merecido el nombre de Sibila de Madrid, adquirido por sus admirables versos, por su felice ingenio y gran prudencia, habiendo sacado de la estampa un libro de diez novelas que son diez asombros para los que escriben deste género, pues la meditada prosa, el artificio dellas y los versos que interpola, es todo tan admirable, que acobarda las más valientes plumas de nuestra España. Acompáñala en Madrid doña Ana Caro de Mallén, dama de nuestra Sevilla, a quien se deben no menores alabanzas, pues con sus dulces y bien pensados versos suspende y deleita a quien los oye y lee. (*La Garduña de Sevilla*, pp. 94–96)

> [in our own time there shines and triumphs, adorned with happy laurels, the genius of María de Zayas y Sotomayor, who has rightly deserved the name of Sybil of Madrid, earned on account of her admirable verse, her felicitous genius and her great prudence, having published a book of ten novellas, which are considered ten marvels by those who write in the genre, since the measured prose, the artistry and the interspersed poems are all so admirable that the most valiant quills of our Spain feel intimidated. She is accompanied in Madrid by Doña Ana Caro de Mallén, a lady from our city of Seville, who is owed no lesser praise, since with her sweet and well-considered verse she excites and delights everyone who hears and reads them.]

Ana Caro Mallén de Soto was mainly known as a poetess, but she also wrote a number of plays, two of which are extant: *El conde Partinuplés* and *Valor, agravio y mujer*. She was not the only female playwright of the period. In 1997 Teresa Scott Soufas published a collection of plays written by women dramatists including Ángela de Azevedo, Ana Caro Mallén de Soto, Leonor de la Cueva y Silva, Feliciana Enríquez de Guzmán and María de Zayas y Sotomayor.[26] Many of these plays 'depict male characters that are unable to fulfil the patriarchal behaviour ascribed to them by society' (McGrath, *La traición*, p. 11) and stress the importance of female friendship, thus presenting alternative models of behaviour that question the contemporary depictions of bitter rivalry.[27] María de Zayas's play, which features a female version of Don Juan — Larson has called it 'simultaneously an inversion, a subversion and a comic copy of Tirso's *Burlador de Sevilla*'[28] — is entitled *La traición en la amistad* and was probably written sometime before 1632.[29]

It is not certain whether these plays were ever put on or just read out at gatherings. Samson states that there is no evidence that they were ever performed. Rodríguez Garrido, on the other hand, claims that Zayas's play was performed for a group of friends, possibly including Lope de Vega and Pérez de Montalbán.[30] This does not imply a contradiction if we accept that the play may have been performed privately without being staged in one of the public theatres (*corrales*). The same applies to plays written by other women playwrights of the period like Sor Juana Inés de la Cruz, whose comedy *Los empeños de una casa*, for example, was performed at the house of Don Fernando Deza, the tax collector of the Viceroy of Mexico.[31]

Speculations about her sexuality

Zayas's friendship with Ana Caro has led Brownlee to speculate about her sexuality, saying the poetess from Seville was 'perhaps a kindred spirit in sexual preference as well as literary taste'.[32] Commenting on a homosexual scene in 'Mal presagio casar lejos', she further writes that 'the sensitivity of the portrayal makes us wonder whether it stems from her own possibly lesbian relationship with another noblewoman' (Brownlee, *Cultural Labyrinth*, p. 52). Taken on their own, these statements would seem far-fetched indeed, but in some of her novellas Zayas appears to give a positive portrayal of at least the possibility of lesbian relationships. Zelima in 'La esclava de su amante' says she had a friend 'cuyo nombre era Leonisa, que me quería con tanto extremo, que comía y dormía en su misma cama' [whose name was Leonisa and who loved me so very much that I ate with her and slept in the same bed] (*Desengaños*, p. 154). And in 'La burlada Aminta' the eponymous heroine is seduced by Jacinto, who is accompanied by his apparently bisexual lover, Flora, who tells him: 'ya sabes que tengo el gusto y los deseos más de galán que de dama, y donde las veo y más tan bellas, como esta hermosa señora, se me van los ojos tras ellas y se me enternece el corazón' [you already know my preferences and desires are more those of a gentleman in love than those of a lady, and when I see such pretty ones as this beautiful lady, I cannot take my eyes off them and my heart melts] (*Novelas*, p. 223).[33]

Even more extreme is the case of Esteban in 'Amar sólo por vencer', where the male protagonist dresses himself up as a woman in order to seduce the young Laurela and spends a year as Estefanía, declaring his love to her as a maid, which causes much mirth. 'Volviéronse a reír, confirmando el pensamiento que tenían de que Estefanía estaba enamorada de Laurela' [They all laughed again, seeing their notion that Estefanía was in love with Laurela confirmed] (*Desengaños*, p. 307) and:

> todas lo juzgaban a locura, antes les servía de entretenimiento y motivo de risa, siempre que la veían hacer extremos y finezas de amante, llorar celos y sentir desdenes, admirando que una mujer estuviese enamorada de otra, sin llegar a su imaginación que pudiese ser lo contrario. (*Desengaños*, p. 309)
>
> [they all thought it was folly and more than anything else they found it entertaining and it made them laugh whenever they saw her playing the refined and over-the-top lover, crying with jealousy and showing disdain, amazed that a woman could be in love with another, without the thought ever crossing their minds that the opposite could be true.]

Based on these and other passages, Lisa Vollendorf goes so far as to say that Zayas 'sanctions love between women,'[34] although in an earlier article she is more nuanced and, in my view, more correct when she writes that:

> the extent to which homoeroticism, particularly female homoeroticism, was intelligible to early modern readers cannot be known with any precision. Nor can we know for sure whether our own readings of early modern sexuality (of any sort) accurately decipher the erotic codes present in the texts.[35]

Nevertheless, her overall opinion seems to be that Zayas portrays lesbian love positively. 'Zayas's endorsement of female homoerotic desire constitutes an equally striking representation of women's intimacy' (Vollendorf, 'Good Sex, Bad Sex', p. 6).

When Lope de Vega mentions Zayas in his *Laurel de Apolo* (1639), he compares her to Sappho:

> de las rosas | Tejed ricas guirnaldas y trofeos | A la inmortal Doña María de Zayas | Que sin pasar a Lesbos ni a las playas | Del vasto mar Egeo | Que hoi llora el negro velo de Teseo | A Safo gozará Mitilenea | Quien ver milagros de muger desea: | Porque su ingenio, vivamente claro | Es tan único y raro.[36]
>
> [from its roses weave garlands and trophies for the immortal Doña María de Zayas; whoever wants to see a woman's miracles without crossing over to Lesbos or the beaches of the vast Aegean Sea, which weeps on account of Theseus's black sail, will enjoy a Mytilenean Sappho: her talent is plain for all to see, unique and rare.]

At various points in her oeuvre, Zayas discusses eminent women writers who have gone before her — as we have seen above — thus inserting herself into a historical-literary pedigree, but she never mentions the poetess from Lesbos. Greer suggests that this may be a form of 'strategic distancing' and adds that the same is true for Sor Juana Inés de la Cruz. I would argue, however, that there are various ways of interpreting the supposed lesbian episodes and that an autobiographical reading is the least convincing interpretation. As with other elements of her novellas, the episodes in question fit the wider framework of her quest for titillation and sensation, on a par with her scenes of torture, rape, dismemberment and assassination.[37] Moreover, her stance on homosexuality is by no means unequivocally positive. The bisexual Flora is an evil character, whereas Esteban's spell as a lovelorn maiden, which some critics have seen as exemplifying Judith Butler's theory of gender-as-performance, causes nothing but laughter, and not the kind of feminine laughter Cixous had in mind, designed to 'smash everything, to shatter the framework of institutions, to blow up the law, to break up the "truth"'.[38] Furthermore, after he has successfully seduced Laurela, his fervent lesbian discourse evaporates and he abandons her, whereupon she is killed by her father — she is crushed under a wall.

If the author can be said to be ambiguous about lesbian desire, she is downright scathing about male homosexuality, as is clear in 'Mal presagio casar lejos', in which Blanca discovers her husband in bed with his page: 'Vio acostados en la cama a su esposo y a Arnesto, en deleites tan torpes y abominables, que es bajeza, no sólo decirlo, mas pensarlo' [She saw her husband and Arnesto in bed, engaged in such awful and abominable pleasures that it is despicable not only to mention them, but to even think about them] (*Desengaños*, p. 360). This is a far cry from Brownlee's 'sensitive portrayal' and can hardly be read as a sympathetic view of homosexuality, even if the activity is described as 'deleite' [pleasure]. Not only do these episodes correspond to her 'gusto tremendista' [taste for the sensational] (Foa, p. 97) but they are also an integral part of her baroque project of juxtaposing contrasting ideas and playing a clever baroque game of *engaño/desengaño* [deceit/ seeing through deceit] and *ser/parecer* [being/appearance]. We are led to believe one thing and then it transpires we have been misled, or that there are multiple possibilities.[39]

Married or not?

It is generally assumed that Zayas never married. In 1903 Serrano y Sanz wrote: 'No he podido averiguar con toda certeza si fue o no casada' [I have not been able to find out with certainty whether or not she was married] (Serrano y Sanz, p. 584). Amezúa and Alborg are two of the few scholars who do not discard the possibility that she *was* married. The former suggest that she might have moved out of Madrid and settled, perhaps married, in Zaragoza, where her first novellas were published. The latter simply states that she was probably married and moved to Zaragoza or Barcelona.[40] As discussed above, had she been married, she would not have moved to Naples with her father, unless she found a husband after she returned to Spain at the age of twenty-six. This supposed spinsterhood, again, has led to all sorts of conjectures. Amezúa assumes she was ugly because other poets only ever praised her talents, not her beauty. 'Fea o hermosa (más bien lo primero, ya que en las poesías que sus admiradores escribieron en laudo suyo nadie la celebró nunca por bella, unánime silencio muy sospechoso)' [Ugly or beautiful (the first being more likely, since in the poetry written by her admirers no one ever celebrated her beauty, and this unanimous silence is most suspicious)] (Zayas, *Novelas* (1948), p. xxii). Rincón follows the same line of reasoning: 'jamás encontró quien loara su belleza [...] ¿Será mucho aventurar que debió ser más bien fea o, al menos, para decirlo con mayor dulzura, poco agraciada?' [she never found anyone who praised her beauty [...]

Would it be too much to surmise that she must have been rather ugly, or at the very least, to put it nicely, a little lacking in grace?] (*Novelas* (1968), p. 11).⁴¹

Barbeito Carneiro, on the other hand, writes that Zayas returned to Spain from Naples 'en plena juventud y, según los indicios, dotada de belleza' [in the first flush of youth and, as far as we can tell, beautiful] (Barbeito Carneiro, *Mujeres y literatura*, p. 162), without explaining what these 'indicios' might be. She continues by saying that Zayas published her second volume when she was in her fifties, an age at which she 'arrastra la suma de muchas experiencias negativas, que la han envejecido y afeado más de los años' [was burdened by many negative experiences, which had made her old and ugly beyond her age] (ibid.). The difference in tone between the two volumes of novellas has been cited as evidence for a bitter experience — a *desengaño* — in love, although in fact, most scholars nowadays agree that it is unreasonable to assume this happened to her when she was in her fifties. As a matter of fact, most scholars who mention this point state that this is the view of *other* critics.⁴²

One poem has come to light, however, that describes her physical appearance in the most unflattering of terms. In 1643, the young Catalan poet Francesc Fontanella described her as a woman with a masculine face and a haughty moustache, who 'semblava a algun cavaller' [looked like some gentleman or other].⁴³ But since the poem is clearly in a parodic vein — the poet describes how he falls asleep out of boredom during a literary competition (*certamen*) and dreams that he visits the moon — not much can be deduced from it, although the poet clearly sees Zayas as a sexually ambiguous creature and a freak of nature.⁴⁴ Fontanella's description of Zayas as a *mujer varonil*, a manly woman or virago in the early modern sense of the word, chimes with Bernardo de Quirós calling Zayas neither a man nor a woman (see above).

However, there may be more at play here than mere misogynist comments by two contemporaries. According to what Thomas Laqueur has dubbed the 'one-sex model' women were seen as biologically and ontologically inferior versions of men.⁴⁵ Due to a different distribution of the cardinal humours, women were thought to be incapable of true creativity; those who were, were considered freaks of nature. This reasoning is clear, for example, in Huarte de San Juan's *Examen de ingenios* (1575), where he writes that: 'la compostura natural que la mujer tiene en el cerebro no es capaz de mucho ingenio ni de mucha sabiduría' [the natural texture of a woman's brain is not capable of much intelligence or wisdom].⁴⁶ And:

> Porque pensar que la mujer puede ser caliente y seca, ni tener el ingenio y habilidad que sigue a estas dos calidades, es muy grande error; porque si la simiente de que se formó fuera caliente y seca a predominio, saliera varón y no hembra; y por ser fría y húmida, nació hembra y no varón. (Huarte de San Juan, p. 252)

> [Because to think that a woman can be hot and dry, or have the intelligence and ability that follow from these qualities, is a grave error; because if the seed from which she was formed had been predominantly hot and dry, she would have become a man and not a woman; but since it was cold and humid, she was born a woman and not a man.]

By describing Zayas as a *mujer varonil* the poet highlights her extraordinariness: her unnatural gift for creation.[47] Zayas was aware of the humoral theories on which these assumptions were based and in her prologue she upturns the traditional thinking by arguing that women might in fact be *more* intelligent on account of their humours:

> Porque si en nuestra crianza, como nos ponen el cambray en las almohadillas y los dibujos en el bastidor, nos dieran libros y preceptores, fuéramos tan aptas para los puestos y para las cátedras como los hombres, y quizá más agudas, por ser de natural más frío, por consistir en humedad el entendimiento. (*Novelas*, p. 160)
>
> [Because if in our youth, rather than giving us cambric for our pincushions and patterns for our embroidery frames, they gave us books and private tutors, we would be as suited for any position — or indeed professorship — as men, and perhaps we would be even more intelligent, since we are by nature colder, and intellect resides in the damp humour.]

Literary production

Five years before Zayas's *Novelas amorosas y ejemplares* ran off the press in Zaragoza, Pérez de Montalbán wrote in his *Para todos* (1632):

> D. Maria dezima Musa de nuestro siglo, ha escrito a los Certamenes con grande acierto, tiene acabada vna comedia de excelentes coplas, y vn Libro para dar a la estampa en prosa y verso de ocho Nouelas exemplares.[48]
>
> [Doña María, tenth muse of our age, who has participated in literary competitions with great success, has finished a *comedia* written in excellent stanzas as well as a book of eight exemplary Novellas, containing both prose and poems, which is ready to go to the printer's.]

From this we can deduce the following. First, it is clear that Montalbán knew what Zayas was going to publish before her work went to the printer's, suggesting a considerable degree of intimacy. Second, Zayas must have written two more novellas between 1632 and 1637. In all likelihood, Zayas wrote the first eight novellas between 1620 and the early 1630s. There is a licence (*licencia*) for her novellas dated 4 June 1626, eleven years before her novellas were actually published. Amezúa assumes that this is a misprint for 1636. Jaime Moll, however, investigated the matter and found that the licence to print must in effect have been issued in 1626, since Dr Juan de Mendieta, who signed it, was no longer in office in 1636.[49] I would add that the idea of a misprint is very unlikely given that in the original the date is spelled out as 'cuatro de junio de mil y seiscientos y veinte y seis.'[50] Let us assume therefore that the *licencias* are indeed from 1626. This means that Zayas had already written some of her novellas at that time and subsequently continued to add to them until she was finally able to publish a collection of ten novellas in 1637. The reason for this delay is easily explained. In 1625 the *Junta de Reformación* proposed to suspend licences for printing *comedias* and novellas, which was accepted by the *Consejo de Castilla* and remained in force until 1634. It seems that Zayas was able to get the ecclesiastical but not the civil approval to publish her work, not until 1635 that is. Two years after that, her novellas were printed in Zaragoza. Although some, like Amezúa, have seen this as evidence that she had taken up residence in the Aragonese capital, it is equally plausible that her Aragonese publicist Escuer (Esquer) had her novellas printed in Zaragoza because the printers in Madrid were busy with back orders after the ban had been lifted.[51]

Olivares and others have suggested that Escuer was probably responsible for the title of the collection, hoping to cash in on the commercial success of Cervantes's *Novelas ejemplares*. Zayas herself never mentions Escuer's title, but usually speaks of the *Honesto y entretenido sarao* (or *Sarao*, or *nuestro sarao*) when she refers to the collection and to *maravillas* [marvels] when she talks about the stories of the first collection. This was also the title on both ecclesiastical *licencias*. Olivares furthermore suggests that Zayas may have been displeased with the decision to change the title, which might explain why she had her second collection published by Inés de Casamayor instead of Escuer. The title of that collection was *Parte segunda del sarao y entretenimiento honesto*, even if there had officially never been a part one. Note how again the title was changed from Zayas's original one, albeit slightly this time. All the same, Pérez de Montalbán talks about 'novelas exemplares', not 'Sarao' (see above), although he might have referred to the genre and not the title per se. It is also worth noting that in 1624 José Camerino, who was active in the same literary circles as Zayas, published a collection of novellas equally called *Novelas amorosas y ejemplares*. One of his stories is entitled 'La soberbia castigada' [Arrogance punished], while Zayas has a tale called 'La inocencia castigada' [Innocence punished]. Furthermore, his novella 'El casamiento desdichado' [The unhappy marriage] has been suggested as the source for 'El traidor de su sangre' by José María Roca Franquesa.[52]

In Barcelona

As we saw above, Zayas appears in a parody written in Barcelona in 1643. Kenneth Brown, who published a paper on the matter, construes this as evidence that Zayas lived in the Catalan capital and that she was active in its literary circles — the Academia de Santo Tomás de Aquino to be precise — and on intimate terms with the poet Fontanella: 'Es seguro que Fontanella tenía mucha confianza con María de Zayas para ofenderla tan impunemente. Si lo contrario fuera verdad, tales conceptos serían de demasiado mal gusto' [It is certain that Fontanella was on intimate terms with María de Zayas to be able to offend her with impunity. Had that not been the case, such notions would have been in really bad taste] (Brown, p. 359). However, to call Zayas a moustachioed virago who hides a sword beneath her petticoats by no means implies a degree of intimacy. Nor would it be the first poem to have been in bad taste — that hardly ever stops anyone from publishing potentially offensive material. But Brown's main point is that Fontanella mocks Zayas alongside other contemporary poets of his Catalan circle. He further suggests that, if she ever left, she returned to Barcelona in 1647 or 1648 to negotiate an edition of her novellas — the *Primera Parte* of her *Sarao* was published in Barcelona in 1646; the second edition of the *Segunda Parte* in 1649 — but this is disputed by Olivares, who points out that the renewed edition of part one was based on the princeps from 1637, while part two was never corrected by the author, making her stay in Barcelona in 1647 unlikely. Still, Olivares accepts that the author may have lived in Barcelona in the 1640s. This assumption is also made by Gamboa, who makes the additional suggestion that Zayas was politically involved with the anti-Olivares party — the Count-Duke of Olivares was Philip IV's favourite and one of the most powerful men in the country until his fall in 1643 — and had become persona non grata in Madrid:

> Aunque desconocemos el paradero de Zayas en los años próximos a su muerte, su relación con Fontanella, y la crítica de los coetáneos de las academias literarias de Madrid [...] me lleva a pensar que su participación política la lleva a los círculos de Fontanella y que no vuelve a Madrid dado que se convierte en persona non grata. (Gamboa, *Cartografía social*, p. 166)

> [Even though we do not know anything about Zayas's whereabouts in the years preceding her death, her relationship with Fontanella and the criticism of her contemporaries in the literary salons of Madrid [...] lead me to think that her political activities brought her closer to Fontanella's circles and that she did not return to Madrid, where she had become persona non grata.]

Gamboa furthermore suggests that the sibyl from Madrid may have ended her days in Perpignan, having gone into exile with other radicals. O'Brien equally follows Brown's assumption that Zayas lived in the Catalan capital: 'That this Castilian author should have been found in physical proximity to the conflict and in the company of Francophile and secessionist Catalans is thought-provoking'.[53] In a broad sense, Zayas is of course very political and critical of what she perceives to be the decline of Spain. Moreover, as Charnon-Deutsch has pointed out, Zayas shares the insight, formulated amongst others by Foucault, that systems of power and control in the private sphere are reflected in larger political spheres.[54] But there is not much evidence for specific partisan leanings in her novellas, although there is one paratext that could potentially point in that direction, namely the fact that the *Desengaños amorosos* is prefaced by a letter from Inés de Casamayor to Jaime Fernández de Silva, the future Duke of Híjar, whose father was one of the leaders of the anti-Olivares grandees (see Greer, *Baroque Tales*). Nevertheless, as Julián Olivares writes, this affair has little to do with Zayas herself, who may not even have been around to see her second volume of novellas published.

Death and disappearance

Around the time of the publication of her *desengaños*, Zayas disappears from the records, which again has led to considerable speculation. Montesa, in his pioneering work on the author, remarked that she corrected the proofs of the *Primera Parte* but not the *Segunda Parte*. Moreover, in Part Two the order of the stories as announced in the frame narrative differs from the actual order, and after the fifth tale the narrator says: 'después de dichos los cuatro desengaños' [after the four *desengaños* have been told] (*Desengaños*, p. 255).[55] The fact that the novellas of the second collection were not 'de nuevo corretas, y enmendadas por su misma Autora' [once more corrected and amended by the Author herself] (*Novelas*, p. 150), as was the case for the second edition of part one, has been blamed on her death.

In an attempt to dig up more detailed biographical material, scholars have brought to light two death certificates (*partidas de defunción*) of women called María de Zayas, both from Madrid. One registers the death, on 11 January 1661, of 'Doña María de Çayas, viuda de Juan Valdés', whose last will and testament is also known, as well as a letter of authorization (*poder*) issued in her name, neither of which she signed herself, because 'aunque savía escrivir, por la grave enfermedad que tenía y tener algo turbada la vista, rogó á testigo lo firmase por ella' [although she was able to read, due to a serious illness and because her vision was clouded, she asked the witness to sign it on her behalf] (Serrano y Sanz, p. 585). The other *partida de defunción* refers to 'D.ª María muger que fué de Pedro Balcazar y Alarcon, en la calle del Relox' [Doña María wife of Pedro Balcazar y Alarcon, from the street of the Clock] and dates from 26 September 1669. In 1972, Felipe Maldonado uncovered another María de Zayas. She was the wife of Don Fernando de Buitrago and appears in a document from 1636. Elsewhere she is called María Ramírez de Zayas.[56] None of these three women is likely to have been the author of the *Honesto y entretenido sarao*.

With regards to Zayas's last years, by far the most common assumption is that she followed the example of her heroines and entered a convent. This, however, constitutes too literal a reading of her novellas. It is true that many of her heroines seek refuge in a nunnery and Lisis, who has organized the story-telling event, is about to be wed at the start of the second part of the *Sarao*, but sees the light and decides to enter the convent as a lay sister (*seglar*). The latter is an important point, because it testifies to her mundane rather than spiritual reasons — women who entered the convent as *seglares* probably did so less out of religious conviction than as a means to escape patriarchy.

The convent has often been described as a space outside of the Symbolic Order (see Greer, *Baroque Tales*) or 'a possible feminine utopia'.[57] Convents were, however, not an entirely feminine space and nuns had male confessors, some of whom, like Teresa de Ávila's, forced them to write down their visions. Vollendorf also sees the convent as a space outside of the narrative, but at the same time describes it as a site of struggle, a paradoxical institution: a feminine space controlled by the male-dominated church (see Vollendorf, *Reclaiming*). Much more can be said about Zayas and the conventual ending of many of her tales, but to assume that she became a bride of Christ just because so many women in her novellas do is to confuse life with literature.

That is not to say that she did *not* end her life in some cloistered community, which was hardly unusual at the time — unfortunately we have no way of checking because most convent records were destroyed in the Civil War (see Montesa and Olivares) — but not because she followed in the footsteps of her heroines or in some way needed to write the *Desengaños* before making up her mind. In this biographical silence, we can only let her work speak for itself. In an interesting last twist, however, for centuries this was not entirely possible, because, as Olivares points out, Zayas's novellas only survived in emasculated form, that is to say, without the prologues and the introduction:

> Los críticos que afirman que *Novelas amorosas y ejemplares* gozó de gran popularidad y que fue un *best-seller* ignoran que el texto que el público leía durante los doscientos años de su máxima popularidad — trescientos años en total — no era el de Zayas, sino una invención de otras manos, de editores masculinos. Al igual que los personajes femeninos, víctimas de abusos físicos y violaciones, representados en las *Novelas*, el texto zayesco sufrió una mutilación, una violación de su cuerpo textual femenino. (*Novelas*, p. 127)
>
> [Critics who claim that the *Novelas amorosas y ejemplares* enjoyed great popularity and that the book was a best-seller gloss over the fact that the text read by the public for two hundred years in which it was at the height of its popularity — out of three hundred years in total — was not by Zayas, but a creation of others, namely male editors. Like the female protagonists in her *Novelas* who suffer physical abuse and rape, Zayas's text underwent a mutilation, a violation of her female textual body.]

What was missing is what many nowadays consider the most appealing and original aspect of her work and without a doubt the main reason for her renewed appreciation since the last decades of the twentieth century: her overtly militant, proto-feminist tone and message.[58] Instead, her novellas survived as macabre tales of gore and violence, a form of pulp fiction.

1.2 A Feminist Phoenix: Fame, Oblivion and Recognition

The trajectory of Zayas's fame is an inverted bell-curve: famous in her time, then slipping down the ladder of literary appreciation in the centuries afterwards — still read in cheap, abridged editions and translated, but no longer praised and admired — and after that, all but forgotten except by the odd Hispanist or voracious readers and erudites like Menéndez Pelayo, until she was gradually rediscovered by literary scholars, especially in the United States, in the last decades of the twentieth century. Scholars often mention the fact that Zayas was a popular novella writer in her day, producing 'instant best-sellers' (Boyer, *Enchantments*, p. xii) that were only rivalled in popularity by Cervantes, Quevedo and Alemán and which retained their appeal for two hundred years. Zayas herself mentions her success in the second part of the *Sarao*, referring to three editions of her book: 'como sucedió en la primera parte de este sarao, que si unos le [*sic*] desestimaron, ciento le aplaudieron, y todos le buscaron y le buscan, y ha gozado de tres impresiones, dos naturales y una hurtada' [as happened with the first part of this *sarao*, where for every handful of people who thought little of the tales, one hundred applauded them, and they all wanted to buy them and still do, and they have been printed three times, two authorized editions and a pirated one] (*Desengaños*, p. 258). Brownlee explains that by exploiting the taste for the sensational she became 'the best-selling author of the Spanish literary scene after Cervantes, Quevedo and Alemán' (Brownlee, *Cultural Labyrinth*, p. 84). The same statement is made by Merrim, who calls her 'the best-selling yet militant feminist Zayas' (Merrim, p. 38) and is echoed by Greer: 'Zayas's novellas were extremely popular in her day' (Greer, *Baroque Tales*, p. 39), although she later concedes that Castillo Solórzano and Pérez de Montalbán were even more popular when judged by the number of editions of their novellas. The likely source for these affirmations is Amezúa's prologue to his edition of her novellas: 'Con excepción de Cervantes, de Alemán y de Quevedo, no hubo acaso ningún otro autor de libros de pasatiempo cuyas obras lograsen tantas ediciones como ella' [With the exception of Cervantes, Alemán and Quevedo, there was perhaps no other author of popular fiction whose works were printed so many times as hers] (Zayas, *Novelas* (1948), p. xxxi). A short article by the Dutch Hispanist Van Praag is also often adduced as evidence of her popularity. 'Después de las novelas ejemplares de Cervantes son las de doña María de Zayas las que lograron mayor difusión en el occidente de Europa' [After the exemplary novellas by Cervantes it's María de Zayas's that were most widely spread in Western Europe].[59] Margarita Nelken suggested that the vogue for Zayas gave rise to a 'school' of feminine novella writers and cites Carvajal as an example. Mariana Carvajal y Saavedra was a widow from Jaén who published a collection of novellas called *Navidades de Madrid y noches entretenidas* in 1663. Long considered inferior to Zayas — Merrim calls the quality of her work 'questionable' (Merrim, p. 83) and I would agree with that — there have recently been attempts to rehabilitate her work.[60]

With regards to Zayas's popularity, it is prudent to make a few remarks. First, Amezúa uses the word 'acaso' [maybe], while Van Praag mentions the number of translations as a measure of her popularity, not Spanish editions. Second, as we have seen at the end of the previous section, Zayas's novellas survived in edited — not to say mutilated — form and lacked the proto-feminism for which she is now best known. Her fame rested more on her ability to shock and titillate than on her feminism. Third, as Rhodes reminds us, the claim she is the best-selling author after Cervantes and Alemán is often repeated, but never substantiated.[61] If Zayas's novellas were printed ten times in the seventeenth century, Pérez de Montalbán's *Sucesos y prodigos de amor* was printed at least nineteen times in the same period — and quickly translated into Italian and French. What should be remembered is that novellas *tout court* were all the rage in the seventeenth century.

Like other works from Golden Age Spain, some of Zayas's novellas were translated into French, English, German and Dutch (often via French).[62] Paul Scarron adapted some of her tales; his story 'La précaution inutile', for instance, is based on 'El prevenido engañado', and his 'Châtiment de la misère' takes 'El castigo de la miseria' as its model. In England, three of Zayas's tales were circulated as works by Cervantes: 'Estragos que causa el vicio', 'El traidor contra su sangre' and 'Al fin se paga todo'. Two further novellas by Zayas — 'La esclava de su amante' and 'La inocencia castigada' — were published anonymously in England.[63] In the eighteenth century Zayas's work was published eleven times in Spanish, leading one critic to suggest 'that her aesthetics had considerable resonance among European readers of pre-Romantic inclination' (Rhodes, *Dressed to Kill*, p. 172).

Between 1847 and 1948 no complete edition of the novellas was available. Greer has linked this decline in popularity to the availability of other women writers, although that probably supposes too much of a gender-consciousness on the part of readers. And even if it were true that women prefer to read women authors, the emergence of a new generation by no means needs to affect the popularity of earlier work; women did not stop reading the Brontë sisters or Jane Austen in the twentieth century because they were able to read books by Virginia Woolf and Iris Murdoch.

The nineteenth century was also the period in which the foundations of Hispanic studies were laid. One of the great early Hispanists was George Ticknor from Boston. In his comprehensive overview of Spanish literature he mentions Zayas and his disparaging comment on one of her stories is often quoted to illustrate his puritanical attitude towards her entire oeuvre. Olivares for example speaks of a 'backlash puritánico' (*Novelas*, p. 127). Goytisolo also refers to the criticism of Ticknor and Pfandl provoked by Zayas's eroticism, while Ordóñez writes that these scholars misread Zayas, labelling her as obscene, immodest, lewd and truculent.[64] To be fair to Ticknor, though, he also calls her a 'sturdy defender of women's rights',[65] and his infamous comment is about one story only and is made in a footnote:

> One of the stories, — *El Prevenido Engañado*, I mean, — though written by 'a lady of the court', is one of the most gross I remember to have read, and was used by Scarron in his 'Précaution Inutile', with little mitigation of its shameless indecency. (Ticknor, p. 166, note 33)

This tale includes an episode in which Fadrique spies on a noblewoman having an affair with an African stable boy and another in which he courts a woman who, as a practical joke, makes him spend the night in bed with her and her 'husband', in reality her cousin Violante, during which he lies as still as a mouse for fear of being found out.

A similarly maligned quotation is one by Pfandl, who at the end of his brief discussion of Zayas poses the question: '¿se puede dar algo más ordinario y grosero, más inestético y repulsivo que una mujer que cuenta historias lascivas, sucias, de inspiración sádica y moralmente corrompidas?' [is it possible to find anything more vulgar and crude, more hideous and repulsive than a woman writing lascivious, obscene, sadistic and morally corrupt stories?].[66] This reads like an outright rejection of her work, but elsewhere he is much more sympathetic, calling her novellas entertaining and interesting: 'Estas novelas no dejan de ser entretenidas y casi siempre son interesantes' [Still, these novellas are entertaining and nearly always interesting] (Pfandl, p. 369). Having said that, his exclamation of '¡Delicioso feminismo!' [Delightful feminism!] (Pfandl, p. xxiv) can easily be construed as condescending.

Before Amezúa's publication of the novellas, Zayas did not attract much academic attention, although there were some early studies, such as the ones by Sylvania Lena, Margarita Nelken and Edwin Place. Right up to the early 1980s scholars were still looking for more biographical information or studying her possible sources. Zayas was generally seen as a *costumbrista* writer whose harrowing tales gave a realistic view of the harsh realities of her era, an approach that has since been abandoned.[67]

As indicated above, an important step in the rediscovery of her novellas was the first complete edition since 1847 by Agustín Amezúa in 1948, with a thorough introduction to her work. Among the criticism published after this edition was an article by Van Praag, who commented on the author's popularity (see above), and by Morby, who discussed the source of one of Zayas's novellas. From the late 1950s, there is also some purely literary interest in the writer. She features in a humorous vignette in Azorín's *Los clásicos redivivos*, in which she is an old spinster who lives alone with her cats. After the scandal caused by 'El prevenido engañado' — the tale that so shocked Ticknor — she has turned her hand to writing newspaper serials (*folletines*).[68] In the early 1960s a selection of her more macabre novellas was translated into English by John Sturrock, who held that the principal attraction of her tales 'lies in their improbable mixture of gothic extravagance and practical feminism' (Zayas, *A Shameful Revenge and Other Stories*, p. v).[69] The same period also saw multiple publications of her novellas in Spanish — Hesse (1965), Rincón (1968) and Martínez del Portal (1973) — and a number of book-length studies on Zayas, both in Spain and abroad.[70]

One of the most influential studies of that period was Juan Goytisolo's essay on Zayas in his *Disidencias*. Although he recognizes the author's conventional approach and her predictable plots, he lauds her description of women as desiring subjects, saying: 'no sólo son deseadas sino que desean, y, si son objeto erótico del varón, éste puede ser igualmente objeto erótico suyo' [not only are they desired, they desire, and if they are the erotic object of a man, the latter can equally become *their* erotic object].[71] In addition, he jettisons the notion of her work as realistic and *costumbrista*. Goytisolo's article opened the door to a new appreciation of Zayas as a feminist and subversive writer. This trend was further developed by scholars like Paul Julian Smith, who drew on French feminist theories and Lacan to analyse Zayas's oeuvre.[72]

From the 1990s onwards, an ever-increasing number of studies on Zayas focused on the feminist aspect of her oeuvre. In 1995 Amy Williams and Judith Whitenack published an important collection of articles on the author.[73] Around the turn of the century, a high-water mark was reached with the publication of three further collections of articles on early modern women-writers including Zayas,[74] a Spanish collection of woman-authored novellas, including work by Zayas,[75] and four monographs: Stephanie Merrim's *Early Modern Women's Writing*, with a chapter on Zayas, Margaret Greer's *María de Zayas Tells Baroque Tales of Love and the Cruelty of Men*, Marina Brownlee's *The Cultural Labyrinth of María de Zayas* and Lisa Vollendorf's *Reclaiming the Body: María de Zayas's Early Modern Feminism*. Merrim, Greer and Vollendorf all write within the feminist tradition, which has arguably become the most prolific field of Zayan studies. Other scholars working in this field are Eavan O'Brien, Yolanda Gamboa, Laura Gorfkle, Yvonne Jehensen, Amy Kaminsky, Teresa Langle de Paz, Mercedes Maroto Camino, Susan Paun de García, Lía Schwarz and many others. Most of the research on Zayas comes from the United States. In Spain, the interest seems to have dried up or else is not reaching a global audience. Olivares's nine-page bibliography at the end of his introduction to the *Novelas* contains more English-language articles or studies devoted to Zayas than Spanish ones; it is a deplorable state of affairs when a Spanish scholar editing the work of a Spanish author for a prestigious Spanish publisher has to rely so heavily on an English-language body of criticism.

Not all criticism and scholarship takes the feminist angle, however. Brownlee's monograph is a good example of a different approach that has evolved in the last few decades, which takes into consideration the literary and cultural background of her oeuvre, highlighting its baroque elements. One of the pioneers in this respect was Marcia Welles, who re-evaluated the *novela cortesana* and Zayas's place within that tradition. Then there appeared a much-referred-to article by Susan Griswold, who views Zayas's feminism as a mere rhetorical game, a literary topos, and nothing more: 'nor can Zayas's work be said, by any stretch of the imagination, to be an intrepid defence of women's rights. At best, feminism and antifeminism are counter-themes which provide an important structuring element to the book' (Griswold, p. 113). She also claims that the focus on Zayas's defence of women's rights detracts from her merits as an artist. Initially, her challenge to treat Zayas as a baroque writer was not taken up by many scholars, but since the 1990s, and especially since the turn of the century, more and more research has been done that highlights this aspect of her oeuvre. As Nancy Lagreca writes: 'Analyses of Zayas's prose have matured from placing undue emphasis on the feminist message and didacticism of the novellas [...] to valuing baroque characteristics of her art, thus recognizing a place for her in the Canon of Spanish Golden Age literature' (Lagreca, p. 567). And in her study on seduction in Zayas, Costa Pascal says that the author 'mérite donc de ne pas être enfermée dans une classification générique ou simpliste où l'écriture d'une femme serait nécessairement celle d'une parole subversive' [therefore deserves not to be confined to a generic or simplistic classification in which the writing of a woman must needs be subversive] (Costa Pascal, p. 219). Scholars who have contributed to this field include Patricia Grieve, Marina Brownlee, Louise Salstad, Nieves Romero Díaz, Nancy Lagreca, Irene Albers, Anne-Gaëlle Costa Pascal and Elizabeth Rhodes.

These two strands of research, the baroque and the feminist, are of course everything but mutually exclusive and some scholars, such as Brownlee, manage to combine both approaches very fruitfully. Indeed, whichever way we look at Zayas's novellas, there is always a need to reconcile her modern-sounding feminism with her baroque outlook and techniques.

1.3 Magic in Zayas: A Brief Overview of the Literature

In the above-mentioned publications, relatively little attention is paid to supernatural or magical elements in Zayas, despite their prevalence, although they have not been entirely absent from the discussion. An assessment typical of earlier scholarship comes from Amezúa, who highlights 'el frecuente y deliberado empleo que hace de lo sobrenatural y maravilloso' [the frequent and deliberate use she makes of the supernatural and the marvellous] (Zayas, *Novelas* (1948), p. xxviii), ascribing it to the fact that the belief in magic was widespread and that she, as a woman, was especially susceptible to such beliefs. Melloni claims that magic was a common literary trope taken seriously by Zayas: 'La Zayas prende terribilmente sul serio [...] la magia e il soprannaturale' [Zayas takes magic and the supernatural terribly seriously] (Melloni, p. 85). The same is stated by Martínez del Portal, while Montesa (*Texto y contexto*) comments that the only thing that sets Zayas's treatment of magic apart is its comparative abundance. Boyer is of the opinion that in Zayas 'magic seems to represent a fashionable and flashy literary device' (Zayas, *Enchantments*, p. xviii). She goes on to say: 'Magic and witchcraft are significant feminist issues in that the persecution of witches was, in fact, a persecution of women' (ibid.). That is a gross oversimplification. Even if in most countries it was predominantly women who were the victims of witchcraft persecutions, to speak of a persecution of women *tout court* ignores the complexities of the matter (for a discussion, see 2.4). Goytisolo too makes mention of Zayas's supernatural episodes, saying they anticipate Gothic literature and are among her best-written passages:

> Los episodios de brujería de *El desengaño amando*, con la viva descripción del gallo con anteojos y la figura humana hecha de cera y, sobre todo, de la posesión carnal de doña Inés gracias a las artes diabólicas de un nigromántico moro, figuran sin duda entre las páginas más logradas de la pluma de la escritora. En ellas (y en algunos pasajes paródicos) el estilo se aligera y desembaraza de los clisés que lastran y dificultan la lectura de sus obras, consiguiendo a momentos una eficacia dramática (o cómica) digna de los mejores escritores de aquel tiempo. (Goytisolo, p. 106)

> [The episodes of witchcraft in 'El desengaño amando', with the vivid description of the blinkered cockerel and the waxen statuette, and above all the carnal possession of Doña Inés by means of the diabolical arts of a Moorish necromancer, are without a doubt amongst the most successful pages written by the author. There (and in some parodic passages) her style becomes lighter and she rids herself of the clichés that encumber her prose and make it difficult to read, pulling off at times a dramatic (or comic) efficiency that is worthy of the best writers of that period.]

None of the studies mentioned so far analyse the magical episodes. A few other critics, however, have offered an insight in Zayas's treatment of the supernatural.

One of the first publications in which the supernatural in Zayas is of central concern is an article by Kenneth Stackhouse called 'Verisimilitude, Magic and the Supernatural in the Novelas of María de Zayas y Sotomayor' from 1978.[76] In his analysis, Zayas wants to provoke *admiratio* by giving a realistic account of supernatural events and her verisimilitude is more moral than psychological, although it is not entirely clear what he means by that. He further points out that 'Zayas's concept of magic and the supernatural, however, lies well within her contemporaries' moral and religious beliefs' (Stackhouse, p. 67). The unreliability of supernatural events is one step removed as the novellas are based on gossip — a word that is associated with the novella itself. And when we go to the source of the story, we often find that it is unreliable. The article further makes the following four claims about magic in Zayas: it is real and efficacious; those who use it pay an extreme penalty; it occurs more abroad than in Spain due to the influence of the Inquisition; and it is temporary, as if by divine dispensation, and powerless when faced with the Virgin. As we shall see, these claims need to be nuanced.

In 1992 Susan Paun de García published an article on magic and power in Zayas in which she refers to Spengler's notion that in the early modern period people saw the world as a struggle between the forces of good and evil and that witch-hunts were a manifestation of this battle.[77] However, in the same period the Inquisition began to perceive witchcraft as a superstition and not as a fact. And while enlightened thinkers as well as members of the Church might doubt the powers of witches and sorcerers, they did not doubt those of the Devil. Her most relevant contribution to the debate, as far as this study is concerned, is the realization that in Zayas there are contrasting attitudes to magic:

> En algunos casos, la magia se ve como impostura, como medio para despojar al crédulo, principalmente para sacarle dinero, y también, a veces como broma pesada. Pero en la mayoría de los casos, la magia se pinta como verdadera. (Paun de García, 'Magia y poder', p. 47)
>
> [In some cases, magic is seen as a fraud, as a means to fleece the credulous, principally to take his or her money, but also sometimes as a prank. But in most cases magic is described as real.]

Judith Whitenack was one of the editors of *The Dynamics of Discourse* and contributed an article on enchantment in one of Zayas's novellas.[78] The article centres on 'La inocencia castigada' in which the protagonist Inés is raped while under a spell and when she is discovered, she ascribes her memories of the ordeal to lewd dreams (*descompuestos sueños*). Whitenack contrasts her experience with that of heroes from romances of chivalry, like Lancelot, who do not remember what happened to them when they were bewitched. She interprets Inés's feelings of guilt vis-à-vis her salacious dreams as manifestations of repressed sexual longing of which she is ashamed. Whitenack adds that Catholic doctrine and popular belief held that men and women have free will, which cannot be overcome, not even by enchantment. As a result, 'someone who is enchanted is in some way susceptible to it, consciously or not' (Whitenack, 'Lo que ha menester', p. 184). Inés must have had deep-seated longings that made her a possible victim of the erotic enchantment, suggesting that Zayas 'may even be casting doubt on the whole notion of erotic enchantment while at the same time making use of the ancient motif' (Whitenack, 'Lo que ha menester', p. 185). We shall return to this novella in 3.4 and to the question of free will in 5.3.

Yvette Cardaillac Hermosilla begins her brief study of magic in Zayas's novellas with the statement that in patriarchal societies women's knowledge was often confined to magical rites and goes on to differentiate between sorcery and diabolical witchcraft.[79] She suggests that Zayas is influenced by the mix of magic and the marvellous in hagiographies and deliberately creates ambiguity. We shall return to the idea of ambiguity throughout this study and to hagiographies in chapter 5.1. Furthermore, she contends that magic is used as a meta-language which imbues the dominant order with ludic or ironic connotations and which constructs a parallel world that questions it:

> La autora acepta el orden establecido, por lo que parece a primera lectura, pero el mundo mágico brota como una protesta implícita, es un germen de revolución social, el temor principal de las autoridades de la época. (Cardaillac Hermosilla, p. 372)
>
> [The author accepts the established order, at least on a first reading; however, the world of magic sprouts up like an implicit form of protest, as a seed of a social revolution, which was the main fear of the authorities of that time.]

Of the Zayan monographs that were published around the turn of the century, Greer's *María de Zayas Tells Baroque Tales of Love and the Cruelty of Men* is the most comprehensive and includes a broad overview of the scholarship up to that point. Her overall approach to Zayas follows Lacan. In the chapter dedicated to the undead and the supernatural she suggests that Zayas reworks magic and death in the defence of women, although it never becomes entirely clear how this works. She also points out that Zayas uses magic more often than Cervantes and introduces supernatural elements in her adaptations of his stories, 'as if she were deliberately reinscribing the tales in the older, magical order' (Greer, *Baroque Tales*, p. 242). She refers to Adorno's analysis of the decline of social systems, which causes paranoia and the search for irrational causes such as astrology or the occult, explaining early modern witch-hunts as an attempt to 'artificially reconstruct a social order that by that time had become obsolete'.[80] We shall return to the early modern 'witch-craze' in 2.4 and see that the situation is more complex than an attempt to reconstruct an obsolete social order. According to Greer, Zayas's supernatural and uncanny episodes are described in detail, setting them apart from the rest of the tales, which are written in an idealistic style. Furthermore, magic is predominantly perpetrated by foreigners and, unusually for such tales, by men: in Greer's words Zayas 'cross-dresses' magic (Greer, *Baroque Tales*, p. 250), projecting its negative power onto a demonized 'other'. The rest of Greer's chapter deals primarily with death and the undead and with women who speak through their martyred bodies. The macabre attention to gory detail and the description of incorruptible, beautiful female cadavers is described as 'a fundamentally masochistic fantasy' (Greer, *Baroque Tales*, p. 281). We shall discuss incorrupt cadavers in chapter 5.2.

Brownlee published *The Cultural Labyrinth of María de Zayas* the same year Greer published *her* monograph. Brownlee addresses the wider cultural context of Zayas, and in particular what she calls her baroque 'polysemy'. She dedicates a chapter to magic, mass printing and mass audience and stresses the shift from the collective and universal to the private. The private is made public, making the reader a kind of voyeur. Zayas is 'committed to exploring the new mass market of private readers with a taste for the sensational, the erotic, and the forbidden' (Brownlee, *Cultural Labyrinth*, p. 77). The author is praised for her knack for reading the market and exploiting its potential, which Brownlee links to the emerging popular press. Brownlee also discusses what she calls the Renaissance 'obsession' with magic and the determination to understand science as a rational discipline as well as 'the seventeenth century's relentless fascination with the epistemology of the supernatural, ranging all the way from apparitions of the Virgin and her miraculous powers, to false ghosts' (Brownlee, *Cultural Labyrinth*, p. 94). She relates this fascination to the topos of appearance versus reality. Furthermore, she mentions the distinction between elite (*culto*) and popular (*vulgo*) readers. She disagrees with Maravall, who sees all baroque literature as kitsch.[81] Instead, she views Zayas's novellas as appealing to various audiences by attracting one kind with her melodramatic tales and another by the *admiratio* caused by the aesthetically pleasing way in which she recounts her complex stories:

> The *Novelas* were clearly designed to have this type of mass appeal, but that is only one aspect of Zayas's literary project. To reduce her twenty tales to 'pretentious and shallow' writing bereft of artistic quality is to distort the polysemy they project. (Brownlee, *Cultural Labyrinth*, p. 89)

In the rest of the chapter, Brownlee analyses a number of novellas that contain magical episodes: 'El jardín engañoso', 'El desengaño amando', 'La inocencia castigada', 'El verdugo de su esposa' and 'La perseguida triunfante'. In these tales Zayas uses the supernatural — magic, necromancy and hagiography — to catch a glimpse of the forbidden, the sensational and the pornographic. All these novellas will be discussed at length in this study.[82]

★ ★ ★ ★ ★

Since the gradual rediscovery and reappreciation of Zayas's oeuvre much has been written about her pro-woman argument, but there is also an increasing body of scholarly work devoted to the baroque aspects of her novellas. However, one of the more salient features of her tales — her deployment of the supernatural — remains relatively under-studied. As we have seen, a number of intelligent and pertinent analyses exist, but none analyses the epistemological shift affecting the belief in the supernatural or discusses the various subcategories of the supernatural. Some studies point to the varied treatment of magic but do not offer a close reading of the novellas that contain spells and acts of sorcery, which shows the extent to which the stories are imbued with indeterminacy. Furthermore, all the studies I have come across take the Devil's act of generosity in one of the novellas at face value and none, as far as I can see, have commented on Zayas's controversial position on free will and its subjugation to the stars. The miraculous is dealt with by some critics, but more often linked to the pornographic and masochistic than to the fantastic. All these questions will be addressed in the remainder of this study, but before turning to the novellas it is crucial to have an understanding of exactly how the supernatural was conceived in seventeenth-century Spain, how it was experienced and dealt with by the authorities, and what role it played in the literature of the period.

Notes to Chapter 1

1. Alonso de Castillo Solórzano, *La Garduña de Sevilla y anzuelo de las bolsas*, ed. by Federico Ruiz Morcuende (Madrid: Ediciones de La Lectura, 1922), pp. 94–95.
2. See Nancy Lagreca, 'Evil Women and Feminist Sentiment: Baroque Contradictions in María de Zayas's "El prevenido engañado" and "Estragos que causa el vicio"', *Revista Canadiense de Estudios Hispánicos*, 28.3 (Spring 2004), 565–82.
3. 'Throughout Spain, women could sign contracts, but their signatures were often discounted' (Lisa Vollendorf, 'Good Sex, Bad Sex: Women and Intimacy in Early Modern Spain', *Hispania*,

87.1 (2004), 1–12 (p. 3). The situation was different for widows, who could act on their own behalf in legal matters. Nevertheless, it seems that women participated actively in legal transactions in cities like Seville; see Mary Elizabeth Perry, *Gender and Disorder in Early Modern Seville* (Princeton, NJ: Princeton University Press, 1990).
4. See Salvador Montesa Peydro, *Texto y contexto en la narrativa de María de Zayas* (Madrid: Dirección General de la Juventud y Promoción Sociocultural, 1979).
5. For the English titles of Zayas's novellas, see the Introduction.
6. Felipe Ximénez de Sandoval, 'Doña María de Zayas y Sotomayor, una escritora fantasma', in *Varia historia de ilustres mujeres* (Madrid: Epesa, 1949), pp. 207–15.
7. Quoted in Manuel Serrano y Sanz, *Apuntes para una biblioteca de escritoras españolas* (Madrid: Sucesores de Rivadeneyra, 1903), p. 584. See also Montesa, *Texto y contexto*, p. 21; and Isabel Barbeito Carneiro, *Mujeres y literatura del siglo de oro: espacios profanos y espacios conventuales* (Madrid: Safekat, 2007), p. 157.
8. See Yolanda Gamboa, *Cartografía social en la narrativa de María de Zayas* (Madrid: Biblioteca Nueva, 2009). In his introduction to the *Honesto y entretenido sarao*, Olivares notes that Kenneth Brown has equally suggested that the name 'çayas', which means 'silversmith', is Judaeo-Spanish, leading him to postulate that Zayas might have had Converso ancestry. See Olivares (ed.), *Honesto y entretenido sarao*, p. lxxx, note 121.
9. Alicia Redondo Goicoechea, 'La retórica del yo-mujer en tres escritoras españolas: Teresa de Cartagena, Teresa de Jesús y María de Zayas', in *Compás de letras. Monografías de literatura española. En torno al yo*, 1 (1992), pp. 49–63.
10. The same assumption is made by José Hesse, who edited the *Novelas (La burlada Aminta y venganza del honor; El prevenido engañado)* (Madrid: Taurus, 1965); Eduardo Rincón, editor of the *Novelas ejemplares y amorosas o Decameron español* (Madrid: Alianza, 1968) and McGrath, who wrote the introduction to *La traición en la amistad* (Newark, DE: European Masterpieces, 2007).
11. In his introduction to the *Novelas* and again in the introduction to the *Honesto y entretenido sarao* he refers to Amezúa's hypothesis as 'poco sostenible' [difficult to maintain] (*Honesto y entretenido sarao*, p. lxxix) because it is based on the assertion that the narrator of 'Al fin se paga todo', which is set in Valladolid, knows the characters involved in the story.
12. Jean Canavaggio, *Cervantes*, trans. by J. R. Jones (New York: Norton, 1986), p. 244.
13. The standard word for priest in Italian is 'prete', not 'prevete'. Ferdinando Galiani, *Vocabulario delle parole del dialetto napoletano, che piu' si scostano dal dialetto toscano* (Naples: Giuseppe-Maria Porcelli, 1789); see <https://archive.org/details/vocabolariodellootscgoog/page/n5>.
14. See for instance Montesa; Olivares in his introduction to the *Novelas*; and Eavan O'Brien, *Women in the Prose of María de Zayas* (Woodbridge: Tamesis, 2010).
15. See Sandra Foa, *Feminismo y forma narrativa: estudio del tema y las técnicas de María de Zayas y Sotomayor* (Valencia: Albatros, 1979).
16. See Josephine Donovan, 'Women and the Framed Novella: A Tradition of Their Own', *Signs*, 22.4 (1997), 947–80 and María Goyri de Menéndez Pidal, *La difunta pleiteada: estudio de literatura comparativa* (Madrid: Librería General de Victoriano Suárez, 1909). Donovan also appears to suggest that Zayas adapted at least one story from Christine de Pisan, which is highly unlikely. See also a recent article by Henry Cohen, 'The Reworking and Incorporation of Two of Marguerite de Navarre's "Heptaméron" *Nouvelles* by María de Zayas y Sotomayor in Her *Novela* "Tarde llega el desengaño"', *Comparative Literature Studies*, 56.1 (2019), 104–32.
17. In addition to Barbeito Carneiro and Foa we could mention Brownlee, O'Brien, Vollendorf and Merrim, who writes that 'María de Zayas reads Marguerite de Navarre with a critical eye' (Merrim, p. xliv). I have not been able to locate the original study by Edwin Place, *María de Zayas: An Outstanding Woman Short-Story Writer of Seventeenth-Century Spain*, University of Colorado Studies, 13 (Boulder: University of Colorado, 1923).
18. In the Cátedra edition the text reads 'estando ausente *del* excelentísimo señor conde de Lemos [...] *de* mi señora, su esposa', which I assume to be an error. In *Honesto y entretenido sarao* (2017) this error has been amended to read as quoted.
19. The same is suggested by Anne-Gaëlle Costa Pascal, who says that 'elle était très liée à la famille du neuvième comte de Lemos' [she had very close ties to the family of the 9th Count of Lemos].

Anne-Gaëlle Costa Pascal, *María de Zayas, une écriture féminine dans l'Espagne du Siècle d'Or: une poétique de la séduction* (Paris: L'Harmattan, 2007), p. 24.
20. María de Zayas, *Novelas amorosas y ejemplares* (Madrid: Aldus, 1948), p. xi.
21. Paun de García, in 'Zayas as Writer: Hell hath no fury', in *María de Zayas: The Dynamics of Discourse* (London: Associated University Presses, 1995), pp. 40–51, is a little more cautious and writes that we do not know which *academia* she frequented, but since Pérez de Montalbán and Castillo Solórzano mention her success in *academias* of Madrid, Mendoza's is a good candidate. Pérez-Erdélyi, in *La pícara y la dama: la imagen de las mujeres en las novelas picaresco-cortesanas de María de Zayas y Sotomayor y Alonso de Castillo Solórzano* (Miami: Ediciones Universal, 1979), claims that Zayas formed part of Medrano's *academia* of from 1617 to 1622 and Mendoza's from 1623 to 1637. See also Olivares's introduction to the *Novelas* and the *Honesto y entretenido sarao*.
22. For this section, see Amezúa's introduction to the *Novelas* (1948) and Olivares's introduction to the *Honesto y entretenido sarao*.
23. See José Antonio Álvarez y Baeza, 'María de Zayas y Sotomayor (Doña)', in *Hijos de Madrid ilustres en santidad, dignidades, armas, ciencias y artes*, 4 vols (Madrid: Cano, 1791, repr. Madrid: Atlas, 1973), IV, 48–49.
24. See María Martínez del Portal's introduction to the *Novelas completas* (Barcelona: Bruguera, 1973). Olivares says this is 'muy probable' (*Honesto y entretenido sarao*, p. xxvii).
25. See Olivares's introduction to the *Novelas*, p. 157, note 8.
26. See Teresa Soufas, *Women's Acts: Plays by Women dramatists of Spain's Golden Age* (Lexington: University Press of Kentucky, 1997). To this list of women dramatists could be added Sor Marcela de San Félix — Lope de Vega's daughter — and Sor Juana Inés de la Cruz as well as the more obscure Bernarda Ferreira de la Cerda, Sor Maria do Ceo, and Juana Teodora de Sousa. See Alex Samson, 'Distinct Dramatists? Female Dramatists in Golden Age Spain', in *A Companion to Spanish women's Studies* (Woodbridge: Tamesis, 2011), pp. 157–72. McGrath, who published Zayas's only extant play (see note 10), gives the same names as well as that of Isabel Rebeca Correa.
27. For more analysis of Zayas's play, see José Antonio Rodríguez Garrido, 'El ingenio en la mujer: "La traición en la amistad" de María de Zayas entre Lope de Vega y Huarte de San Juan', *Bulletin of the Comediantes*, 49.2 (1997), 357–73; Robert Bayliss, 'Feminism and María de Zayas's Exemplary Comedy, "La traición en la amistad"', *Hispanic Review*, 76.1 (2008), 1–17; Valerie Hegstrom, 'The Fallacy of False Dichotomy in María de Zayas's "La Traición en la amistad"', *Bulletin of the Comediantes*, 46.1 (1994), 59–70; Nieves Romero Díaz, 'En los límites de la representación: la traición de María de Zayas', *Revista Canadiense de Estudios Hispánicos*, 26.3 (2002), 475–92; Mercedes Maroto Camino, 'María de Zayas and Ana Caro: The Space of Women's Solidarity in the Spanish Golden Age', *Hispanic Review*, 67 (1999), 1–16.
28. Catherine Larson, 'Gender, Reading, and Intertextuality: Don Juan's Legacy in María de Zayas's *La traición en la amistad*', *INTI: Revista de Literatura Hispánica*, 40–41 (1994), p. 129.
29. There has been some debate about the date of composition. For a discussion see McGrath's introduction and above all Rodríguez Garrido ('El ingenio en la mujer').
30. Rodríguez Garrido furthermore points out that by the time the play was performed, Zayas had probably already written 'El juez de su causa', which deals with the same topic as Lope de Vega's *Las fortunas de Diana*, one of his novellas for Marcia Leonarda. In 1619, he had also written a play called *El juez de su causa*, although it was not published until 1647.
31. See the introduction to *Los empeños de una casa*, ed. by García Valdés (Madrid: Cátedra, 2010), p. 53.
32. Marina Brownlee, 'Genealogies in Crisis: María de Zayas in Seventeenth-Century Spain', in *Generation and Degeneration: Tropes of Reproduction in Literature and History from Antiquity through Early Modern Europe* (Durham, NC: Duke University Press, 2001), p. 192.
33. Marcia Welles sees Flora's sexuality as the result of her diabolical, dualistic nature, a facet of the Terrible Mother. See Marcia Welles, 'María de Zayas and her *novella cortesana*: A Re-Evaluation', *Bulletin of Hispanic Studies*, 55 (1978), 301–10.
34. Lisa Vollendorf, *Reclaiming the Body: María de Zayas's Early Modern Feminism*, North Carolina Studies in the Romance Languages and Literatures (Chapel Hill: University of North Carolina, 2001), p. 186.

35. Lisa Vollendorf, 'The Future of Early Modern Women's Studies: The Case of Same-Sex Friendship and Desire in Zayas and Carvajal', *Arizona Journal of Hispanic Cultural Studies*, 4 (2000), 265–84 (p. 270).
36. Lope de Vega, *El laurel de Apolo* (London: Leclere y Compañía, 1824), ll. 184–85.
37. See Nadia Avendaño, 'La violencia masculina en los "Desengaños amorosos" de María de Zayas', *The South Carolina Modern Language Review*, 5 (2006), 38–53.
38. Hélène Cixous, 'The Laugh of the Medusa', *Signs*, 1.4 (Summer 1976), 875–93 (p. 888). See also Judith Butler, *Gender Trouble* (London: Routledge, 1990). For more on Judith Butler and Zayas, see Deanna Mihaly, 'Socially Constructed/Essentially Other: Servants and Slaves in María de Zayas' *Desengaños amorosos*', *Romance Languages Annual*, 10.2 (1999), 719–25.
39. For more discussion on this narrative strategy, see Brownlee (*Cultural Labyrinth*).
40. See Juan Luis Alborg, 'La novela corta: Zayas, Céspedes, Lozano', in *Historia de la literatura española*, II (Madrid: Gredos, 1970), pp. 498–504.
41. In her introduction to her edition of the novellas, María Martínez del Portal ascribes the latter comment wrongly to Amezúa instead of Rincón.
42. See Paun de García, 'Zayas as Writer: Hell hath no fury'; José M. Roca Franquesa, 'Ideología feminista en doña María de Zayas', *Revista de la Facultad de Filología*, 26 (1976), 293–311; Salvador Montesa Peydro, 'Significado de la estructura barroca de la novelas de Doña María de Zayas y Sotomayor', *Analecta malacitana*, 3 (1980); and Julia Farmer, 'Inscribing Victory: Rivalry and Mise en Abyme in María de Zayas's Novella Collections', *MLN*, 126.2 (2011), 245–58.
43. Quoted in Kenneth Brown, 'María de Zayas y Sotomayor: escribiendo poesía en Barcelona en época de guerra (1643)' *Dicenda. Cuadernos de filología hispánica*, 11 (1993), 355–60.
44. The imagined voyage to the moon appears to have been a fairly common theme in the seventeenth century. Francis Godwin wrote *The Man in the Moone* in the 1620s and Cyrano de Bergerac his *Histoire comique des États et Empires de la Lune* around 1650.
45. See Thomas Laqueur, *Making Sex: Body and Gender from the Greeks to Freud* (Cambridge, MA: Harvard University Press, 1990).
46. Juan Huarte de San Juan, *Examen de ingenios*, in *Electroneurobiología* 3.2 (1996), 1–322 (p. 25).
47. According to Mariscal (*Contradictory Subjects*), Teresa de Ávila was also referred to as a *mujer varonil*. For an elaborate study of the *mujer varonil*, see Melveena McKendrick, *Woman and Society in the Spanish Drama of the Golden Age: A Study of the Mujer Varonil* (Cambridge: Cambridge University Press, 1974).
48. Juan Pérez de Montalbán, *Para todos. Exemplos morales, humanos y divinos*, fol. 353^v.
49. See Jaime Moll, 'La primera edición de las "Novelas amorosas" de María de Zayas y Sotomayor', *Dicenda*, 1 (1982), 177–79.
50. In his introduction to the *Honesto y entretenido sarao* Olivares suggests that Escuer changed the date on both *licencias* to make the novellas look more recent. His reasoning is that if Mendieta issued his licence on 4 June 1626 (not 1636, when he was no longer in office), then Valdivieso must have given his out on 2 June 1626 (two days earlier), not 2 June 1636 (ten years later).
51. This is what Olivares suggests in his introduction to the *Novelas*. See also Don W. Cruickshank, 'Literature and the Book Trade in Golden Age Spain', *The Modern Language Review*, 73.3 (1978), 799–824. Willis suggests Zayas called her tales 'maravillas' instead of 'novelas' to avoid the ban, which forbade the publication of *novelas* and *comedias*, but that is unlikely and even if she did, the ruse was unsuccessful. See Angela Willis, 'Fleeing the Model Home: María de Zayas Rewrites the Rules of Feminine Sensuality and "Honra" in the Boccaccesca "Novela Cortesana"', *Letras Femeninas*, 35.2 (Winter 2009), 65–89.
52. See María Dolores López-Díaz, 'Un novelista poco conocido: José Camerino y sus *Novelas amorosas*', *Revista de filología*, 8 (1992), 291–98; and José María Roca Franquesa, '"Aventurarse perdiendo" (Novela de Doña María de Zayas y Sotomayor)', in *Homenaje al Excmo. Sr. Dr. D. Emilio Alarcos García*, 2 vols (Valladolid: Sever-Cuesta, 1965), II, 401–10.
53. Eavan O'Brien, 'Personalizing the Political: The Habsburg Empire of María de Zayas's "Desengaños amorosos"', *Bulletin of Hispanic Studies*, 88.3 (2011), 289–305 (p. 290).
54. See Lou Charnon-Deutsch, 'The Sexual Economy in the Narratives of María de Zayas', in *María de Zayas: The Dynamics of Discourse* (London: Associated University Presses, 1995), pp. 117–32.

55. The inconsistencies appear to have been rectified in Yllera's edition, where the comment is made after the fourth *desengaño*.
56. See Felipe Maldonado, 'Otra María de Zayas... y van cuatro', *Estafeta literaria*, 501 (October 1972), 10–13.
57. Eavan O'Brien, 'Female Friendship Extolled: Exploring the Enduring Appeal of María de Zayas's Novellas', *Romance Studies*, 26.1 (2008), 43–59 (p. 50). See also Nina Cox-Davies, 'Re-Framing Discourse: Women Before their Public in María de Zayas', *Hispanic Review*, 71.3 (2003), 325–44.
58. Simerka says she finds the prefix 'proto' in 'proto-feminism' condescending, even though she uses it herself at various points in her article. See Barbara Simerka, 'Feminist Epistemology and Premodern Patriarchy, East and West: "The Kagero Diary" by Michitsuna's Mother and the Novellas of María de Zayas', *Letras Femininas*, 35.1 (Summer 2009), 149–67.
59. J. A. van Praag, 'Sobre las novelas de María de Zayas', *Clavileño* 15 (1952), 42–43 (p. 43).
60. Mariana Carvajal y Saavedra, *Navidades de Madrid y noches entretenidas*, ed. by Dámaso Chicharro (Jaén: Instituto de Estudios Giennenses, 2005). For recent articles on her, see Lisa Vollendorf, 'The Future of Early Modern Women's Studies'; Rosa Navarro Durán, 'La "rara" belleza de las damas en las novelas de María de Zayas y Mariana de Carvajal', *Belleza escrita en femenino*, ed. by Àngels Carabí and Marta Segarra (Barcelona: Universitat de Barcelona, 1998), pp. 79–86; and Eavan O'Brien, 'Verbalizing the Visual: María de Zayas, Mariana de Carvajal, and the Frame-Narrative Device', *Journal of Early Modern Cultural Studies*, 12.3 (2012), 116–41.
61. See Elizabeth Rhodes, *Dressed to Kill: Death and Meaning in Zayas's 'Desengaños'* (Toronto: University of Toronto Press, 2011).
62. One Dutch collection in the Koninklijke Bibliotheek in The Hague is called *De verliefde en niet minder treurige als ook vermakelyke gevallen* [The lover and other no less sad and also amusing affairs] (Amsterdam: Bouman, 1731), which comprises six novellas by Zayas plus two tales that are wrongly attributed to her, namely 'De gelukkige schilder' [The happy painter] and 'De baetzugtige vrouw' [The selfish woman]. Van Praag says the Dutch versions appear to have been translated from French — even though the title page claims they have been translated from Spanish by 'een voornaem liefhebber' [an important admirer] — and that compared to Zayas, they are 'mucho más lúbricas' [much more obscene] (Van Praag, p. 43).
63. The first was published as *A Letter from Madrid* in weekly supplements in *The British Mercury* in 1712–13, while the second was adapted in the second volume of Aubin's *The Illustrious French Lovers*, itself a translation of *Les illustres françaises* by Charles Challes. See Elizabeth Rhodes, *Dressed to Kill*, p. 171.
64. See Elizabeth Ordóñez, 'Woman and Her Text in the Works of María de Zayas and Ana Caro', *Revista de estudios hispánicos*, 19.1 (1985), 3–15. In her introduction Boyer misquotes Ticknor, writing: 'Although written by a lady of the court, the work is the filthiest and most immodest that I have ever read'. She does not reference the quotation and I suspect she translated it from Amezúa's Spanish rendition back to English without consulting the original, making him sound harsher in his condemnation ('gross' becomes 'filthy and immodest').
65. George Ticknor, *History of Spanish Literature*, 4th edn, 3 vols (Boston, MA: Houghton, Mifflin and Company, 1863), III, 166.
66. Ludwig Pfandl, *Historia de la literatura nacional española en la edad de oro*, trans. by Jorge Rubió Balaguer (Barcelona: Sucesores de Juan Gili, 1933), p. 370.
67. See Sylvania Lena, 'Doña María de Zayas y Sotomayor: A Contribution to the Study of her Works', *Romantic Review*, 14 (1923), 193–232; Margarita Nelken, 'La novela, el teatro y la licencia de la pluma', in *Las escritoras españolas* (Barcelona: Labor, 1930; repr. Madrid: horas y HORAS, 2011), pp. 151–65, which has a section called 'Las novelas amorosas y ejemplares de María de Zayas y la escuela cínica'; Edwin Morby, 'The *Difunta pleiteada* Theme in María de Zayas', *Hispanic Review*, 16 (1948), 238–42; Ricardo Senabre Sempere, 'La fuente de una novela de Doña María de Zayas', *Revista de filología española*, 46 (1963), 163–72.
68. Azorín, *Los clásicos redivivos* (Madrid: Espasa-Calpe, 1958).
69. This is more nuanced than Kenneth Stackhouse suggests when he writes that Zayas's tales have been rejected on account of their superstition, an attitude that 'persists into the twentieth

century with her English translator's dismissal of her tales as mere "Gothic extravaganza"'; Kenneth Stackhouse, 'Verisimilitude, Magic, and the Supernatural in the *Novelas* of María de Zayas y Sotomayor, *Hispanófila*, 62 (1978), 65–76 (p. 67).

70. In Spain, Montesa Peydro (*Texto y contexto*) and Irma Vasileski, *María de Zayas y Sotomayor: su época y su obra* (New York: Plaza Mayor, 1972); in Italy, Foa (*Feminismo y forma narrativa*) and Alessandra Melloni, *Il sistema narrativo di María de Zayas* (Turin: Quaderni Ibero-Americani, 1976); and in Germany, Hans Felten, *Maria de Zayas y Sotomayor. Zum Zusammenhang zwischen moralistischen Texten und Novellenliteratur* (Frankfurt: Klostermann, 1978).
71. Juan Goytisolo, 'El mundo erótico de María de Zayas', in *Disidencias* (Barcelona: Seix Barral, 1977), p. 97.
72. Paul Julian Smith, 'Writing Women in Golden Age Spain: Saint Teresa and María de Zayas', *MLN*, 102.2 (1987), 220–40; *Writing in the Margin: Spanish Literature of the Golden Age* (Oxford: Clarendon Press, 1988) and *The Body Hispanic* (1989).
73. Amy Williamsen and Judith Whitenack (eds), *María de Zayas: The Dynamics of Discourse* (London: Associated University Presses, 1995).
74. Monika Bosse, Barbara Potthast and André Stoll (eds), *La creatividad femenina en el mundo barroco: María de Zayas — Isabel Rebeca Correa — Sor Juana Inés de la Cruz*, 2 vols (Kassel: Reichenberger, 1999); Anita Stoll and Dawn Smith (eds), *Gender, Identity, and Representation in Spain's Golden Age* (London: Associated University Presses, 2000); and Gwyn Campbell and Judith Whitenack (eds), *Zayas and Her Sisters*, II: *Essays on Novelas by 17th-Century Spanish Women* (New York: Global Publications Binghamton University, 2001).
75. Evangelina Rodríguez Cuadros and Marta Haro Cortés (eds), *Entre la rueca y la pluma: novela de mujeres en el Barroco* (Madrid: Biblioteca Nueva, 1999).
76. Kenneth Stackhouse, 'Verisimilitude, Magic, and the Supernatural'.
77. Susan Paun de García, 'Magia y poder en María de Zayas', *Cuadernos de ALDEEU*, 8 (1992), 43–54.
78. Judith Whitenack, '"Lo que ha menester": Erotic Enchantment in "La inocencia castigada"', in *María de Zayas: The Dynamics of Discourse*, ed. by Amy Williamsen and Judith Whitenack (London: Associated University Presses, 1995), pp. 170–91.
79. Yvette Cardaillac Hermosilla, 'La magia en las novelas de María de Zayas', in *La creatividad femenina en el mundo barroco hispánico: María de Zayas — Isabel Rebeca Correa — Sor Juana Inés de la Cruz*, 2 vols (Kassel: Reichenberger, 1999), I, 354.
80. Theodor Adorno, *The Stars Down To Earth and Other Essays on the Irrational in Culture* (London: Routledge, 1994), p. 165.
81. In his seminal study Maravall defines kitsch as 'una cultura vulgar, caracterizada por el establecimiento de tipos, con repetición standardizada de géneros, presentando una tendencia al conservadurismo social respondiendo a un consumo manipulado' [a people's culture characterized by the creation of types, with standardized repetition of genres, presenting a tendency towards social conservatism and responding to manipulated consumption] (José Antonio Maravall, *La cultura del Barroco* (Barcelona: Ariel, 1975), p. 184).
82. Ingrid Matos-Nin also published a monograph and a number of articles on the supernatural in Zayas. See bibliography.

CHAPTER 2

Witches and Watermelons: The Supernatural in Early Modern Spain

> We do therefore hereby signify to all in general (and to the surviving sufferers in special) our deep sense of, and sorrow for, our errors, in acting on such evidence to the condemning of any person; and do hereby declare, that we justly fear that we were sadly deluded and mistaken; for which we are much disquieted and distressed in our minds; and do therefore humbly beg forgiveness. (From the recantation of the Salem village jurors, 1693)[1]

In one of Zayas's novellas a witch called Lucrecia hexes her lover by putting blinkers on a cockerel and chaining it up in the attic. In another, a Muslim necromancer fashions an effigy of a married woman so that a man besotted with her can lure her to his bed and have his wicked way with her. In yet another tale, an unhappily married woman who is the victim of domestic abuse seeks out a sorceress and is told to collect the hair and teeth from a corpse for a spell. When she is at a roadside chapel to do this, her brother receives a telepathic warning and comes to her rescue. There is also the story of a would-be adulterer on his way to a rendezvous who is addressed by a man swinging from a gallows who offers to go in his stead. The hanged man is murdered, for a second time it would appear (but see 5.1), by the jealous husband and returns from the dead to explain what happened. Elsewhere a lover sees the corpse of his beloved, who has been killed by her brother, bathed in an unnatural light, the blood still flowing from her wounds even though she has been dead for nine hours. Her blood is said to be flowing still a year later when she is relocated to a new tomb. The *Novelas amorosas* and *Desengaños amorosos* are replete with such marvellous and miraculous episodes, their intent being to shock and amaze the reader.

When Zayas describes supernatural events in her novellas, she does so in an age when the thaumaturgical order was being reassessed. This process was part of a larger epistemological shift that took place in the seventeenth century, a period that is sometimes hailed as the birth of the clockwork universe. This change did not take place overnight nor did it affect all parts of society in equal measure. Nevertheless, it is clear that claims and explanations regarding supernatural events that were commonly accepted in the sixteenth century were no longer taken seriously one hundred or so years later, at least not by the cultured elite:

> The change may be best expressed by saying that in the sixteenth century the claims of a would-be prophet would always be seriously investigated, even if ultimately exposed as groundless, but by the eighteenth century the majority of educated men concurred in dismissing them *a priori* as inherently ridiculous.[2]

The seventeenth century also saw large-scale witch-hunts in many parts of Europe in which tens of thousands of women were burnt at the stake. Spain was spared the worst of the excesses, in large part due to the sceptical attitude of the Inquisition; witchcraft was believed to be possible in theory, but by and large the Holy Office was reluctant to accept the evidence with which it was presented in individual cases. With regards to sorcery, which is not quite the same as witchcraft (as we shall see below), inquisitors often accused the practitioners of fraud, but showed themselves lenient in their sentences.

Studying the supernatural episodes in Zayas requires understanding what the supernatural meant for the author and her readers and adopting what anthropologists call an emic — as opposed to an etic — perspective.[3] Sorcery, deals with the Devil, miracles, disembodied voices and pristine cadavers play an important part in Zayas's oeuvre, but such events are far from absent from the works of her contemporaries, which is why it pays to have a brief glance at how magic and witchcraft are dealt with in Golden Age literature before analysing her novellas. But let us start by asking ourselves what we talk about when we talk about the supernatural.

2.1 The Natural, Preternatural and Supernatural Orders

So far, I have used the word 'supernatural' as if its definition were self-evident and unproblematic. Supernatural episodes in Zayas are stories involving sorcery, diabolical pacts, miracles, discarnate voices, and so forth. These are all events or manifestations that, in the words of the *Oxford English Dictionary*, are 'attributed to some force beyond scientific understanding or the laws of nature'. *Merriam Webster*'s definition equally stresses the transcendental origin of supernatural events, but fails to distinguish between God and the Devil as their ultimate source, defining them as 'being, having reference to, or proceeding from God or a god, demigod, spirit, or infernal being'.

To the educated early modern mind, however, there was a crucial difference between the supernatural *sensu lato* (in the broad sense of the word) and the supernatural *sensu stricto* (in the narrow sense of the word), the latter being the exclusive domain of God, who alone can contravene the laws of Creation. Wedged in between the supernatural and the natural order we find the preternatural order. This is strictly speaking an extension of the natural order and subject to the same laws, except that it contains the *extra*-ordinary — in the etymological sense of the word — and everything that causes wonder and amazement. Amongst other things, the preternatural comprises monsters, freaks and other outlandish creatures and phenomena, and as such it corresponds to the period's vivid interest in teratology. The preternatural order is also called the marvellous, the amazing or the prodigious order, and preternatural operations are known as marvels or wonders (*mira*). It is the theatre of operations par excellence of the Devil, who can perform prodigious feats that may appear to exceed the bounds set by nature but in fact never do. As the theologian Wolleb put it: 'Mali Angeli mira faciunt, sed miracula facere nequeunt. Miracula enim sunt opera, omnem creaturarum potentiam superantia' [Evil Angels can do wonders, but not work miracles, for miracles are works exceeding all powers of creatures].[4] Being a fallen angel who has been around since before the Creation, the Devil has awesome powers and a vast knowledge of the workings of the universe. By moving objects at astonishing speeds, for example, he can trick us into believing something has vanished altogether, even though this is strictly speaking impossible; and by stirring a corpse, he can make us believe it has been brought back to life. But that would require breaking the laws of nature, and this can only happen in the miraculous order, also called the order of grace, whose operations are known as miracles (*miracula*), which can only be performed by or through God; this is the supernatural *sensu stricto*.[5] The Spanish friar Castañega, who wrote a treatise on superstition and witchcraft, warns his readers that:

> nunca jamás hemos de decir que sea milagro cosa que naturalmente, aunque por virtudes a nosotros ocultas, se pueda producir, porque el milagro es obra que la virtud natural no tiene fuerzas para obrarla.[6]

> [we should never call something a miracle that can occur naturally, albeit through powers hidden from us, because a miracle is something that natural powers lack the virtue to accomplish.]

As a truly baroque agent of deception and illusion, the Devil makes us believe he can carry out miraculous deeds, when all he can do is create marvels. Moreover, he makes people believe that he can be summoned to do their will, with the result that the deluded victim is twice deceived, first by thinking that he or she can summon and command the Devil, and second by taking his preternatural legerdemain to be a miracle.

This division into a natural, preternatural and supernatural order goes back to St Thomas Aquinas.[7] Amongst others it is referred to by Pedro Ciruelo, who, like Castañega, wrote a treatise on superstition:

> *Cualquier cosa que nuevo se hace en el mundo, tiene causa o causas de donde procede. Estas son en tres maneras, y no puede haber otras fuera de ellas: porque procede de causas naturales que tienen virtud para hacerla, o procede de Dios que milagrosamente obra sobre curso natural, o procede de los ángeles, buenos o malos, que se juntan con las causas naturales.*[8]

> [*Anything new that is done in the world has a cause, or causes, from which it stems*. There are three ways something can happen, and there cannot be any other: because it either stems from natural causes that have the virtue to do so, or it comes from God, who miraculously operates above the natural course of things, or it stems from good or bad angels who ally themselves with natural causes.]

In his *relectio* on magic pronounced in Salamanca in 1540, the friar Francisco de Vitoria says that most marvels achieved by magi are 'falsas, fingidas y creídas sólo por la frivolidad de la gente' [false, feigned and believed only because people are frivolous].[9] But, citing Biblical evidence, he acknowledges that magic worked by immaterial forces is not beyond the realm of possibility. He distinguishes between evil angels, good angels and God as the source of these operations, although he adds that humans (Christians) too may work miracles by virtue of *gratiae gratis data*.[10]

The details of the three orders were further worked out in Martín del Río's influential *Investigations into Magic*, published in 1595. Interestingly, the Spanish Jesuit acknowledges that for many people — then as now — there is no distinction between the supernatural and the preternatural:

> This order does not go beyond the boundaries of the natural order, but is said simply to go beyond reasonable explanation. People (most people, at any rate) are not aware of this and so they usually call it 'supernatural' too, in the widely accepted meaning of the term. But the more accurate and more meaningful term is *preternatural*. (Del Río, p. 57)

The lexicographer Covarrubias hints at a similarly broad use of the Spanish term 'milagro' (miracle) in his dictionary from 1611:

> *Latine miraculum, quidquid admirationem affere potest, quasi sit contra naturem, portentum, prodigium, monstrum, hoc grammatici.* Pero en rigor milagros se dicen aquellos que tan solamente se pueden hacer por virtud divina. Largo modo, decimos acá milagros, cualquiera cosa extraordinaria y admirable, como decir 'Fulano ha hecho milagros', id est ha hecho cosas tan grandes que no se esperaban dél.

> [In Latin 'miraculum', to wit, all that can cause wonder, as if it were something unnatural or prodigious, a portent, an omen, thus say the grammarians. But strictly speaking miracles are only those events that can come about by divine power. Broadly speaking, we call miracles anything that is extraordinary and wondrous, like when we say 'so-and-so has done miracles', meaning that he has done great things that were not expected of him.]

This echoes what Vitoria says: 'Y aunque los latinos empleen el nombre de milagro para significar cualquier hecho sorprendente y admirable, los teólogos sólo lo usan en ese sentido dicho y con razón' [And although the Latins use the term 'miracle' to refer to anything that is surprising and causes wonder, theologians only use it with the aforesaid meaning and with good reason] (Vitoria, p. 97).

Although the preternatural is actually a sub-order of the natural, many people treat it as identical to the supernatural and fail to see the crucial difference between *mira* and *miracula*. They are therefore deceived (*engañado*) and only a correct understanding of the difference between the two will lead to the scales falling from their eyes so that they realize what is real and what is not and thus become un-deceived (*desengañado*). What is more, the baroque opposition between being (*ser*) and appearance (*parecer*) is not restricted to the natural order, but lies, in effect, at the heart of the opposition between the preternatural and the supernatural. Only a full cognizance of the thaumaturgical order will make us appreciate the true power of God and see through the Devil's deception.

The following anecdote could serve as an example of Del Río's reasoning. When the author was living in Belgium, he heard the story of a man who was said to have had sex with a cow. The animal subsequently gave birth to a human boy with bovine leanings, such as grazing and chewing the cud. Del Río concludes that this must have been the Devil's handiwork: the Evil One made the cow look pregnant, snatched a boy from somewhere and dropped him near the cow. The boy, believing he was born from a cow, developed the aforementioned traits in his imagination. Del Río does not accept that the boy was *actually* cow-born, which would contravene the laws of Creation (and, indeed, procreation), nor does he dismiss the story as an old wives' tale, but instead he reinterprets the facts of the story so they fall within the remit of the preternatural. The belief in the Devil's existence is never in doubt and the arch-deceiver is assumed to have used his prodigious powers to create the impression that a cow had given birth to a boy, although it never becomes clear what the purpose of this deceit might have been. Apart from his preternatural speculations, Del Río's story also shows some insight into the psychology behind autosuggestion. The medieval philosopher Nicholas Oresme formulated a similar belief when he proposed that the hearer of a curse is affected by the physical properties of the word, not their significance, and that the resulting disturbance in the imagination is what affects the body.[11]

In the example above, it appears that the Devil took the initiative to fool the people. More often, however, people claimed to arrogate preternatural powers on their own initiative, appealing directly or indirectly to God's sempiternal adversary. The action of influencing the world around us by bringing about something that exceeds (appears to exceed) the bounds of nature through conjurations, spells, potions, hexes, curses, charms, philtres, effigies and so forth is known as magic.

2.2 Magic: A Bird's-eye View

The history of magic is diffuse and complex; indeed, one could argue that there is no history of magic at all, only a history of magical practices or attitudes to magic.[12] Magic has been described variously as 'the bastard sister of science', since it is based on the same principles of cause and effect, albeit misguided; as filling a gap in human knowledge, especially in situations we cannot fully control; as springing from the same fountain as religion, namely *mana*, the Melanesian name for the spiritual force inherent in all things; and much more besides.[13] According to James George Frazer's monumental study on religion and fertility rites, magic thinking preceded religion and is rooted in the belief that we humans can impose our will on the world, provided we perform the correct ritual. He distinguished between two kinds of magic: sympathetic (which functions like a simile) and contagious (which is based on the notion of prior contact). Among the myriad examples offered by Frazer, let the following suffice:

> In the island of Saghalien, when a woman is in labour, her husband undoes everything that can be undone. He loosens the plaits of his hair and the laces of his shoes. Then he unties whatever is tied in the house or its vicinity. In the courtyard he takes the axe out of the log in which it is stuck; he unfastens the boat, if it is moored to a tree, he withdraws the cartridges from his gun, and the arrows from his crossbow. (Frazer, p. 193)

The idea behind the husband's actions is obvious enough: everything is done to ensure the baby's unobstructed passage through the birth canal. If a cartridge is stuck in the barrel of a gun, this may hinder the baby's birth, because there is a magical link between the birth canal and the barrel; they influence each other at a distance through analogous operations. A similar principle underlies the common superstition of placing an open pair of scissors under the bed of a woman in labour. The usual explanation is that it 'cuts the pain in half', although it is at least as likely that the scissors were originally thought to assist the passage of the infant by 'cutting through' any impediments. The survival of such beliefs — if they can be called that — shows that one system of thought is never fully superseded by the next; vestiges and practices often remain as a kind of substratum.

María Helena Sánchez Ortega, who studied love magic in early modern Spain by looking at inquisitorial records (*relaciones de causas*), found a wealth of amorous spells that follow the pattern of analogous thinking and sympathetic magic. In one type of conjuration, salt or alum was thrown into the fire with the words: 'Que así te has de quemar, se queme el corazón de Fulano porque me venga a ver' [Just as you must burn, may the heart of so-and-so burn, so that he will come and see me] (Sánchez Ortega, p. 66). In another spell, a woman would twist the cotton or linen she had used to clean herself after intercourse into a wick and then light it in an oil lamp, uttering the words: 'Como arde esta torcida, arda el corazón de Fulano' [Just as this twisted cloth burns, may the heart of so-and-so burn] (Sánchez Ortega, p. 81). Others used even cruder spells: 'Furioso vienes a mí, furioso vienes a mí, tan fuerte como un toro, tan fuerte como un horno, tan sujeto estés a mí como los pelos de mi coño están a mí' [Furious you come to me, furious you come to me, as strong as a bull, as hot as an oven, may you be as attached to me as the hairs of my cunt are to me] (Sánchez Ortega, p. 67). Sometimes such incantations involved sacred imagery: 'Tan humilde, tan sujeto, vengas a mí, como mi señor Jesucristo subió al santo árbol de la cruz, a morir por ti y por mí. Amén' [May you come to me as humble, as submissive, as my Lord Jesus Christ when he climbed the Holy Tree of the Cross to die for you and me. Amen] (Sánchez Ortega, pp. 69–70). Santa Elena was invoked with regularity because of her association with the nails of the True Cross — thus having the power to 'pin a man down'. A certain witch-like Marta was also often called upon:

> Marta, Marta, a la mala digo, que no a la santa, a la que por los aires anda, a la que se encadenó. [...] Otra Marta, no la buena ni la santa, sino la mala y la endemoniada, la que los infiernos manda.[14]
>
> [Marta, Marta, the evil one I mean, not the saintly one, the one who flies through the air, the one who was chained up. [...] The other Marta, not the good or saintly one, but the evil one, the wicked one, the one who commands hell.]

Although less explicitly formulated, this magic thinking is evident in the spells alluded to in Zayas. In 'El desengaño amando y premio de la virtud' an Italian-born witch casts a spell on her lover by means of a blinkered and chained cockerel in the attic of their house. The animal analogizes Lucrecia's lover, who only has eyes for her and is bound to her. The spell is undone when the blinkers are lifted.

In 'La inocencia castigada' Diego has a Moorish necromancer fashion an effigy of his beloved Inés, whose body he can summon by burning a candle on top of the statuette. Just like the women with their salt or twisted cloths, we can imagine this act being accompanied by the incantation 'just like the candle on this image of my beloved burns…'.

St Augustine held that all pagan gods are demons and that magic is perforce a diabolical activity. In spite of this, the idea developed or persisted that not all magic was diabolical but that there was also such a thing as *natural* magic. Renaissance magicians were convinced that it was possible to harness the hidden or occult forces of the universe to a good end. This version of magic was called theurgy and was tied up with the Neoplatonic worldview, first formulated by Plotinus (205–70 CE) and revived in the Renaissance by Marsilio Ficino (1433–1499), who traced the occult teachings back to the legendary Hermes Trismegistus — a supposed Egyptian sage thought to be a contemporary of Moses. According to this theory, the universe is imbued by a *spiritus mundi* connecting everything to everything else. The magus Cornelius Agrippa taught that there were three kinds of magic: natural magic, concerned with occult sympathies between substances; celestial or mathematical magic, which dealt with astral influences; and ceremonial magic, which directed itself to the supercelestial world of angelic spirits.[15] Del Río calls Agrippa 'the Archmagician' (Del Río, p. 72) and firmly rejects his kind of magic: 'Since there is no such thing as theurgy or "white" magic, it follows that all this magic of wonders is nothing other than *goetia* and "black" magic' (ibid.). He explains that Agrippa believed that it was possible to compel demons to obey us and it is easy to see why he was scornful about such a suggestion.

In one of Zayas's stories, 'El castigo de la miseria', we are introduced to a bogus version of the Renaissance magus who conjures up the demon Calquimorro, in reality a cat with its tail set on fire (see 3.1). Like the Neoplatonic astrologers, Zayas was convinced of the influence of the stars on our lives. The difference is that in her case she is not attempting to harness the forces of natural magic for good (or evil) ends, but uses it to convey her profound, fatalistic pessimism. In fact, some of her narrators even go so far as to claim that the stars are more powerful than our free will (see 5.3).

Some have seen theurgy and *goetia* as corresponding to 'high magic' and 'low magic' (see Kieckhefer), but it simply will not do to equate 'high magic' with white magic and 'low magic' with black magic. After all, the key difference is intention, which is hardly dictated by social status or learning. That is not to say that philosophically grounded magic and folk magic are identical. There are scholars who maintain that the latter is a mere corruption — even perversion — of the former.[16] But this is based on the false assumption that popular culture must needs be derivative. Black magic is often rooted in folk tradition and orally transmitted, going back to half-remembered pseudo-science (see Scarre and Callow). Keith Thomas observed that some folk healers may have had books on magic, but that they learnt their techniques from a relative or a neighbour. Their knowledge had come down to them from the Middle Ages and had links with both Anglo-Saxon and classical practice:

> Even when the cunning man's procedures are recognizable as debased reflections of Neoplatonic or hermetic theories there is usually little to suggest that he was aware of this descent. His was a stereotyped ritual, not an application of previously worked-out theory. (Thomas, p. 272)

In addition, folk magic had no lofty pretensions; it was a means to an end. The knowledge upon which it relied was held in the collective memory of each community, forming 'a rich medley of indigenous beliefs, practices and rituals'.[17] The omnipresent folk healers were 'multi-faceted practitioners of magic who healed the sick and the bewitched, who told fortunes, identified thieves, induced love, and much else besides' (Davies, *Cunning-Folk*, p. vii). They were often consulted when one suspected witchcraft, even though they themselves were at risk of being persecuted as witches.[18] Cunning-folk were also known as wise men or wise women, charmers, blessers and conjurers in Britain, and as *sabias, santiguadores, curanderos, saludaderos* and *ensalmadores* in Spain. After a visitation of the Basque valleys the inquisitor Salazar refers to a 'copia de santiguadores y ensalmadores de todos géneros de estados' [abundance of blessers and conjurers of all kinds and backgrounds] in those lands.[19] This is echoed in one of Zayas's tales where it is said that in Naples it is easy to contract the services of sorceresses because there are so many of them. They are portrayed as duplicitous schemers who are only out to line their pockets with their credulous victims' money (see 3.2).

The ubiquity of folk healers and superstitious practices led to a number of Spanish treatises on superstition. After a few cases of suspected witchcraft, the Bishop of Calahorra charged Fray Martín de Castañega with the task of writing the *Tratado de las supersticiones y hechicerías*, which was published in Logroño in 1529. Apart from denouncing some rather innocuous forms of superstition, like the excommunication of locusts, he also writes a great deal about witches, describing them as members of a diabolical anti-church. Better known than Castañega's work is the treatise on superstition and fraudulence by Pedro Ciruelo published in 1538. He deals with pretty much the same material, writing about witches (*brujas* and *jorguiñas*) who travel through the air to meet the Devil, true and false astrology, the evil eye — which he says is either natural or caused by witchcraft — and people who conjure clouds and excommunicate vermin. Francisco de Vitoria's lecture from 1540 equally mentions *saludadores*, although the friar indicates he has not made up his mind about them: 'no veo claro qué pensar y decir de ellos' [I do not really know what to think or say of them] (Vitoria, p. 89). They lead disreputable lives and although their proceedings are not superstitious per se, they are not sufficiently religious to be saintly or credible. On the whole, therefore, he says:

> mucho me temo que sean impostores que no tengan eficacia alguna; y si alguna tuvieren me temo que sea más del demonio que de Dios. Pero digo esto no de modo definitivo, puesto que las gracias se dan para el bien común. Bien puede suceder que el Señor quiera impartir su misericordia a los hombres por medio de esas personas, sean como sean. (Vitoria, p. 89)
>
> [I rather fear that they are imposters who have no efficacy at all; and if they ever did, I am afraid it is the Devil's work and not God's. But I do not say this in

a definitive way, since grace is given for the benefit of all. It may well happen that the Lord wants to bestow his mercy on mankind by means these people, no matter what they are like.]

This attitude is typical of the doubt that surrounded much of magic and witchcraft. We shall come back to this indeterminacy in 2.7.

The most important group of practitioners of magic with regards to Zayas and her novellas are those involved in amatory magic, which was more or less the exclusive domain of women, although renegade priests have sometimes been linked to the practice too.[20] Their main objective was to make people fall in love through love philtres, spells or incantations, or to retain a lover's or husband's affections. Rather than being love-struck fools, these women were being pragmatic since they relied on male support (see Sánchez Ortega). Ruggiero, who studied amatory magic in early modern Venice, explains why many women turned to black magic to get what they wanted. The body, and therefore sexuality, was dominated by the Devil, whereas the soul was God's province. So if you wanted to have any control or power over the body, it was only logical you should turn to the Devil, even if you remained bound to God for spiritual matters. This is part of what he calls the 'rich and eclectic creativity of popular cultures that must explain the complex, apparent illogic of everyday life' (Ruggiero, p. 98). The use of black magic and diabolical incantations is further complicated by the fact that spells did not merely involve demons, but often also appealed to Christian imagery or saints, as we saw in the example quoted above.

Magic and its practitioners are far from absent from the literature of early modern Spain. To get an idea of the literary landscape in which Zayas was operating, let us cast a brief glance at how magic and sorcery are portrayed in some of the works of her contemporaries.

2.3 Magic and Sorcery in Golden Age Literature

In Golden Age plays there are occasional appearances of magicians, astrologers or characters who strike deals with the Devil. Some of these *comedias* are run of the mill and unremarkable. Ana Caro's *El conde Partinuplés*, Lope de Rueda's *Armelina*, Calderón's *El jardín de Falerina* and his *El astrólogo fingido*, Alarcón's *La prueba de las promesas*, *El anticristo*, and *Quien mal anda en mal acaba* are some examples. Other plays, like Calderón's *Las cadenas del demonio* and especially *La vida es sueño* and *El mágico prodigioso*, are much more powerful and thoughtful reflections on the preternatural. As we shall see in later chapters, in Zayas the lack of theological and philosophical subtlety is compensated by a variety of treatment; in her work we have a bogus magician (see 3.1) as well as men who make pacts with the Devil (see 4.4 and 4.5).

A number of Golden Age plays and novellas deal with the phenomenon of ghosts. Again, these revenants range from moderately successful creations — for example Calderón's *El galán fantasma*, Castillo Solórzano's *La fantasma de Valencia* — to hair-raising appearances, like Tirso's stone guest in *El burlador de Sevilla*, or eerie apparitions, like the shadow (*sombra*) in Lope de Vega's *El caballero de Olmedo*, who warns the eponymous hero of his impending death. Looking ahead, we shall see the same eeriness in various novellas by Zayas, where it is more fully worked out than in Lope de Vega (see 5.2). There are two novellas in which ghosts do play a role, one being an actual penitent soul from Purgatory, the other a fake phantom (see 3.3).

The most common occurrence of preternatural activity in Golden Age literature, as in Zayas, is love magic. Its archetypical practitioner is Celestina. Fernando de Rojas's enormously popular *Tragicomedia de Calisto y Melibea (La Celestina)*, published in 1499, gave rise to a vast number of continuations and parodies.[21] In the original, a sorceress and procuress called Celestina puts a spell on a girdle she gives to Melibea to make her fall in love with Calisto. The magic thinking is clear enough and very common — the girdle will 'bind' her to Calisto. In one of her articles, Valbuena has suggested an additional metaphorical reading, namely that just as Melibea must unwind the girdle, just so will she lose her virginity.[22] Moreover, the girdle has been soaked in snake oil, with all the associations that entails — the serpent as the seducer of Eve, as a phallic animal, and so on. But Celestina does much more than merely apply a magical lubricant to a belt; her room is filled to the rafters with objects associated with black magic, such as the skin of a black cat, a paper covered with letters written in the blood of a bat, a piece of rope, presumably from a gallows, and much else besides. What is more, she invokes the help of the Devil, thinly disguised as Pluto, even threatening him should he not accede to her demands. 'Conjúrote, triste Plutón, señor de la profundidad infernal, emperador de la corte dañada [...] Si no lo hazes con presto movimiento, tendrásme por capital enemiga' [I conjure you, dismal Pluto, lord of the infernal depths, emperor of the damned court [...] If you don't do it forthwith, I shall be your arch-enemy] (*La Celestina*, p. 158). And when the spell works she thinks she has successfully forced the Devil to do her bidding: '¡O diablo a quien yo conjuré, cómo compliste tu palabra en todo lo que te pedí!' [Oh Devil conjured by me, how well you have kept your word and done everything I asked of you!] (*La Celestina*, p. 171). This goes to show the extent of her deception. Not only does she put her faith in *goetia*, she compounds this by believing she is in control. Celestina conformed to a certain type of sorceress, combining her love magic with procuring, prostitution and 'the restoration of virgins'.[23]

Lope de Vega's play *El caballero de Olmedo*, already referred to, equally features a Celestinesque sorceress cum procuress called Fabia, who gives a shoestring and a 'seasoned' letter to Inés to make her fall in love with Alonso. Like Rojas's antiheroine, she invokes the Devil: '¡Apresta, | fiero habitador del centro!' [Prepare yourself, fierce dweller of the centre!] (ll. 393–94). And likewise, she is convinced of the efficacy of her spell: '¡Oh, qué bravo efeto hicieron | los hechizos y conjuros!' [Oh what a wonderful effect the spells and conjurations had!] (ll. 816–17). Up to this point, Fabia follows her model Celestina very closely. At the end of the play, however, Rodrigo attributes powers to Fabia that go beyond those of a mere cauldron-stirring love-sorceress and part-time procuress:

> Fabia, que puede trasponer un monte;
> Fabia, que puede detener un río
> y en los negros ministros de Aqueronte
> tiene, como en vasallos, señorío;
> Fabia, que deste mar, deste horizonte,
> al abrasado clima, al Norte frío
> puede llevar un hombre por el aire.
> (*El caballero de Olmedo*, ll. 2320–26)

> [Fabia, who can move mountains — Fabia who can hold a river back — and who, over Acheron's dark retainers, — holds sway as if they were her vassals — Fabia, who from this sea, this horizon — to scorching climes, to the frozen North — can transport a man through the air.]

In Cristóbal de Villalón's *El Crótalon* the narrator is warned of similarly powerful sorceresses, who are said to have the ability to metamorphize men and change the course of the stars:

> Y luego como comenzamos a caminar por Navarra fue [*sic*] avisado que las mugeres en aquella tierra eran grandes hechiceras encantadoras, y que tenían pacto y comunicación con el demonio [...] eran poderosas en pervertir los hombres y aun convertirlos en bestias y piedras si querían [...] mandan el sol y obedeze, a las estrellas fuerzan en su curso, y a la luna quitan y ponen su luz conforme a su voluntad.[24]

> [And as soon as we began to walk through Navarre we were warned that the women of those lands were great sorceresses and enchantresses, and that they had a pact with the Devil and communicated with him [...] and that they had great skills in perverting men, even converting them to animals and stones if they wanted to [...] they command the sun, and it obeys; they force the course of the stars, and they give and take the light from the moon, as they see fit.]

The Navarrese setting is no coincidence, since of all the provinces of the Peninsula the Basque region (including Navarre and the Pyrenees) was the one most commonly associated with witchcraft. Castañega wrote his treatise in reaction to a witchcraft trial in the diocese of Calahorra y la Calzada in La Rioja on the border with Navarre. In Vélez Guevara's *El diablo cojuelo* the eponymous lame Devil shows Cleofás 'una vieja, grandísima hechicera' [an old and very great sorceress] who is applying flying ointment 'para hallarse en una gran junta de brujas que hay entre San Sebastián y Fuenterrabía' [in order to go to a large reunion of witches that is celebrated between San Sebastián and Fuenterrabía].[25] And in Cervantes's canine picaresque novella 'El coloquio de los perros' one of the witches says: 'Tres días antes que muriese habíamos estado las dos en un valle de los Montes Perineos en una gran jira' [Three days before she died the two of us had been to a valley in the Pyrenees, at a large outdoor feast], an obvious reference to a witches' sabbath.[26] We shall return to this *novela ejemplar* later. At this point, though, we ought to say something about the difference between witches and sorceresses.

2.4 *Hechiceras* (Sorceresses) versus *brujas* (Witches)

Although at a first glance the terms 'witch' and 'sorceress' may seem synonymous and fully interchangeable, strictly speaking Celestina and her brood are *hechiceras* (sorceresses), not *brujas* (witches). Modern English usage does not clearly differentiate between 'sorceress' and 'witch', and in the English translations of one of the most famous texts on witchcraft, the *Malleus maleficarum*, the key word 'maleficum' is translated as 'sorcery' by Mackay and as 'witchcraft' by Summers.[27]

But for the author of *La Celestina* and his contemporaries, as Cárdenas Rotunno points out in an article on the tragicomedy, 'in consonance with prevailing, popular literature, the terms "bruja" and "hechicera" signalled substantially separate entities'.[28] The word 'bruja' is not used once in Lope de Vega's play discussed above. The same is true for *El Crótalon*, which only mentions 'magas' and 'hechiceras'. In Rojas's wonderful work, the term 'bruja' appears only once and applies to Celestina's best friend Claudina. And even there, as Cárdenas Rotunno has noted, she is only *accused* of being a witch: 'le levantaron que era bruxa' [they accused her of being a witch] (*La Celestina*, p. 198), and she is forced to make a false confession: 'la hizieron aquella vez confesar lo que no era' [on that occasion they made her confess to being what she was not] (*La Celestina*, p. 199).

In Cervantes's 'El coloquio de los perros', by contrast, we are introduced to three women who are said to be both 'bruja' and 'hechicera'. The greatest of the three, Camacha de Montilla, has the power to control the weather and transport people through the air: 'Ella congelaba las nubes cuando quería, cubriendo con ellas la faz del sol, y cuando se le antojaba, volvió sereno el más turbado cielo; traía los hombres en un instante de lejas tierras' [She would freeze the clouds when she wanted to, covering the face of the sun with them, and when she felt like it, even the stormiest skies would turn serene; in the blink of an eye she would transport men from faraway places] (*Novelas ejemplares*, II, 337). In addition, she can transform men into animals, which is why Cañizares, one of the other witches, thinks that the dog Berganza is her friend Montiela's bewitched son.

So far, nothing new. The threesome appear to be weather-altering, demon-conjuring *hechiceras* of the same ilk as Fabia and the Navarrese *magas* of *El Crótalon*. But when we are first introduced to Cañizares, the fact that 'bruja' and 'hechicera' are not synonymous is made quite clear: 'Fuese la gente maldiciendo a la vieja, añadiendo al nombre de hechicera el de bruja' [The people went off, cursing the old woman, calling her not just a sorceress, but a witch to boot] (*Novelas ejemplares*, II, 336). After her friend Montiela is executed as a witch — 'al fin murió bruja' [in the end she died a witch] (*Novelas ejemplares*, II, 338) — Cañizares attempts to give up *hechicería*, but finds it impossible to relinquish *brujería*: 'he querido dejar todos los vicios de la hechicería en que estaba engolfada muchos años había, y sólo me he quedado con la curiosidad de ser bruja, que es un vicio dificultísimo de dejar' [I've wanted to give up all the vices of sorcery I'd been mixed up in all those years, and my only fancy now is that of being a witch, which is a vice that is extremely difficult to give up] (*Novelas ejemplares*, II, 338). Cárdenas Rotunno claims that this shows that for Cervantes 'hechicería' carries a greater semantic charge than 'brujería', implying that the former is the more evil of the two. I disagree. For Cañizares, *hechicería* is an activity that can be given up at will, but through *brujería* the Devil has such a strong hold over her, that she cannot possibly abandon it, even if she wanted to. Cañizares has been so befuddled by the Horned One that it is impossible to leave his service: 'Con todo esto, nos trae tan engañadas a las que somos brujas, que, con hacernos mil burlas, no le podemos dejar' [What with all that, he has deceived us witches to such an extent, by playing a thousand tricks on us, that we cannot leave him] (*Novelas ejemplares*, II, 339). What is more, they take part in witches' sabbaths where they meet their billy goat (*cabrón*):

> Vamos a verle muy lejos de aquí, a un gran campo, donde juntamos infinidad de gente, brujos y brujas, y allí nos da de comer desabridamente, y pasan otras cosas que en verdad y en Dios y en mi ánima que no me atrevo a contarlas, según son sucias y asquerosas, y no quiero ofender tus castas orejas. (*Novelas ejemplares*, II, 339)

> [We go and see him very far away from here, in a large field where a huge number of us get together, warlocks and witches alike, and there he offers us foul food to eat, and other things take place that, for the sake of the truth and God and my soul, I don't dare tell you, lest I offend your chaste ears, that's how disgusting and revolting they are.]

What makes them *brujas* in addition to *hechiceras* is that they are part of a Satanic sect. That is also why in *El diablo cojuelo* the only time the word 'bruja' is mentioned is when the witches all get together in the Basque country, presumably to attend a witches' sabbath.

For much of their history, there had not been much to distinguish a *bruja* (also known as *xorguiña* or *jorguiña*) from an *hechicera* (or *maga*), but with the emergence of a new type of witch in the early modern period — of the Devil-worshipping variety — the difference became an important one. The typical *hechicera* worked alone and in an urban setting. Her main task was to perform love magic with the help of potions and spells. She was not averse to conjuring up the Devil and skulking about cemeteries at night to collect ingredients for her dark arts. The *bruja*, by contrast, was a rural creature, in Spain predominantly associated with the Basque region. She was a member of a Satanic sect, whose members travelled long distances through the air to meet the Lord of Hell and commit unspeakable evil.[29] The sorceress-witch is of all times and known on all continents, whereas the Devil-worshipping witch is unique to early modern Europe and its colonies. It is true that Evans-Pritchard, who studied the Azande in the early twentieth century, also distinguishes between witches and sorcerers — witches are born as witches and have a 'witch substance' in their body and over time suck the soul out of their victims, whereas sorcerers cause immediate and serious harm by means of spells they have had to learn — but he was transposing African notions to English.[30] Another difference, which is often overlooked, is that *hechiceras* were undoubtedly real, whereas *brujas* were almost certainly figments of the imagination. And lastly, it was *brujas* who were burnt at the stake in their tens of thousands (not millions as has been claimed by some), not *hechiceras*.[31]

In the early modern period it was widely assumed that the end of time was nigh, and it had been prophesied that this would be heralded by the coming of the Antichrist and general apostasy. That explains why Castañega writes about the two churches of this world: the Catholic Church with its sacraments, and the diabolical church with its 'execraments'. In a brilliant study of this phenomenon, Stuart Clark explains how witches were a diabolical form of Bakhtinian misrule, the expression of an eschatological expectation, a necessary evil and a complete inversion of all that Christianity stood for. Witches did everything backwards ('fair is foul, and foul is fair'): they celebrated black masses, ate revolting food, worshipped the Evil One, and, in general, strove to bring down Christendom. This topsy-turvydom is described with some relish and in great detail in the *Relación de Logroño* (1611), a news sheet that appeared in the wake of one of the best-known witchcraft trials ever to take place in Spain. The *Relación de Logroño* was printed a year before the publication of Cervantes's novellas, which were written between 1590 and 1612, and I conjecture that 'El coloquio de los perros', which appears as the last of the *Novelas ejemplares*, was also written last, after Cervantes had heard about the witches of Navarre and read about them in this *relación* or a similar text, using it as a platform to investigate the discourse surrounding witchcraft, just as his novella 'Rinconete y Cortadillo' is, amongst other things, an exploration of the jargon and culture of the Sevillian underworld.

From being an irksome superstition of the people, denounced but not persecuted by the Church, witches had become a sprawling, clandestine and highly nefarious (albeit purely imaginary) sect, the arch-enemies of the common weal. This explains why statespeople and lawyers like Jean Bodin and King James I wrote demonological treatises. These works should not be dismissed as quirks and aberrations; instead they formed part of a mindset that made possible the large-scale trials. 'They described and accounted for contemporary problems in what seemed an accurate way and presented attractive solutions to them' (Clark, p. 686).

The 'witch-craze' did not strike everywhere with the same force. The vast majority of the executions — about seventy-five percent — took place in German-speaking lands.[32] Other centres of widespread persecution were Scotland and parts of France. Despite the fame of the self-styled 'witch-finder general' Matthew Hopkins in seventeenth-century Essex and the infamous trial in Salem, witch-hunts were relatively rare in Old and New England and almost absent in the United Provinces, Italy, and Spain. A number of explanations for the uneven distribution have been put forward, but the most compelling account of regional variation hinges on the presence or absence of central judicial control. Where central control was weak, there was a risk that local magistrates might give in to popular pressure and trials could turn into 'village inquisitions'. Where central judiciary control was strong, witchcraft trials were more likely to be thrown out by the courts. In Spain and Italy witchcraft fell under the remit of the Inquisition, which exerted a strong central control. This explains why these lands saw 'surprisingly few witchcraft trials' (Scarre and Callow, p. 25).[33]

Witches, then, did not play a large part in the collective Spanish imagination and were mainly associated with the Basque region and surrounding areas.[34] Like most of her contemporaries, Zayas steers clear of Satan-worshipping *brujas* and confines herself to urban *hechiceras* of the Celestina type and other practitioners of black magic. Nevertheless, the controversy surrounding witchcraft and the Inquisition's stance towards it shed light on the indeterminacy surrounding the preternatural, which is fully exploited by Zayas. This is why it is worth examining the attitudes of the Holy Office with regards to witchcraft and sorcery.

2.5 Inquisitorial Responses to Witchcraft and Magic

In 1637 Deodato Scaglia wrote *La Prattica di procedere con forma giudiciale nelle cause appartenenti alla Santa Fede*, a document which contains guidelines for the Roman Inquisition. It shows the cautious attitude of the Holy Office vis-à-vis confessions made by witches:

> We do not rush headlong, especially in the matter of these nocturnal games, to believe and proceed as if the crime were fully established; but, rather, the prudent judge weighs various questions: is the confession plausible or does it contain features that are impossible and contrary to nature, as is the case, for example, where a woman confesses that she has been in person at night participating in one of these covens and yet had not left her husband's bed; or when she asserts that she physically left the house without passing through any door or window.[35]

This approach stands in stark contrast to that of the instigators of the witch-hunts in Baden-Württemberg and Bavaria, where perhaps as many as 9000 people were executed as witches in the first half of the seventeenth century.[36]

By and large, the Spanish Inquisition proceeded along the same lines as its Roman counterpart, but that did not prevent the occasional trial from taking place. The majority of these took place in the Basque country and Navarre, which saw witchcraft trials in 1507, 1517 and the 1520s (see Scarre and Callow). As a result of these events, the Inquisition convened a meeting in Granada in 1526 during which a vote was taken to decide if witches really attended sabbaths or if they only went there in their imagination. Six inquisitors thought they really did attend, while four — including the future Inquisitor General, Valdés — were convinced that it was all in their imagination (Kamen, *The Spanish Inquisition*; Tausiet, *Urban Magic*). Henceforth, the Suprema would show itself reticent when it came to sentencing witches and acted swiftly if a local tribunal executed people accused of witchcraft. Spain did have one notorious trial of witches, however, which was the indirect result of mass persecutions in the Labourd organized by Pierre de Lancre, who believed that devils from all over the world had congregated in that particular corner of France.[37] In Spain it all started when the twenty-year-old María de Ximildegui returned to Zugarramurdi after having lived for four years in Ciboure, across the border in France. She claimed to be a member of a sect of witches and accused others in the village of the same. Many of the accused eventually confessed under duress and the Inquisition was alerted. They sent Inquisitor Valle on a visitation with the aim to root out suspected witches. As was the custom, whenever he visited a village or town, an edict of grace was read out from the pulpit, inciting the congregation to declare knowledge of anyone who had trespassed against the faith. These edicts contained vivid descriptions of the activities of which witches were accused, and with our modern understanding of psychology we can see how they formed the framework for subsequent (self-) accusations and confessions.[38] All in all, more than 5000 people were suspected of witchcraft and around 2000 were eventually charged with the crime. Eventually, however, only six people were burnt at the stake — plus another five in effigy — at an auto-da-fé celebrated in Logroño on 7 and 8 November 1610.[39] Of the three inquisitors on the tribunal, one had voted against the death sentence. His name was Alonso Salazar Frías, the youngest of the three and a protégé of Sandoval y Rojas, the Inquisitor General.

When rumours of a recrudescence of witches were seeping out of the Baztán Valley, Salazar went on an elaborate tour of eight months, after which he returned to Logroño carrying with him no fewer than 5600 folios of documentation. In his investigation Salazar found that many people wanted to retract their earlier confession. What is more, he realized that the phenomenon of witches was new: 'No hubo brujos ni embrujados en el lugar hasta que se comenzó a tratar y escribir de ellos' [There were no witches or bewitched in the place until they began to be talked and written about] (quoted in Henningsen, *El abogado*, p. 382). Salazar knew that in France a 'witch-craze' had fizzled out after the Bishop of Bayonne, the erudite Bertrand d'Echaux, had forbidden the people to talk or write about the matter.[40]

Although Salazar did not deny the possibility of witchcraft, he found that there was no concrete evidence on which to base a conviction: 'No he hallado certidumbre ni aun indicio de que colegir algún acto de brujería que real y corporalmente haya pasado' [I have not found anything certain nor any indication which would lead me to deduce that any acts of witchcraft have actually and corporally taken place] (quoted in Henningsen, *El abogado*, p. 366). From looking at the inquisitorial records, he was aware that the institution had always shown restraint with regards to witchcraft and he set out to write a series of recommendations to the Suprema. In this, he was supported by Venegas, the Bishop of Pamplona, who wrote the following to the Inquisitor General on 4 March 1611:

> Y ahora, por mayor, digo a Vuestra Señoría Ilustrísima que siempre he tenido por cierto que en este negocio hay gran fraude y engaño, y de tres partes de lo que se dice, las dos no son verdaderas. (quoted in Henningsen, *The Salazar Documents*, p. 189)

> [And now I am telling Your Illustrious Grace outright that I have always believed that in these matters there is much fraudulence and deception, and that two thirds of what they say is untrue.]

During his visitation, Salazar carried with him a copy of Pedro de Valencia's treatise *Discurso acerca de los cuentos de las brujas*, written at the behest of Sandoval in 1611 in the wake of the auto-da-fé in Logroño. Pedro de Valencia, like Salazar, acknowledges the existence of witchcraft, but finds that witches claim to do impossible things and recommends that their supposed deeds not be published: 'no conviene que las relaciones de tales confesiones y delitos, verdaderamente nefandos, se impriman, ni aun se reciten en público' [it is not fitting that the tales of such confessions and crimes, which are truly heinous, be printed, nor that they be read out in public].[41] Based on his findings Salazar wrote recommendations that became known as the *Instrucciones de Logroño*, which were introduced in all the other tribunals and were even known by the Roman Inquisition. However, it is important to underline that:

> Salazar's long memorial was a victory neither for humanism nor rationalism, but quite simply for the laws of evidence. As a trained lawyer (*letrado*) he was interested less in the theological debate over the reality of witchcraft than in the material problem of having to arrest people on the basis of unsupported hearsay. (Henningsen, *El abogado*, p. 274)

Although some have seen Salazar as 'un auténtico precursor de los hombres ilustrados del siglo XVIII' [a true precursor of the enlightened men of the eighteenth century],[42] he was closer to Montaigne in spirit and simply loath to condemn someone to the stake if he was not absolutely certain a crime had been committed: 'Après tout c'est mettre ses conjectures à bien haut prix, que d'en faire cuire un homme tout vif' [After all, it is putting a very high price on one's conjecture to roast a man alive for them].[43]

If witchcraft trials were a comparative rarity in Spain, we have already seen that there were plenty of *hechiceras*, *saludadores*, *santiguadores*, *ensalmadores*, and other practitioners of folk magic. Here too the Inquisition showed a remarkably lenient attitude. In 2000 Rafael Martín Soto published *Magia e Inquisición en el antiguo reino de Granada*, in which he describes the activities of the Inquisition with regards to 'magic crimes' as recorded in the archives of the Granadan tribunal. In all, a mere 7.2% of the cases involved magic. In the sixteenth century only 1% of cases mention witchcraft, but this goes up to 10% in the seventeenth century. For the same period, we see a decrease of cases dealing with Moriscos (from 43% to 14%) but an increase in cases involving suspected Judaizers (from 10% to 38%), which was probably due to the influx of converted Jews (*marranos*) from Portugal after 1580.

In the wake of the Council of Trent the Church was involved in a drive to stamp out superstitions, which were considered a threat to the Church's monopoly (see Clark). The same motivation underpins the treatises by Castañega and Ciruelo mentioned before. Blasphemy, folk healing, amatory magic, divination and treasure hunting all fell under the rubric of superstition. Many of the convicted were sentenced to public shaming (*salir a la pública vergüenza*), often with the administration of one to two hundred lashes and exile from the city or town for a stipulated number of years. Punishments were harsher for recidivists. On occasion, the Inquisition would absolve defendants because they could not see any heresy in their actions. Martín Soto cites the case of a 'possessed' women who masturbated continuously and who introduced sundry objects into her vagina, including crucifixes. Her case was suspended and she was urged to find a new confessor to direct her soul and persuade her to give up her vice (*vicio*). In the convent of Santa Clara de la Paz in Antequera obscene rituals were held between men and women, both professed and lay. They would gather to adore the Devil, who would copulate with one of the women present. There were claims that participants could freely go from cell to cell and fly away after having applied a special ointment. After the ceremony there was a banquet and all participants engaged in sexual activities. Many nuns became pregnant and tried to abort; some gave birth and subsequently killed their infants, using their blood for ointments. Eventually the Inquisition got involved; they sent some of the culprits away and then offered a general amnesty provided that everyone confess their sins.

In dealing with these 'crimes' the Inquisition regularly used the term 'sortílega' [fortune-teller] instead of 'hechicera', often in conjunction with the epithet 'embustera' [mendacious] or 'supersticiosa' [superstitious]. In many instances the defendants acknowledged that it was all fake: 'todo era mentira [...] pues solo era un invento para sacar dinero, ya que era muy pobre' [it was all a lie [...] it was only something I made up to fleece people, seeing as I was very poor] (Martín Soto, p. 139). For many, it seems, magic was a modus vivendi and did not result from a true belief in its efficacy: 'sólo Dios puede saber las cosas por venir, y no creyó que dicha oración tuviese virtud para obrar los efectos que aconsejó a la mujer, y que todo[s] sabe[n] que es embuste' [only God has knowledge of things to come, and she did not believe that the aforesaid prayer had the power she pretended to the woman that it had, and everyone knows it to be make-believe] (Martín Soto, p. 355). In part, Zayas evinces the same sceptical attitude, although none of the leniency, when she portrays some of the women involved in love magic as imposters (see 3.2). Even when the efficacy of the magic spell is borne out by the story, the sorceress in question is still referred to as full of lies and tricks (see 3.3).

The inquisitorial stance may appear modern and enlightened but, as Henningsen has argued, this sceptical attitude is the result of the 'old-fashioned' Aristotelian — as opposed to the 'modern' Neoplatonic — teaching at Salamanca, that is to say it is a product of Spain's Catholic orthodoxy and conservatism:

> The healthy, sensible attitude of the Spaniards to the witch problem was thus not a matter of being 'ahead of their time', but rather of being 'behind' the general development of philosophy. This is the Spanish paradox. (Henningsen, *The Salazar Documents*, p. 13)

Moreover, many inquisitors were trained as canonical lawyers, not as theologians, and were therefore trained to look for evidence.[44]

The Church authorities showed pragmatic scepticism with regards to magic and witchcraft, the belief in which was gradually being eroded. This erosion was part of a larger epistemological shift, a kind of intellectual watershed changing the way in which the natural and supernatural were seen and experienced, although it must be stressed that it was a gradual process, and one which did not affect everyone to the same extent.

2.6 The Seventeenth-Century Epistemological Shift

In *The Order of Things*, Foucault attempts to lay bare the archaeological strata of our knowledge, which he sees as a succession of internally coherent systems of thought and ways of seeing the world called 'epistemes', each of which constitutes a rupture with the one that preceded it. In the Renaissance episteme, he explains, the universe was conceived of as a book replete with signs that awaited interpretation, even if this was not as straightforward as one might suppose. The difficulty lies in what Foucault describes as a parallax: hermeneutics (uncovering the meaning of signs) and semiology (the body of knowledge necessary to know what a sign is) were superimposed in a way that rendered the interpretation of signs opaque. Reading a sign is never direct and unmediated, but always at one remove. Sympathies, conveniences, emulations, resemblances and similitudes were all interlinked in non-predictable and non-transparent ways. In the Renaissance, the key epistemic notions were resemblance and similitude; to write the history of a plant or animal was to describe its elements and organs, its virtues and uses, but also the legends and stories that surrounded it, its place in heraldry, what the Ancients recorded of it or travellers might have said of it, and so forth. This was not because science was hesitating between rational vocation and naïve tradition; it was because signs and signatures were part and parcel of the things themselves. Nature and antiquity were both fields and spaces that required interpretation; divination and erudition were part of the same hermeneutics. As a result, 'sixteenth-century knowledge condemned itself to never knowing anything but the same thing' (Foucault, p. 34).

An integral part of this worldview was the existence of natural magic; the universe was assumed to be filled with occult forces, sympathies and antipathies, the 'virtudes a nosotros ocultas' [virtues hidden to us] referred to by Castañega (see 2.1). Common examples of these notions are the belief that a corpse would start bleeding in the presence of its murderer, or that a wound could be cured by applying a salve that came from the weapon that caused it. Likewise, it was thought that snakes cannot abide the shadow of the ash tree — according to legend the Cross was made from this type of wood — or that tarantulas and scorpions hate each other.[45] In 1633 the Spanish Jesuit Eusebio Nieremberg published what was essentially a compendium of classical learning on this topic, the *Oculta Filosofia de la Sympatia y Antipatia de las Cosas*, in which he explains the workings of these hidden forces of attraction and repulsion:

> Sympatia y Antipatia, como hablan los Griegos; esto es vna secreta conformidad, y auersió que parece, ò ay en las cosas con que se executan efetos admirables por lo extraordinario, y anomalo, que tienen a la vista, y lo inuisible, y oculto de sus causas. (Nieremberg, *Oculta Filosofia*, fol.1^r)
>
> [Sympathy and Antipathy, as the Greeks call it; this is a secret conformity and aversion that is apparent, or exists, in things, and that creates effects that are wondrous because of what we perceive as extraordinary and anomalous, and because of the hidden and invisible nature of their causes.]

Perhaps the most emblematic figure to emerge from this period is the Renaissance magus. These were men like Giovanni Pico della Mirandola (1463–1494), Heinrich Cornelius Agrippa von Nettesheim (1486–1535) — dubbed 'the Arch-magician' by Del Río — and Paracelsus (1493–1541). Other famous intellectuals who devoted their studies to the occult were John Dee (1527–1608), Giambattista della Porta (1535–1615) and Robert Fludd (1574–1637). These men inspired a number of well-known literary characters such as Marlowe's Doctor Faustus, based on a historical figure, and Shakespeare's Prospero, but also protagonists of Golden Age fiction like Illán in Alarcón's *La prueba de las promesas*.

Although Foucault has been taken to task for his sweeping generalizations, obscurantist language and circular reasoning — using examples as illustration instead of evidence — as well as giving untoward prominence to a marginal group of hermetic writers, he nevertheless provides us with a compelling model for the history of thought in the early modern period.[46] He describes how in the course of the seventeenth century the Renaissance episteme was replaced by what he calls the Classical Age: the era of taxonomy and tabulation. In his inimitable prose, the French thinker explains that the universe was no longer replete with signs, whether we knew about them or not, but that there was no sign unless it was recognized as such, because a sign 'can be constituted only by an act of knowing' (Foucault, p. 65). The pre-ordained and pre-existing system of divine hieroglyphics evaporated. Turning to Spanish literature, Foucault cites Don Quixote as the negative image of the Renaissance world that was about to disappear, a world where 'resemblances and signs have dissolved their former allegiance; similitudes have become deceptive and verge upon the visionary or madness' (Foucault, p. 53). More important for this investigation is what he has to say about the baroque as a period of epistemological crisis, describing it as an era in which:

> the chimeras of similitude loom up on all sides, but they are recognized as chimeras; it is the privileged age of *trompe-l'œil* painting, of the comic illusion, of the play that duplicates itself by representing another play, of the *quid pro quo*, of dreams and visions; it is the age of the deceiving senses; it is the age in which the poetic dimension of language is defined by metaphor, simile, and allegory. (Foucault, p. 57)

Other examples that could be taken from Spanish literature and art to sustain this idea are legion, from Velázquez's *Las meninas* (with which Foucault starts his book) to Lope de Vega's *Lo fingido verdadero* (in which an actor becomes the role he plays) to Calderón de la Barca's *La vida es sueño* and Góngora's poetry. And although Zayas's prose lacks the scintillation of Cervantes's wit and the dazzling quality of Góngora's poetry, she nevertheless constructs a polysemous, intricate narrative labyrinth where readers' senses are deceived. Her work is baroque too in its morbid fascination, the obverse of the festive baroque.

When the philosophers of the Enlightenment looked back at the early modern period, it seemed to them that in the course of the seventeenth century witchcraft prosecutions had disappeared like phantoms of the night fleeing the blinding rays of Reason. But this is a triumphalist account and we should not see the decline of witchcraft prosecutions as the direct corollary of the emergence of the 'clockwork universe'. The ideas formulated by Descartes and Newton took time to percolate down to the people and there is a significant gap in time before they were taken up by the population at large. It is also well known that Newton himself took a lively interest in astrology and alchemy. Instead, what took place was a more gradual process during which, as happened in Spain with Salazar, the evidence for the old worldview simply no longer seemed convincing, constituting a crisis which would lead to the development of a new paradigm.[47]

2.7 'Betwixt Charybdis and Scylla': The Indeterminacy of Magic

At the time that Zayas was writing her tales of sorceresses and necromancers, the old epistemological system was crumbling and its sands were shifting. Characteristic of this 'tired episteme' — or pre-paradigmatic crisis — is the indeterminacy surrounding magic and the preternatural. Determining whether something was supernatural *sensu stricto* or preternatural demanded exceptional (navigational) skills, as James I explains in his treatise on demonology:

> And by these meanes shall we saill surelie, betuixt *Charybdis* and *Scylla*, in eschewing the not beleeing of them altogether on the one part, least that drawe vs to the errour that there is no Witches: and on the other parte in beleeuing of it, make vs to eschew the falling into innumerable absurdities, both monstruouslie against all Theologie diuine, and Philosophie humaine.[48]

This wavering attitude did not mean outright rejection; the existence of the Devil was beyond dispute, and witches were thought to constitute a genuine threat:

> Evil spirits are on the loose, seeking to take possession of foolish and deluded souls. Never have there been as many witches as there are today, and the main reason for this is the faintness of and contempt for the Catholic faith [...] Idolatry and witchcraft go together, as innumerable Jesuit testimonies from India illustrate. (Del Río, p. 27)

> We have seen heresy flourishing in Belgium and we see swarms of witches laying waste the whole of the North, like locusts. (Del Río, p. 29)

Despite the undeniability of the Devil and his minions, demonologists like Del Río refused to accept any old story at face value; we have seen, for example, how he reinterprets the story of the cow-born boy as a preternatural trick (see 2.1). He eloquently sums up his attitude as follows: 'Whoever maintains that every effect is the result of trickery, or believes that every effect is real, should be regarded as a water-melon rather than a human being' (Del Río, p. 78). So within a clearly delineated, post-Tridentine, Catholic intellectual framework, he urges us to be sceptical. Pedro de Valencia was likewise convinced of the gravity of the threat of witches, but stresses that they confess to do things that can scarcely be believed:

> como en aquellas confesiones, supuesto que en el todo fuesen verdaderas, se mezclan particularidades tan poco provables i casi increíbles, muchas personas, no pudiendo inducirse a creerlas, juzgarán por ellas que todo el hecho es vanidad, ilusión i sueño. (Valencia, p. 235)

> [since those confessions, supposing that on the whole they are true, include particulars that are so unlikely and well-nigh incredible, that many people, unable to convince themselves of their truth, will on account of these facts dismiss them altogether as vain illusions and dreams.]

Far from being an all-out sceptic, the Spanish humanist is afraid that because some of the elements of the confessions are so outlandish, there are those who might reject witchcraft altogether. The outrageous claims are in fact a diabolical ruse: witches mix incredible things with truth so that they will not be believed at all. After discussing whether or not people can be transported by angels or devils, Pedro de Valencia states that in individual cases it is legitimate and recommendable to doubt and that we should always prefer a naturalistic explanation:

> Esto en lo universal del dogma. Pero en lo particular del hecho, en cada caso es mui lícito, i aun prudente i devido, el dudar — en las cosas que pueden acontescer de muchas maneras — de quál dellas acontesció la de que se trata. I la presunción está siempre por la vía ordinaria, humana i natural. (Valencia, p. 236)

> [This as far as the universality of the dogma is concerned. But in the particulars of each case, it is most legitimate and even prudent and necessary to be doubtful; things can occur in many ways, and we must establish how the event in question occurred. And the assumption must always be that it happened in the normal, human and natural way.]

When Salazar, who had read Pedro de Valencia's treatise, wrote his *memoriales*, he showed himself impatient with people who invoked the Devil's preternatural powers. What was important, he claimed, was to assess whether or not we should believe people based on their ludicrous claims:

> Y tampoco mejora con averiguar que el Demonio puede hacer esto y aquello, repitiendo cada paso sin provecho la teoría de su naturaleza angélica; y que también digan los doctores por asentadas estas cosas, que sólo sirven ya de fastidio inútil, pues nadie las duda; sino en creer que en el caso individuo [*sic*] hayan pasado como los brujos las dicen de cada acto particular, por las dudas que dejé apuntadas y porque ni ellos han de ser creídos, ni el juez dar sentencia, sino en lo que exteriormente traiga verdad perceptible igual para cuantos la oyeren — pues no lo es para ninguno: volar cada paso una persona por el aire, andar cien leguas en una hora, salir una mujer por donde no cabe una mosca, hacerse invisible a los presentes, no se mojar en el río ni en el mar, estar a tiempo en la cama y en el aquelarre. (quoted in Henningsen, *El abogado*, p. 409)

> [Nor does it help to argue that the Devil can do this, that and the other, reiterating all the time and without any benefit the theory of the Devil's angelic nature; and also that learned men have taken these things to be well established, because this is a useless nuisance, since no one doubts this; we should consider whether we believe that, in each and every individual case, things happen the way witches say they do, and I have made clear my doubts on the matter, which is why they should not be believed, nor should any judge sentence them, except if the truth can be established by a third party and in such a way that anyone can check it, because what they claim is quite something: people flying through the air all the time, travelling a hundred leagues in one hour, women leaving their houses through holes too small for a fly to get through, making oneself invisible to everyone else, not getting wet when crossing rivers or seas, and being at the same time both in bed and attending a witches' sabbath.]

We have already seen that in 1526 the Inquisition voted on whether or not witches could fly to their sabbaths and that four of ten inquisitors voted against the proposition. We see the same hesitancy and ambivalence in Castañega and Ciruelo, who both write that sometimes witches actually fly to sabbaths, while at other times the Devil merely implants the idea in them. Almost a century later things were no clearer. The witches tried in Logroño were thought to attend sabbaths, sometimes in the flesh, sometimes only in their dreams: 'itém que [...] muchas veces van espiritual y mentalmente en sueños, aunque otras veces vayan corporalmente' [also that [...] many times they go there spiritually and mentally in dreams, although at other times they go physically] (quoted in Henningsen, *El abogado*, p. 238). Covarrubias's definition of 'bruxa' likewise displays this indeterminacy:

> *Bruxa*, cierto género de gente perdida y endiablada, que perdido el temor a Dios, ofrecen sus cuerpos y sus almas al demonio a trueco de una libertad viciosa y libidinosa, y unas veces causando en ellos un profundísimo sueño les representa en la imaginación ir a partes ciertas y hacer cosas particulares, que después de despiertos no se pueden persuadir sino que realmente se hallaron en aquellos lugares y [sic] hicieron lo que el demonio pudo hacer sin tomarlos a ellos por instrumento. Otras veces realmente y con efeto las lleva a parte donde hacen sus juntas, y el demonio se les aparece en diversas figuras, a quien dan la obediencia, renegando de la santa fe que recibieron en el bautismo.

> [*Witch*, a certain type of people that have gone astray and are possessed by the Devil; having lost their fear of God, they offer their bodies and souls to the Devil in return for a sinful and libidinous freedom, and the Devil sometimes causes them to fall into a profound sleep during which they imagine that they visit certain places and do certain things, and when they wake up, they insist that they really visited those places and did what the Devil demanded that they do of their own free will. On other occasions, he really takes them to places where they meet, and the Devil appears to them in various guises, and they pledge obedience to him, reneging the holy faith they received in baptism.]

Note, incidentally, how the lexicographer starts with the gender-neutral 'gente' [people] and 'ellos' [they], but then 'slips into' the feminine 'las' [them] when he writes: 'las lleva a parte donde hacen sus juntas' [he really takes them to places where they meet], that is to say, the gender-neutral witches become women precisely when they attend the sabbath.

In 'El coloquio de los perros', when Cañizares explains to Berganza how she meets the Devil, she gives another textbook explanation of this uncertainty:

> Hay opinión que no vamos a estos convites, sino con la fantasía en la cual nos representa el demonio las imágenes de todas aquellas cosas que después contamos que nos han sucedido. Otros dicen que no, sino que verdaderamente vamos en cuerpo y en ánima; y entrambas opiniones tengo para mí que verdaderas, puesto que nosotras no sabemos cuándo vamos de una o de otra manera, porque todo lo que nos pasa en la fantasía es tan intensamente que no hay diferenciarlo de cuando vamos real y verdaderamente. (*Novelas ejemplares*, II, 339–40)

> [Some say that we don't actually go to those meetings, but only in our imagination, with the Devil conjuring up the images of all those things we later say happened to us. Others disagree and say we truly attend the sabbath in body and soul. Personally I think they are both right, since we don't know whether we attend in one way or in another, because everything that happens

in our imagination is so intense that it is impossible to tell whether we are there for real or not.]

We have already seen that other aspects of the preternatural too were marked by dubiety. Francisco de Vitoria admitted that he had not made up his mind about *saludadores* (see 2.2), and some of the people involved in magical practices confessed that it was all a lie (see 2.5). Their clients on the other hand probably believed that black magic worked, although even here we cannot be sure. One of the women studied by Ruggiero, for example, was asked by the Inquisition if she believed in her spell. She replied that if it was effective, she did, and if it was not, she did not.

In the seventeenth century the border between the natural and the preternatural had become unstable. Many things once thought possible, at least in theory, were hesitantly and inconsistently recategorized as impossible and therefore inexistent, or else a natural cause was found. Faced with the mechanistic explanations of the universe the Church had to redefine its sense-of-the-impossible. In this process, the triple ordering of natural-preternatural-supernatural was maintained but the preter- and supernatural were significantly reduced in scope and only applied to rare and remote occurrences. Consequently, the preserve of the preternatural and supernatural slowly shrank (see Campagne). In addition, the borders of the supernatural had to be patrolled and policed.

As a direct result of the Reformation and the subsequent confessional rivalry in Europe, God's wondrous interventions had been exposed as cultural constructs. Stuart Clark sees this realization, which also affects magical thinking, as the cause of the eventual demise of the belief in witchcraft. He writes that as early as 1653 Sir Robert Filmer expressed the view that witchcraft was what we now refer to as a cultural construct when he pointed out that if, according to Del Río, a witch had to renounce the Virgin, then only Catholics could be witches. This strategy, though, had its dangers and created a slippery slope, since the problem of establishing hard and fast criteria to distinguish between natural and supernatural phenomena had a 'corrosive effect on the status of the miraculous in general' (Keitt, p. 179). Miracles were subjected to a bureaucratization and episcopal investigations and had in effect become legal as well as cultural constructs: 'In this juridical context, miracles no longer provided irrefrangible proof of Christian doctrine or the sanctity of an individual, but were themselves in need of proof' (Keitt, p. 180). This resulted in circularities, as visions for example were evidence of virtue, but the virtue of the visionary became key evidence in order to establish the validity of visions; true revelations were not given to dishonest women, who were accused of 'inventing the sacred with strange singularities' (ibid.).

In the literature of the period we see the same indeterminacy surrounding the preternatural. As we have seen, in 'Coloquio de los perros' Cañizares admits that she does not know whether or not they actually meet the Devil. More generally, Cervantes deftly creates a multi-layered narrative where no one knows *what* to believe. Cañizares tells her story to a dog, who is telling his tale to a fellow canine — neither of whom is sure whether what is happening to them and if the fact that they can talk is real or a dream — and these two dogs are overheard by Campuzano, who is recovering from a bout of fever, after having been cruelly deceived by a woman, while he in turn is telling what has befallen him to a comrade he meets outside a hospital. And the whole narrative is the closing tale of a collection of novellas whose author boasts he has *invented* all of them: 'mi ingenio las engendró, y las parió mi pluma' [begotten by my imagination and by my quill brought into this world] (*Novelas ejemplares*, I, 52).[49]

Calderón likewise plays on the belief and disbelief in ghosts. In *El galán fantasma* many characters take Astolfo to be a ghost; he is assumed to have been murdered by his rival but has survived and secretly meets his beloved in her garden, which he enters via a hidden tunnel. The *gracioso* Candil, however makes light of the superstition, saying that 'en mentira de fantasmas nada en mi vida he creído' [I have never in my life believed in the lie that there are ghosts] (*El galán fantasma*, p. 88). In *La dama duende*, it is the servant Cosme who is the credulous one. His master Manuel has moved in with an old friend. Unbeknownst to him, his friend's sister, a beautiful young widow, lives in a secret room adjacent to his and has fallen in love with him. While he is out, having locked the door, she sneaks in from her hiding place. She leaves him a letter and the room in a mess. On their return, the *gracioso* thinks there are sprites or hobgoblins (*duendes*) at play and the following dialogue ensues:

DON MANUEL:	[...] pero, no, Cosme, creer cosa sobrenatural.
COSME:	¿No hay duendes?
DON MANUEL:	Nadie los vio
COSME:	¿Familiares?
DON MANUEL:	Son quimeras
COSME:	¿Brujas?
DON MANUEL:	Menos
COSME:	¿Hechiceras?
DON MANUEL:	¡Qué horror!
COSME:	¿Hay súcubos?
DON MANUEL:	No
COSME:	¿Encantadoras?
DON MANUEL:	Tampoco
COSME:	¿Mágicos?
DON MANUEL:	Es necedad
COSME:	¿Nigromantes?
DON MANUEL:	Liviandad
COSME:	¿Energúmenos?
DON MANUEL:	¡Qué loco!
COSME:	¡Vive Dios que te cogí! ¿Diablos?
DON MANUEL:	Sin poder notorio
COSME:	¿Hay almas en purgatorio?
DON MANUEL:	¿Que me enamoren a mí? ¿Hay más necia bobería? (ll. 1071–91)

[DON MANUEL: [...] but not, Cosme, to believe in anything supernatural. COSME: Are there no goblins? — No one's ever seen them. — What about familiar spirits? — A mere illusion. — And witches? — Even more so. —

Sorceresses? — How awful! — Do succubuses exist? — No. — Enchantresses? — Neither. — Magicians, then? — You're being silly. — Necromancers? — Nonsense. — Can people be possessed? — That's madness. — Thank God I ran into you! What about devils? — Not with any real power. — Are there souls in Purgatory? — Falling in love with me? Have you ever heard of anything so foolish?]

Apart from a healthy scepticism within the bounds of the Catholic faith — devils and Purgatory are not denied — this passage also shows and the split between *vulgo* belief and *culto* scepticism, something equally exploited by Zayas, although not always for comical purposes.

★ ★ ★ ★ ★

At the time when Zayas was writing her novellas the belief in the supernatural *sensu lato* was in a state of flux. The old episteme was being eroded but had not been replaced by a new one. The pervading sense surrounding the supernatural was one of indeterminacy. The supernatural *sensu stricto* was brought under control and miracles were in danger of becoming classified as cultural constructs. Although the belief in the Devil was very real and witches were thought to exist, Spain was spared the worst of the early modern 'witch-craze' thanks in large part to the cool-headed attitude of the Inquisition, which also dismissed other practitioners of folk magic as frauds and imposters. Great minds like Del Río and Valencia advocated a doubting, sceptical stance when it came to the preternatural.

In the literature of the period there are references to astrologers, Celestina-type sorceresses and Basque witches. The attitude is often sceptical and the effect almost always comical. In Zayas not only do the occurrences of marvellous and miraculous events abound, but the tone and approach are much more varied, and while some of her stories are comical and light-hearted, others are dark and disturbing. This multivalent approach is particularly clear when we study the episodes involving magic.

Notes to Chapter 2

1. Quoted in Alan Kors and Edward Peters (eds), *Witchcraft in Europe, 400–1700: A Documentary History* (Philadelphia: University of Pennsylvania Press, 2001), p. 429.
2. Keith Thomas, *Religion and the Decline of Magic* (London: Penguin), p. 173.
3. See Malcom Gaskill, *Witchcraft: A Very Short Introduction* (Oxford: Oxford University Press, 2010).
4. Quoted in John Steadman, 'Milton and Wolleb Again (Paradise Lost, I, 54–56, 777)', *The Harvard Theological Review*, 53.2 (April 1960), 155–56.
5. For more on *mira* and *miracula*, see Gaskill; Geoffrey Scarre and John Callow, *Witchcraft and Magic in Sixteenth- and Seventeenth-Century Europe* (Basingstoke: Palgrave, 1987); Stuart Clark, *Thinking with Demons: The Idea of Witchcraft in Early Modern Europe* (Oxford: Oxford University Press, 1997); and above all Martín del Río, *Investigations into Magic*, trans. and ed. by P. G. Maxwell-Stuart (Manchester: Manchester University Press, 2000).
6. Martín de Castañega, *Tratado de las supersticiones y hechicerías* (Madrid: De la luna, 2001), p. 53.
7. See Fabián Alejandro Campagne, 'Witchcraft and the Sense-of-the-Impossible in Early Modern Spain: Some Reflections Based on the Literature of Superstition (ca. 1500–1800)', *Harvard Theological Review*, 96.1 (2003), 25–62.

8. Pedro Ciruelo, 'Tratado por el cual se reprueban las supersticiones y supercherías', in *Brujería y exorcismos en España. Textos fundamentales*, ed. by Servando Gotor (Zaragoza: Lecturas Hispánicas, 2014), p. 111.
9. Francisco de Vitoria, *Sobre la magia*, ed. by Luis Frayle Delgado (Salamanca: San Esteban, 2006), p. 57.
10. Theologians distinguish between *gratiae gratis data* (also known as *charismata*): special and extraordinary powers given by God for the spiritual benefit of the recipient, and *gratiae gratum facientes*: actual grace granted for our salvation. See <http://www.newadvent.org/cathen/10350a.htm> [accessed 12 February 2017].
11. See Richard Kieckhefer, *Magic in the Middle Ages* (Cambridge: Cambridge University Press, 1989).
12. This point was made by Ronald Hutton in a paper he presented at a conference on Magic and the Supernatural in the Medieval and Early Modern Period held at Cardiff University (21 July 2015).
13. The 'bastard sister of science' quote comes from James George Frazer, *The Golden Bough. A new abridgement* (Oxford: Oxford University Press, 1994), p. 46. On the 'gap in human knowledge' hypothesis, see Bronislaw Malinowski, *Magic, Science and Religion and Other Essays* (London: Souvenir Press, 1948). On *mana*, see Marcel Mauss, *A General Theory of Magic*, trans. by Robert Brain (London: Routledge, 1950).
14. Rafael Martín Soto, *Magia e Inquisición en el antiguo reino de Granada* (Málaga: Arguval, 2000), p. 112.
15. See Frances Yates, *The Occult Philosophy in the Elizabethan Age* (London: Routledge, 1979).
16. See Rafael Martín Soto, *Magia e Inquisición*, chapter 1.
17. Owen Davies, *Cunning-Folk: Popular Magic in English History* (London: Hambledon Continuum, 2003), p. x.
18. See Keith Thomas. See also Alan Macfarlane, *Witchcraft in Tudor and Stuart England* (London: Routledge, 1970).
19. Quoted in Gustav Henningsen, *The Salazar Documents: Inquisitor Alonso de Salazar Frías and Others on the Basque Witch Persecution* (Leiden: Brill, 2004), p. 263.
20. See María Tausiet, *Urban Magic in Early Modern Spain. Abracadabra Omnipotens* (Basingstoke: Palgrave Macmillan, 2014); and Guido Ruggiero, *Binding Passions: Tales of Magic, Marriage, and Power at the End of the Renaissance* (Oxford: Oxford University Press, 1993).
21. Examples of continuations are Feliciano de Silva's *La Segunda Celestina*; Gaspar Gómez de Toledo's *La Tercera Celestina*; Sancho de Muñón's *La tercera Celestina o La Tragicomedia de Lisandro y Roselia*; Sebastián Hernández's *La Policiana*; as well as *La Selvagia*, *La Eufrosina* and *La Florinea*. See Marcelino Menéndez Pelayo, 'Artes mágicas, hechicerías y supersticiones en los siglos XVI y VII', in *Brujería y exorcismos en España: textos fundamentales*, ed. by Servando Gotor (Zaragoza: Lecturas Hispánicas, 2014), pp. 23–70. A clear parody is Pablos's mother in Quevedo's *La vida del buscón*.
22. See Olga Lucía Valbuena, 'Sorceress, Love Magic, and the Inquisition of Linguistic Sorcery in Celestina', *PMLA*, 109.2 (1994), 207–24.
23. In Quevedo's *La vida del buscón* Pablos meets a woman who is not unlike his witch-like mother and of whom it is said: 'hubo fama que reedificaba doncellas' [rumour had it she restored virgins] (*La vida del buscón*, p. 45), her main activity being 'contrahacer doncellas' [counterfeiting virgins] (*La vida del buscón*, p. 97).
24. Cristóbal Villalón, *El Crotalón* (Biblioteca Virtual Universal, 2003), p. 42; online at <http://www.biblioteca.org.ar/libros/89158.pdf>.
25. Luis Vélez de Guevara, *El diablo cojuelo* (Barcelona: Crítica, 1999), p. 23.
26. Miguel de Cervantes, *Novelas ejemplares I & II*, ed. by Harry Sieber (Madrid: Cátedra 1980), p. 340.
27. Heinrich Kramer, *The Hammer of Witches: A Complete Translation of the 'Malleus Maleficarum'*, trans. by Christopher S. Mackay (Cambridge: Cambridge University Press, 2006) and *The Malleus Maleficarum*, trans. by Montague Summers (New York: Dover Publications, 1928).
28. Anthony Cárdenas Rotunno, 'Rojas's "Celestina and Claudina": In Search of a Witch', *Hispanic Review*, 69.3 (2001), 277–97 (p. 278).

29. For more on the urban/rural dichotomy, see Julio Caro Baroja, *The World of the Witches* (London: Phoenix, 2001); Tausiet (*Urban Magic*); Martín Soto; Owen Davies, 'Urbanisation and the Decline of Witchcraft: An Examination of London', in *The Witchcraft Reader*, ed. by Darren Oldridge, 2nd edn (London: Routledge, 2008), pp. 353–66; María Lara Martínez, *Brujas, magos e incrédulos en la España del siglo de oro: microhistoria cultural de ciudades encantadas* (Cuenca: Alderabán, 2013); and José Ignacio Carmona Sánchez, *La España mágica: mitos, leyendas y curiosidades pintorescas* (Madrid: Nowtilus, 2012).
30. E. E. Evans-Pritchard, *Witchcraft, Oracles, and Magic among the Azande*, abridged and with an intro. by Eva Gillies (Oxford: Clarendon Press, 1976).
31. In feminist circles the number of victims of the 'burning times' that is sometimes quoted is unrealistically high. In her book *Our Blood* (New York: Perigree Books, 1976) Andrea Dworkin claims the number of the victims of what she termed 'gynocide' was a staggering nine million. In popular fiction, high numbers are still quoted (five million in Dan Brown's *The Da Vinci Code*). Serious historians offer much lower estimates. Scarre and Callow (1987) put the total number of victims at around 40,000, excluding victims of random violence and lynching. Darren Oldridge (2008) estimates the number of executions at 50,000, while Gaskill (2010) states that the combined estimates for Europe, Scandinavia and America vary between 90,000 and 100,000 trials in the period between 1400 and 1800, the worst years being from 1560 to 1630. Anne Llewellyn Barstow, in *Witchcraze: A New History of the European Witch Hunts* (London: HarperCollins, 1994), suggests a total of perhaps 200,000 accusations leading to 100,000 executions. See also Jane Davidson, *Early Modern Supernatural: The Dark Side of European Culture, 1400–1700* (Santa Barbara, CA: Praeger, 2012).
32. See Wolfgang Behringer, 'Weather, Hunger and Fear: Origins of the European Witch-Hunt in Climate, Society and Mentality', in *The Witchcraft Reader* (London: Routledge, 2002; 2nd edn 2008), pp. 74–85; and Darren Oldridge, *The Devil: A Very Short Introduction* (Oxford: Oxford University Press, 2012).
33. See William Monter, 'Witchcraft, Confessionalism and Authority', in *The Witchcraft Reader* (London: Routledge, 2002), pp. 198–204. See also Brian Levack, 'The Decline of Witchcraft Prosecutions', in *The Witchcraft Reader* (London: Routledge, 2002; 2nd edn 2008), pp. 341–48. For other hypotheses, see Erik Midelfort, 'Heartland of the Witchcraze', in *The Witchcraft Reader* (London: Routledge, 2002; 2nd edn 2008), pp. 99–106; and Christina Larner, 'Was Witch-Hunting Woman-Hunting?', in *The Witchcraft Reader* (London: Routledge, 2002; 2nd edn 2008), pp. 253–56.
34. In the modern Spanish mind, Galicia is also associated with witches (*bruxas*), but I have not found any evidence in seventeenth-century texts that would confirm this was the case in early modern Spain too.
35. Deodato Scaglia, quoted in John Tedeschi, 'The Question of Magic and Witchcraft in Two Unpublished Inquisitorial Manuals of the Seventeenth Century', *Proceedings of the American Philosophical Society*, 131.1 (1987), 92–111 (p. 106).
36. See Lyndal Roper, *Witch Craze: Terror and Fantasy in Baroque Germany* (New Haven, CT: Yale University Press, 2004).
37. See Jane Davidson, *Early Modern Supernatural*; Gerhild Scholz Williams, 'Pierre de Lancre and the Basque Witch-Hunt', in *The Witchcraft Reader* (London: Routledge, 2002; 2nd edn 2008), pp. 180–84. See also Caro Baroja (*The World of Witches*) and Lara Martínez.
38. It is not uncommon for a witch-craze to start with the accusations or confessions of children or adolescents who dream about witches; see Levack ('The Decline of Witchcraft Prosecutions'). In Germany and Sweden a number of mass trials were started by the accusations of children (see Henningsen, *El abogado*). Gaskill points out that in Salem, which was also sparked by accusations of teenage girls, the conflict between Indians and settlers in the mid-1670s caused anxiety and that in people's imagination demons and native warriors had merged.
39. In other words, only 0.3% of the accused were eventually burnt at the stake. Perhaps those who claim hugely inflated numbers of victims of the 'witch-craze' — often for ideological reasons — are misled by the large numbers of accusations (instead of executions).
40. See also Toby Green, *Inquisition* (London: Pan Books, 2007).

41. Pedro de Valencia, *Discurso acerca de los cuentos de las brujas*, Obras completas, VII (León: Universidad de León, 1997), p. 256.
42. Manuel Fernández Álvarez, *Casadas, monjas, rameras y brujas: la olvidada historia de la mujeres españolas en el Renacimiento* (Madrid: Espasa, 2010), p. 384.
43. Michel de Montaigne, *Les Essais* (Paris: Livre de Poche, 2001), pp. 1604–05.
44. See José Luis Betrán Moya, 'El mundo mágico de Julio Caro Baroja', *Historia Social*, 55 (2006), 79–111.
45. Corpses that bled when their killer was nearby were widely reported (Clark; Mauss). Del Río thinks that the cause of this is that a 'hidden, mysterious quality is imprinted upon the body and remains there after death' (Del Río, p. 49). The weapon-salve caused great controversy in the 1630s (Thomas; Clark). The example of the snake comes from Reginald Scot, and that of the tarantula from Nieremberg's *Oculta Filosofia de la Sympatia y Antipatia de las Cosas* (Madrid: Emprenta del Reyno, 1633; repr. Whitefish, MO: Kessinger Legacy Reprints, 2010).
46. For a balanced appreciation of Foucault, see Gary Cutting, *Michel Foucault's Archaeology of Scientific Reason* (Cambridge: Cambridge University Press, 1989); for a much more critical view, see George Huppert, '*Divinatio et Eruditio*: Thoughts on Foucault', *History and Theory*, 13.3 (1974), 191–207.
47. See Thomas Kuhn, *The Structure of Scientific Revolutions* (Chicago, IL: University of Chicago Press, 1962).
48. James I, *Demonology* (Edinburgh: Robert Waldegrave, 1597; repr. San Diego: The Book Tree, 2002), p. 42.
49. A similar claim is made by Castillo Solórzano: 'lo que te puedo asegurar es que ninguna cosa de las que en este libro te presento es traducción italiana, sino todas hijas de mi entendimiento' [what I can assure you is that nothing of what I present to you in this book is a translation from Italian, they are all daughters of my imagination] (Alonso de Castillo Solórzano, *Tardes entretenidas*, 9 (Madrid: Librería de los bibliófilos españoles, 1908), p. 13).

CHAPTER 3

Slippery Sorcery

> Es un mundo exaltado, maravilloso y sobrenatural, con apariencias nocturnas de fantasmas, sueños fatídicos, conjuros y embrujos eróticos, pactos diabólicos, raptos, estupros y asesinatos. (Joaquín del Val)[1]
>
> [It is an exalted, marvellous and supernatural world, with nocturnal appearances of ghosts, premonitory dreams, erotic spells and conjurations, diabolical pacts, abduction, rape and murder.]

In the previous chapter we saw that attitudes to the supernatural were changing in the seventeenth century and that the discourse surrounding it became pervaded by doubt. In no other writer from the period is the indeterminacy more explicitly played out than in Zayas. When we look at her treatment of sorcery and witchcraft it becomes clear that the author embraced a multifarious approach. She neither denies nor confirms the possibility of magic; sometimes she treats it with irony and light-hearted scepticism, whereas in other instances magic — whether efficacious or not — is deployed in unsettling tales of rape and abuse. I do not claim that Zayas consciously exposes the contradictions of a shifting episteme but rather that she reflects and exploits the uncertainty and ambivalence vis-à-vis the supernatural *sensu lato*. By showing multiple facets of magic one could say that she sits on the epistemological fence. This strategy fits in well with her overall aim to cause *admiratio* by her baroque enterprise where the reader is led into a narrative labyrinth of apparent contradiction. Modern readers are sometimes surprised at her daring descriptions of sex, violence and sorcery and wonder how 'she got away with it'. By far the most likely answer is that the censors — and her public — read her tales as they were intended: a series of novellas where things are not always what they seem, and where for many views that are presented (magic is real, women are innocent) the opposite can be found (magic is a sham, women are evil), all of which has been brought under the umbrella of a notional morality of warning and exemplarity, however shallow and hackneyed that conceit had become and perhaps always had been. That is why in the *Aprobación* and the *Licencia* the censors state that the tales contain nothing 'contra nuestra Santa Fe ni buenas costumbres, antes gustosa inventiva y apacible agudeza digna de tal Dama' [against our Holy Faith nor good customs, but rather pleasing creativity and gentle intelligence, worthy of such a Lady]. Zayas's exploitation of the indeterminacy surrounding the preternatural becomes clear when we compare and contrast four novellas that feature magic.

3.1 Fraudulent Magic in 'El castigo de la miseria'

In 'El castigo de la miseria' Marcos loses his fortune after he has been tricked by Isidora, who pretends to be a rich young widow. The morning after their wedding night he discovers she is almost twenty years older than she had given herself out to be, with her face full of wrinkles and wearing a wig and false teeth, some of which Marcos finds in his moustache when he wakes up. Shortly afterwards, Marcela, one of the maids, disappears, and with her Marcos's fortune. Isidora, her 'cousin' Agustinico — in reality her young lover — and another maid also take to their heels and flee to Barcelona. Some time later Marcos bumps into Marcela, who promptly bursts into crocodile tears and promises to help him find his lost treasure by taking him to a magician who will perform a ceremony. Her real intention, however, is to play a prank and shake him down for his last *reales*: 'ella se determinó a engañarle y estafarle lo que pudiese' [she decided to trick him and fleece him for all he was worth] (*Novelas*, p. 283). Marcos agrees to come with her, claiming he is not the least bit afraid of demons: 'era ver un demonio ver un plato de manjar blanco' [seeing a demon was the same as seeing a dish of blancmange] (*Novelas*, p. 284). After an elaborate sham ceremony, involving a fake grimoire and some mumbo-jumbo, someone deliberately sets fire to the tail of a cat and lets it loose on Marcos, whose face is badly scratched as a result. The hapless victim faints, convinced he was confronted not with merely one demon but with a whole legion. The authorities are informed, the imposter thrown in jail and Marcos interrogated. It soon transpires that he has been had; the magician was a charlatan and the grimoire nothing but a battered old copy of *Amadís de Gaula*, a famous romance of chivalry of the kind that drove Don Quixote to madness. This causes much mirth and Marcos leaves with the laughter of the people at court still ringing in his ears. He is seen as the most cowardly man in town, having lost his fortune to boot. Back home he receives a letter from Isidora, mocking him cruelly. After that, he is taken ill and dies, at least in most editions — in the first edition he actually commits suicide; this alternative ending will be discussed in the next chapter.

One likely source for this story is novella XX from *Il Novellino* by Masuccio. In that tale we read that Iacomo Pinto is in love with a lady. He is persuaded by his friend Loisi to consult the famous Misser Angelo, 'lo più gran nigromante che oggi sia sopre la terra' [the greatest necromancer now alive on earth],[2] who promises to conjure up the demon Barabas. When warned of the dangers, the youth confidently replies he feels ready to go to hell and back: 'Io vo' che tu sappi che io anderei insino a l'inferno' [I want you to know that I'd go to the very depths of hell] (*Il Novellino*, p. 184). Since the idea is to fleece Iacomo, he is asked to bring a sword that has killed a man, a castrated ram and some capons. The fraudulent sorcerer draws a circle and pretends to utter a spell: 'fingindo de dire soi incantesimi con strani atti de testa e de boca' [pretending to say his incantations with strange movements of the head and mouth] (*Il Novellino*, p. 185). Iacomo is afraid but gathers his nerve and calls the demon three times. At each time, Loisi, who is dressed as the Devil, makes a terrible din. The two prankster are rolling on the ground laughing: 'erano del gran riso quasi indebiliti' [they were almost knocked out by laughter] ((*Il Novellino*, p. 186).

The youth is asked to hand over the sword, the ram and the capons, after which he takes to his heels. Later Loisi tells his friend what happened. Iacomo punishes Misser Angelo, sells his belongings and goes off to war, but instead of dying he gets rich and in the end rewards the pranksters.

The novella equally owes a clear debt to Cervantes. First of all, the beginning of the plot is reminiscent of 'El casamiento engañoso'. In both stories a gullible man is deceived by false appearances and driven by his lust for money, not by love or even concupiscence. Second, the tale is told with wit and irony and is a perfect companion piece to the other story of the evening, that of the naïve Fadrique who searches in vain for the perfect wife: 'El prevenido engañado'. Both stories are narrated by male participants in the *sarao* and together with the equally male-narrated 'Al fin se paga todo' these tales fit Emilia Pardo Bazán's description of Zayas's oeuvre as 'la picaresca de la aristocracia' [the aristocratic picaresque], although this is much less apposite when applied to her entire oeuvre.[3] Maroto Camino has made the claim that the male-narrated novellas have been more successful than the female-narrated ones, although she does not adduce any evidence. But if Scarron's adaptations into French, which in turn were translated into other languages, are anything to go by, then there is some truth in her assertion, since these three above-mentioned tales were precisely the ones he chose for his renditions.[4]

Sandra Foa considers all characters in the novella to be caricatures, and this should not surprise in a novella that has obvious comical elements. Marcos is described as being as thin as an asparagus and Zayas spends a great deal of time recounting his miserly actions. Another clear parody is the false magician:

> Y luego el astuto mágico se vistió una ropa de bocací negro y una montera de lo mismo, y tomando un libro de unas letras góticas en la mano, algo viejo el pergamino para dar más crédito a su burla, hizo un cerco en el suelo y se metió dentro con una varilla en las manos, y empezó a leer entre dientes murmurando en tono melancólico y grave, y de cuando en cuando pronunciaba algunos nombres extravagantes y exquisitos que jamás habían llegado a los oídos de don Marcos. (*Novelas*, p. 285)

> [And then the astute magician donned a cape of heavy black lining cloth and a cap of the same material, and taking a book written in blackletter on rather old parchment in one hand and, to add credibility to his prank, drawing a circle on the floor, he placed himself in the centre, took a wand in his other hand and began to read, muttering something under his breath in a melancholy and serious voice, sometimes pronouncing outlandish and exotic names that Marcos had never heard before in his life.]

The fake magician is a humorous, bogus version of the Renaissance magus (see 2.6). The esoteric tradition that is mocked here was on the wane and may never have had much currency in Spain in the first place, but there were plenty of people — predominantly men, a fair few of them lower clergy — who resorted to this kind of magic in order to find treasures. In this novella Zayas describes a preternatural activity light-heartedly. Not only is the magic ceremony a hoax, but the victim cuts a pathetic, ridiculous figure. In 'El castigo' the fake ceremony is performed by a man; amatory magic, by contrast, was almost entirely a female domain, as is the case in the fifth novella.

3.2 A Wily Sorceress and a Haunted Roadside Chapel in 'La fuerza del amor'

'La fuerza del amor' is set in Naples where the beautiful Laura is courted assiduously by Diego after he sees her at a ball. He wins her hand in marriage but very soon begins to lose interest and returns to his erstwhile lover Nise. When Laura protests and weeps, he beats her brutally. Her brother Carlos intervenes and would have killed Diego had Laura not stopped him. Unable to see her suffer, her father and brothers abandon her to her fate and return to their home in Pietra Bianca.[5] In her despair Laura seeks out a sorceress in order to win back Diego's love. The 'wily sorceress' (*taimada hechicera*) sends her to a roadside shrine (*humilladero*) at the outskirts of town to collect the beard, hair and teeth of a hanged man — the corpses of executed criminals having been brought to the shrine to decompose on iron hooks over a pit. Before she sets out she rails at the misfortunes of love, decrying her feminine condition and imprecating Diego for his male perfidy. When she enters the pit her brother receives a telepathic warning and jumps on his horse, which stops dead in its tracks when it reaches the shrine. He takes her back to Pietra Bianca, but she refuses to return to Diego and decides to enter the convent of the Immaculate Conception as a lay sister (*seglar*). Her husband leaves to join the army and is soon blown up by a mine; she takes the habit and lives piously ever after.

Historically, many of the women involved in love magic were prostitutes, lovers of friars or else women of 'loose morals', but some of them were married. In her research, Sánchez Ortega found a good number of women who, like Laura, were beaten and abused by their husbands. In one instance, a woman claims she was fed ground-up glass by her spouse in an attempt to kill her. Having recourse to black magic was not seen as apostasy by these women. To truly reject Christ and worship the Devil would involve cutting loose all anchors: family, Church, and neighbourhood or village. Very few if any of those involved in love magic would fit the category of complete renegades. Rather, in this poetics of the everyday, flesh slides into spirit, good into evil, evil into good, as Ruggiero so eloquently puts it (Ruggiero, p. 107). Laura's plight and her recourse to sorcery therefore perfectly fit an established pattern.

The sorceress asks Laura to collect hair and teeth from a cadaver. These were very common ingredient in spells — Tello in *El caballero de Olmedo* is told to do the same by Fabia — because they were thought to contain a person's life spirits, a notion based on contagious magic. Throughout the story it is made clear, however, that magic is an imposture just as in 'El castigo de la miseria'. But there is a considerable difference in tone. Where the tale of Marcos's pathetic miserliness and his comeuppance is comical, Laura's is a harrowing tale of wife battery, abandonment and impotent rage at her lot. The wily sorceress is clearly out to trick Laura out of her money and has no effective magic to offer — her only objective is to 'bleed' Laura's purse (*sangrar la bolsa*). The narrator peppers her tale with references to 'supersticiones' [superstitions], 'apariencias de verdades' [apparent truths], 'invenciones' [inventions], 'enredo' [scheme], and the 'común engaño de personas apasionadas' [common deceit of love-struck people]. She calls the sorceress 'embustera' [imposter], 'falsa enredadora' [false trickster], and 'taimada hechicera' [wily sorceress]. We are left in no doubt that Laura's despair has led her astray and she has fallen into a trap, vainly seeking a magic solution to her problems: 'oyendo decir que en aquella tierra había mujeres que obligaban con fuerzas de hechizos a que hubiese amor' [having heard that in those lands there were women who use spells to force people to love each other] (*Novelas*, p. 361). The scene at the chapel is described in macabre detail. A mile out of town, the shrine stands a little bit away from the main road to Pietra Bianca (see 1.1) and is surrounded by a pit on all sides:

> A estado de hombre, y menos, hay puestos por las paredes garfios de hierro, en los cuales, después de haber ahorcado en la plaza los hombres que mueren por justicia, los llevan allá y cuelgan en aquellos garfios; y como los tales se van deshaciendo, caen los huesos en aquel hoyo que, como está sagrado, les sirve de sepultura. (*Novelas*, p. 365)

> [At about the height of a man, and sometimes lower, there are iron hooks sticking out of the wall. After criminals who have been sentenced to death have been publicly hanged, their corpses are brought here and suspended from these hooks. As their bodies decompose, the bones fall into the pit, which, being consecrated ground, serves as their tomb.]

The situation becomes even more eerie when her brother receives a telepathic warning that she is in danger:

> Estando don Carlos acostado en su cama al tiempo que llegó Laura al humilladero, despertó con riguroso y cruel sobresalto, dando tales voces que parecía se le acababa la vida [...] vuelto más en sí, levantándose de la cama y diciendo: 'En algún peligro está mi hermana', se comenzó a vestir [...] a la una se halló enfrente del humilladero, donde paró el caballo de la misma suerte que si fuera de bronce o piedra. (*Novelas*, p. 366)

> [Don Carlos was fast asleep in his bed when Laura arrived at the roadside chapel, but suddenly he woke up with a terrible and cruel fright, shouting so loudly that it seemed he was dying [...] Having recovered his senses, he got up and said: 'My sister is in some kind of danger', and got dressed [...] At one o'clock, as he rode past the roadside chapel, his horse stopped in its tracks and refused to move, as if it were made of bronze or stone.]

This uncanny episode complicates the reading of the story as a merely sceptical account of magic. Moreover, what happens is referred to as 'un caso portentoso' [a portentous case] (*Novelas*, p. 368). So despite presenting magic as an imposture, Zayas manages to create an otherworldly atmosphere (for more discussion on the fantastic in Zayas, see 5.2).

Laura may have been saved, but she does not return to her husband. Her ordeal came about because she was abandoned by her father and brother and brutally beaten by her husband — precisely the people who were supposed to love and protect her. She embodies the predicament of women under patriarchy. This explains why instead of fearing the salvific implications of her recourse to black magic, she rails against her position as a woman, repeating almost verbatim what Zayas says in her prologue:

> ¿Por qué, vanos legisladores del mundo, atáis nuestras manos para las venganzas,

imposibilitando nuestras fuerzas con vuestras falsas opiniones, pues nos negáis letras y armas? El alma ¿no es la misma que la de los hombres? Pues si ella es la que da valor al cuerpo, ¿quién obliga a los nuestros a tanta cobardía? Yo aseguro que si entendierais que también había en nosotras valor y fortaleza no os burlaríais como os burláis; y así, por tenernos sujetas desde que nacemos vais enflaqueciendo nuestras fuerzas con los temores de la honra y el entendimiento con el recato de la vergüenza, dándonos por espadas ruecas y por libros almohadillas. (*Novelas*, p. 364)

[Why, vain legislators of the world, do you tie our hands and prevent us from avenging ourselves, hamstringing us with your false opinions since you deny us learning and arms? Is not our soul the same as a man's? And if it is the soul that gives our bodies courage, what is it that compels us to such cowardice? I assure you that if you understood that in us too there is courage and strength, you would not cheat on us the way you do; from the day we are born, you subject us and weaken our strength with fears about honour, and our intelligence with modesty and shame, giving us distaffs instead of swords and pincushions instead of books.]

This is why Hernández Pecoraro sees Laura's descent into the pit as a metaphorical descent into hell, even if strictly speaking the protagonist does not enter the pit nor touch the cadavers.[6] Instead, she spends three hours in the chapel unable to go through with what she has set out to do: 'jamás consiguió su deseo, desde las diez que serían cuando llegó allí, hasta la una' [she never managed to get what she wanted, from around ten o'clock, when she arrived, until one o'clock] (*Novelas*, p. 366). But Laura's three hours in the vicinity of the corpses constitutes a harrowing experience and I agree with Hernández Pecoraro that Laura dies a metaphorical death and is resurrected and reborn, having come to the decision never to return to her husband and turn her back on her family. Her reconciliation is not with a patriarchy that condemns her to a degrading existence but with the feminine sphere of the convent. This tallies with Greer's conviction that Zayas's project is aimed at implanting 'the conviction that heterosexual union is *not* the desired goal but a fatal trap for most women, and that true happy endings can only be found by sublimating desire for any corporeal male and rejoining the mother in the feminine world of the convent' (Greer, *Baroque Tales*, p. 340).

When Laura decides to seek out a sorceress, the narrator tells us that this is a cinch because in Naples there are many such women and the Inquisition is not there to put a stop to these practices:

Hay en Nápoles, en estos enredos y supersticiones, tanta libertad que públicamente usan sus invenciones, haciendo tantas y con tales apariencias de verdades que casi obligan a ser creídas. Y aunque los confesores y el virrey andan en esto solícitos, como no hay el freno de la Inquisición y los demás castigos, no les amedrentan. (*Novelas*, p. 361)

[There is in Naples, as far as these superstitions and schemes are concerned, so much freedom that they go about their business openly, and these acts are so frequent and seem so real that one is almost compelled to believe them. And although the confessors and the Viceroy are trying to tackle the problem, seeing as the Inquisition is not there to curb it, these people are not scared.]

There are a few noteworthy elements here. First, there are the references to superstitions and 'apariencias de verdades' [apparent truths] that are so typical of the seventeenth-century approach to magic. Next, the narrator makes a clear effort to align herself with the Spanish authorities and the Church, stressing that the Viceroy and the confessors are trying to remedy the situation, but that they are simply overwhelmed by the sheer number of false witches and hampered by the absence of the Holy Office. The situation in Naples appears to be very similar to the one in Rome in 1645, as described by Scipione Mercurio in *De gli errori popolari d'Italia*:

> This plague is so widespread here where I am writing that without any consideration or fear, almost everyone for a headache, or other infirmity, first goes to visit the *malefica* or witch to be signed by her, and for childbirth ailments, for tertiary or quartan fevers, for wounds or dislocations, and even for syphilis they go to be signed by these really witches, who, with less infamous name are called *segnaresse*. (quoted in Tedeschi, 'The Question of Magic', p. 100)

Since the Spanish Inquisition was established in Castile and Aragon in 1478 there had been a number of attempts to introduce it to other parts of the empire. King Ferdinand tried to set up a branch of the tribunal in Naples, but to no avail. Charles V attempted the same, although with less vigour, and was equally unsuccessful. In 1547 there were revolts when the people thought that the Spanish Inquisition was about to be active in the city. At the time his successor was on the throne, the people 'had [...] lost none of their horror of the Spanish institution and, when Philip II endeavoured to force it upon Milan, their fears were aroused that it might be imposed upon Naples'.[7] The king was forced to assure his subjects 'that he had no intention of introducing the Spanish Inquisition and that trials for heresy should be conducted in the ordinary way as heretofore' (Lea, pp. 86–87). This sounds as though there was no Inquisition at all in Naples, just as Zayas suggests, but in fact, as elsewhere in Italy, there was an episcopal Inquisition that operated in Naples and which had gradually been brought under the control of the papal (Roman) Inquisition by the seventeenth century (see Kamen, *The Spanish Inquisition*). But even if there *had* been the 'freno de la Inquisición' (literally: the bit or curb of the Inquisition), it would probably not have made any difference. In the previous chapter we have seen examples of the Holy Office's leniency with regards to sorcery and that Alonso de Salazar's recommendations to the Suprema counselling reticence in matters of witchcraft were known by the Roman Inquisition. We also saw that Italian inquisitors were advised not to 'rush headlong' into these matters (see 2.5), even though we are dealing with *hechiceras* here and not *brujas*. Apart from showing that Zayas aligns herself with the authorities and the Church, the passage is proof that the Holy Office was not universally feared by Spaniards, despite the famous proverb 'del Rey y de la Inquisición, chitón' [about the King and the Inquisition, best to keep quiet]. Henry Kamen has suggested that the Inquisition was more accepted in Castile than elsewhere, but never enthusiastically supported (nor universally feared), adding that the Reformation made it appear more natural and acceptable and that it fulfilled a social role 'as guardian against heresy, as keeper of public morality, as arbiter between factions, as tribunal for small causes' (Kamen, *The Spanish Inquisition*, p. 82).

In the two novellas discussed so far, magic is not treated as real, but either as a comic sham ceremony or as the shady scheming of a heartless fraud. I shall now turn to two tales in which magic is described as perfectly efficacious, even after being tested by the authorities; within the confines of the story there is no doubt that what happens *is* the result of a spell. But as in the previous two tales, the tone differs from one novella to the other. Although the contrast is not as stark, the spell in one of the stories is explicitly referred to as a funny detail, whereas the heroine in the other suffers a fate even more harrowing than Laura's.

3.3 A Funny Spell in 'El desengaño amando'

The sixth *novela amorosa* of Zayas's collection, 'El desengaño amando y premio de la virtud', is set in Toledo and tells the story of Fernando, an inveterate gambler and womanizer who falls in love with Juana, who is initially courted by Octavio. After some assiduous wooing with poetry and music, Fernando wins her over under the promise of marriage and Octavio leaves town. After having his wicked way with her, however, he is reluctant to marry her, pretending that his widowed mother does not agree with the match. Not having any family, Juana turns to her friend Lucrecia. But the latter also falls in love with Fernando and writes him a letter to that effect. Suspecting foul play, Juana decides to take on her rival 'con las mismas armas' [with the same weapons] (*Novelas*, p. 382). She enlists the help of a student from Alcalá who gives her two rings with green gems that contain genies who are able to tell him whom she will marry, provided she wears the rings a certain way when she interrogates Fernando about his plans. After the interrogation she should take off the rings. Juana follows the instructions and gives the rings to her maid for safekeeping. The maid surreptitiously puts them on as she does the washing. When the student returns, Juana gives the rings back, whereupon the genies beat the living daylights out of him for allowing them to be drenched. They tell him that he and Juana will both go to hell, after which they seem to disappear. Juana takes in the badly beaten student, who renounces the dark arts, although Juana still manages to persuade him to teach her a spell to make her ex-lover Octavio come back to her. She thinks he is alive and well in his native Italy, where she told him to go when a duel threatened to break out between Fernando and himself. Unbeknownst to Juana, however, he has died and when she conjures him up, it is his ghost that appears to harangue her. Juana mends her ways and enters the convent of the Immaculate Conception. Meanwhile, Fernando has amassed huge gambling debts and his roving eye is caught by the young Clara, whom he marries mainly because of her supposed wealth. But after four years and having fathered two daughters, he runs off with Lucrecia to Seville, where they live as man and wife. Although courted by a well-meaning marquis, Clara decides to follow them. She is hired as a maid by Fernando and Lucrecia, who do not recognize her. She is keen to find out what Lucrecia's secret is, and one day her mistress asks her to feed a cockerel that lives in a large chest in the attic. The animal is chained-up and wears blinkers. When she takes them off, Fernando recognizes his wife and starts to weep. Lucrecia knows her game is up and sticks a great needle into a waxen effigy of Fernando. Then she takes a knife and stabs herself in the heart, dropping dead onto the floor. The authorities are informed and an investigation is mounted. In order to verify Clara's story, they put the blinkers on the cockerel, and, sure enough, Fernando has no idea who she is. After that, they doff the blinkers and Fernando recognizes his wife once more, weeping bitter tears. The procedure is repeated various times and the magistrates are convinced of the efficacy of the spell. Fernando and Clara are declared innocent and will not face a prison sentence, unlike the female slaves of the household who are deemed to have been complicit. Fernando remains fatally ill from the effects of the spell. He is taken back to Toledo, where he dies, leaving Clara free to marry her suitor the marquis. They live happily ever after and the two daughters she had with Fernando enter the convent of the Immaculate Conception to join Juana.

Of all the novellas in Zayas's collection, this is the one where magic is most central to the plot. There are three distinct episodes; the first is that of the magic rings, then there is the conjuration of Octavio's ghost, and lastly we have Lucrecia's spells. The ring-dwelling *demonios* are imps or hobgoblins rather than Satan's servants, even if they claim to be able to foresee the future. With reference to the green stones, Matos-Nin says they are emeralds, which were thought to have magical properties, stating that: 'La crítica moderna piensa que esta es una idea ridícula y falta de lógica',[8] without however indicating which critics have said this. After that, Laura uses a spell to make Octavio come to her. When his ghost appears, rattling his chains and surrounded by licking flames, it is not because the spell was effective, but because 'aunque el demonio es padre de mentiras y engaños, tal vez permite Dios que diga alguna verdad en provecho y utilidad de los hombres, para que se avisen de su perdición' [even though the Devil is the father of lies and deceit, sometimes God may permit him to speak the truth for the benefit of the people so that they may be warned of their damnation] (*Novelas*, p. 387).

Martín del Río discusses ghosts in his *Investigations into Magic*, saying that only God has the power to release souls from Purgatory but that in fact he will never allow it: 'To think that he would do so because of the prayers and incantations of magicians is impious' (Del Río, pp. 71–72). Necromancers who claim they can summon up souls are fraudulent. According to Ciruelo, one of the ways the Devil manifests himself is by pretending to be 'algún alma ensabanada que dice que anda en pena' [some sheet-covered soul saying it is in Purgatory] (Ciruelo, p. 110). But sometimes God allows souls to appear to us 'tomando cuerpo fantástico del aire' [assuming a fantastical, aerial body], albeit 'muy de tarde en tarde' [very occasionally] (Ciruelo, p. 203). Francisco de Vitoria too stresses the rarity of the event, although he does not want to exclude it entirely. He condemns the custom of asking souls from Purgatory for help, saying the apparitions are largely false: 'Y si algunas fueran verdaderas, serían obra de los mismos demonios' [And should some of them be real, they would be the work of demons] (Vitoria, p. 93). Zayas's description of Octavio's ghost is therefore strictly conventional, although the event is supposed to be rare. This very real ghost forms a neat contrast with the fake ghost that appears in 'El imposible vencido' (see 5.1).

The novella's most elaborate description of magic involves the 'artes y conjuros' [arts and spells] by Lucrecia. When we are first introduced to her we are told that she is Italian, though 'tan ladina y españolada como si fuera nacida y criada en Castilla' [so sly and Hispanized that it seemed she had been born and raised in Castile] (*Novelas*, p. 380). She is over forty-eight years old but still attractive and reputed to be a 'grandísima hechicera' [very great sorceress]. She only uses her craft for her own benefit and keeps it a secret. We are told that Lucrecia uses her magic to seduce Fernando and that when the latter decides to marry Clara, there is a lull in her spell, probably due to an oversight on the Italian sorceress's part: 'no estaba [Fernando] tan apretado de los hechizos de Lucrecia' [Fernando suffered the effect of Lucrecia's spells less] (*Novelas*, p. 390). But when she finds out he has married another she is furious and casts a nasty spell on him:

> Supo Lucrecia el casamiento de don Fernando a tiempo que no lo pudo estorbar por estar ya hecho; y por vengarse, usando de sus endiabladas artes, dio con él en la cama, atormentándole de manera que siempre le hacía estar en un ¡ay!, sin que en más de seis meses que le duró la enfermedad se pudiese entender de dónde le procedía. (*Novelas*, p. 392)

> [Lucrecia found out about Don Fernando's marriage too late to prevent it, as it had already taken place; and to avenge herself she used her devilish arts and attacked him in his bed, tormenting him in such a way that he was forever crying out in pain, and in the more than six months that his illness lasted he never found out where it came from.]

Then there is the famous episode with the blinkered cockerel. What he wears are described as 'unos antojos' (*Novelas*, p. 403), referred to by some critics as glasses (Greer, *Baroque Tales*; Matos-Nin, *Lo sobrenatural*), while Brownlee calls it a blindfold (*Cultural Labyrinth*). The true meaning, however, is that of blinkers. In his dictionary Covarrubias defines 'antojos' first as 'cravings' (as in modern Spanish) and then as spectacles or glasses ('anteojos' in modern Spanish) and then adds: 'antojos de caballo, estos le ponen no para que vea sino para que esté quedo y no se espante' ['antojos de caballo' are what they put on horses, not so that they might see better, but so they are quiet and do not scare]. Zayas makes this reading perfectly clear by adding: 'a modo de los de caballo, que le tenían privada la vista' [like a horse's, depriving him of his sight] (*Novelas*, p. 403). The logic behind the spell is evident and based on sympathetic magic: just as the cockerel is chained and blinkered, just so is Fernando tied to Lucrecia, only having eyes for her and not his wife.

Lucrecia's magic can also be read metaphorically. Fernando may have been merely seduced by Lucrecia. We still use the language of magic to refer to seduction. We speak of someone's charm and say we are *encantado* or *enchanté* when we meet someone; we sing about men or women putting a spell on us, so that we end up 'bewitched, bothered and bewildered'. Likewise, we can be spellbound, fascinated (subjected to the evil eye) or obsessed (originally a demonological term) by someone (see Whitenack, 'Lo que ha menester' and Kieckhefer). Zayas makes this link between seduction and magic explicit in a number of other novellas. In 'La perseguida triunfante', for example, Federico says: 'Y no te espantes que tema

a un hombre enamorado en presencia de una mujer hermosa, que es un hechizo la
hermosura que a todos mueve a piedad' [And do not be amazed that I fear a man in
love to be in the presence of a beautiful woman, because beauty is a spell that moves
all to devotion] (*Desengaños*, p. 451). We are also told that Lucrecia is past the prime
of her youth and does everything in her power to keep herself attractive:

> aún no había perdido la belleza que en la mocedad había alcanzado de todo
> punto, animándolo todo con gran cantidad de hacienda que tenía granjeado en
> Roma, Italia y otras tierras que había corrido, siendo calificada en todas por
> grandísima hechicera. (*Novelas*, p. 380)
>
> [she had not yet lost the beauty she had reached to perfection in her youth,
> enhancing it with the great wealth she had acquired in Rome, elsewhere in
> Italy and in other countries she had passed through, being labelled in all of them
> as a very great sorceress.]

This can be read as follows: she successfully enhances her beauty by means of the
great wealth she has amassed and *as a result* she is labelled (*calificada*) a sorceress
wherever she goes. It suggests Lucrecia has powers of seduction akin to those of
Cleopatra — 'Age cannot wither her, nor custom stale her infinite variety'.[9] Zayas
adds that 'esta habilidad no era conocida de todos, porque jamás la ejercitaba en
favor de nadie, sino en el suyo' [this ability was not known by all, because she never
applied it on anyone else's behalf, only her own] (*Novelas*, p. 380), implying she
does not share her beautifying secrets with anyone. This metaphorical reading is
made problematic by the fact that Lucrecia is nick-named Circe (three times) and is
alluded to have made a pact with the Devil, although that too could be interpreted
metaphorically. At one point, Fernando feels torn between the embers of his love
for Juana and Lucrecia's charms and spells:

> aquí le tiraba alguna voluntad, que aún había algunas brasas entre las muertas
> cenizas, y acullá los encantos y embustes, estaba parado en la calle, batallando
> con amor y hechizos, sin saber dónde acudir; mas al fin podía más Lucrecia, o
> por mejor decir el demonio, a quien ella tenía muy de su parte. (*Novelas*, pp.
> 381–82)
>
> [he was pulled hither by his desire — there were still some embers among the
> dead ashes — and thither by her spells and tricks, making him stand still in the
> street, torn between love and a hex, not knowing which way to go; but in the
> end Lucrecia won out, or, to be more precise, the Devil, who was very much
> on her side.]

This acknowledgement of the Devil's agency behind Lucrecia's preternatural
powers is in line with the theological conviction that any act of black magic relies
on a diabolical pact, be it explicit or implicit. As Del Río writes: 'All magical
operations rest, as on a foundation, upon a pact made between the magician and an
evil spirit' (Del Río, p. 73).

When Lucrecia realizes her game is up, she takes 'una figura de hombre hecha
de cera' [a statuette of a man made from wax] (*Novelas*, p. 404) and sticks a great
needle into its head, pushing it down through its body before throwing it into the
fire. Again, the voodoo doll is a very common instrument in black magic and the

thinking behind the action is clear enough. Fernando remains fatally wounded, although he has the opportunity to repent. His contrition and confession may save his soul but he cannot overcome the effects of the spell. This lends some poetic justice to the narrative, even though it is unusual, since magic is supposed to disappear with the demise of its source. After his death, Clara marries the marquis, giving the novella a fairy-tale ending.

The overall tenor of the novella is upbeat. The evil sorceress Lucrecia gets what is coming to her, the fickle Fernando pays the price for his treachery although he is allowed to clear his conscience and die confessed, Juana is saved, and Clara is rewarded by her marriage to a rich and doting husband. The audience too experiences the tale as a happy one and refers to Lucrecia's secret in the attic as 'el gracioso suceso del gallo con antojos' [the funny event with the blinkered cockerel] (*Novelas*, p. 408).

3.4 Voodoo Rape in 'La inocencia castigada'

If 'El desengaño amando' is on the whole a positive story, quite the reverse is the case for 'La inocencia castigada'. In that novella Diego falls in love with the beautiful Inés, whose husband is away on an extended business trip to Seville. Despite his best efforts she refuses to give in to his advances. His unhappiness is noticed by a neighbour, who proceeds to deceive him. She borrows one of Inés's dresses and makes a prostitute wear it, tricking Diego into believing he has finally conquered her. The deceit is found out and the woman severely punished. In his despair, Diego turns to a Moorish necromancer who creates a waxen effigy of Inés that will give him control of her. All the spurned lover needs to do is to light the candle on the head of the statue and his beloved will come to his bed. The spell works a treat. After being raped under a spell Inés returns home; when she wakes up she complains about 'descompuestos sueños' [lewd dreams]. The abuse goes on for a month until one night Inés is found sleepwalking in the street by her brother and the Corregidor [magistrate], who follow her and witness her slipping into Diego's bed. Diego remembers not to blow out the candle and tells Inés to go home. He then confesses his crime and Inés is so desperate she asks her brother to kill her for having been 'mala' [bad]. The Corregidor decides to test the enchantment and concludes she is not to blame. But her sister-in-law convinces her brother and her husband, who has returned from Seville, that she faked the spell. They wall her up in a very narrow space where she spends the next six years, standing in her own excrement and covered in worms. The authorities lock up Diego and, after having some difficulty in tracking him down, send the Moor to an inquisitorial dungeon in Madrid. When Inés is finally rescued, after a neighbour hears her moan and pray piteously, she has gone blind. Her husband, brother and sister-in-law are punished and she is put in a convent.

In this tale Diego is first subjected to a baroque test of truth and appearance, which he fails, taking the prostitute wearing Inés's dress to be Inés herself. Then he turns to a magician, 'habiendo oído decir que en la ciudad había un moro, gran hechicero y nigromántico, le hizo buscar, y que se le trajesen, para obligar con encantos y hechicerías a que le quisiese doña Inés' [having heard that in the city there was a Moor, a great sorcerer and necromancer, he sent for him to force Inés to love him by means of spells and sorcery] (*Desengaños*, p. 276). Etymologically, a necromancer is someone who consults the spirits of the dead, like the witch of Endor, through whom Saul tried to communicate with the departed prophet Samuel.[10] But in early modern Europe 'the conjuring of demons came to be known as necromancy' (Kieckhefer, p. 152) and it was the name for an *explicit* form of demonic magic. Zayas's 'nigromante agareno' ['Mohammedan' necromancer] is said to have some hold over the Devil, which is not difficult for him being a non-Catholic: 'como ajenos de nuestra católica fe, no les es dificultoso, con apremios que hacen al demonio' [since they do not profess the Catholic faith, this is not difficult for them, with the demands they make on the Devil] (*Desengaños*, p. 276). He proceeds to make a waxen statue of Inés with a candle on her head.[11] The sympathetic magic is once more evident: as this candle is burning, just so will Inés burn for Diego. Moreover, her heart is pierced by a golden arrow. After Diego has been discovered, the spell is tested rigorously by a magistrate:

> Que algo más quieta la desdichada dama, mandó el Corregidor, sin que ella lo supiera, se saliesen fuera y encendiesen la vela; que, apenas fue hecho, cuando se levantó y se salió adonde la vela estaba encendida, y en diciéndole que ya era hora de irse, se volvía a su asiento, y la vela se apagaba y ella volvía como de sueño. Esto hicieron muchas veces, mudando la vela a diferentes partes, hasta volver con ella en casa de don Diego, y encenderla allí. (*Desengaños*, p. 281)

> [When the unfortunate lady had calmed down a little, the magistrate ordered them to leave the room and light the candle without her being aware, and no sooner had they done just that than she got up and left the room to go to where the burning candle was, and when they told her it was time to go, she returned to her seat and when they extinguished the candle, she came to her senses, as if waking from a dream. They did this many times, placing the candle in various places, even taking it back to Don Diego's house, where they lit it.]

The fate of Diego and the Moor has led to some confusion. Matos-Nin (*Lo sobrenatural*) claims the Moor is the Devil himself because she says he disappears without a trace, even though in reality he is eventually caught. Patsy Boyer mistranslates the relevant passage so that it reads as if *Diego* is never seen again instead of the Moor.[12] It is only in the first instance that it seems the necromancer has vanished; he is apprehended and sent to an inquisitorial cell in Madrid and never seen again. The Spanish is not entirely clear, but this is how I read the passage:

> El Corregidor otro día buscó al moro que había hecho el hechizo; mas no pareció. Divulgóse el caso por la ciudad, y sabido por la Inquisición, pidió el preso, que le fue entregado con el proceso ya sustanciado, y puesto cómo había de estar, que llevado a su cárcel, y de ella a la Suprema, no pareció más. (*Desengaños*, p. 282)

> [The next day the magistrate subpoenaed (literally: looked for) the Moor who had cast the spell, but he did not appear. The case became known all over town, and when the Inquisition got wind of it, they demanded the prisoner be

transferred to them, which they did, after he had already been sentenced (*in absentia*), and they put him where he ought to be, and after he had been moved to their cell, and from there to the Suprema, he was never seen again.]

Whitenack devoted an article to this novella and in her view Inés is plagued by lewd dreams and guilt-ridden because somehow she was susceptible to the spell. She blames her desire on her being (sexually) neglected by her husband. The novella is introduced by the notion that women who do not get 'lo que ha menester' [what they need] are led to 'bajezas' [vile acts], leading men to lose their honour and women to lose their life. Furthermore, she refers to the conviction that free will cannot be subdued by enchantment (for more discussion, see 5.3). This suggests that Inés failed to use her free will to avoid her being raped, which might explain why she wants to die for having been 'mala' [bad]. Still, it would go too far to lay the blame at her door. Let us not forget that the novella is called 'La inocencia castigada'. In contrast to her earlier expression of guilt, from within the extremely narrow confines of her cell she bemoans her fate and insists on her innocence:

> ¿Señor, no castigarás? Pues cuando tú envías el castigo, es a quien tiene culpa, y aun entonces es con piedad: mas estos tiranos castigan en mí lo que no hice, como lo sabes bien tú, que no fui parte en el yerro por que padezco tan crueles tormentos. (*Desengaños*, pp. 284–85)
>
> [Lord, won't you punish them? You only punish those who are guilty, and even then it is with clemency: but these tyrants punish me for something I did not do; as you know, I had no part in the crime for which I am suffering such cruel torments.]

And when a friendly neighbour discovers her and asks her what she has done to deserve her ordeal, Inés replies: 'no tengo culpa; mas son cosas muy largas y no se pueden contar' [I am not to blame: but it is a long story and impossible to tell] (*Desengaños*, p. 286). She clearly believes she is blameless and the story emphasizes the power of the enchantment over her free will since she is 'forzada de algun espíritu diabólico' [forced by some diabolical spirit] (*Desengaños*, p. 277).[13] What appears to be at stake is Inés's utter powerlessness and abandonment, which is given voice through an irrational fear of magic. In Friedman's words: 'When Zayas resorts to the supernatural in this novella and throughout the collection, she seems to imply that, in a world of social negotiations, reason cannot suffice.'[14] Victorino Polo, too, argues that in 'La inocencia castigada' the introduction of the *nigromántico* changes the story completely, since the human plane is abandoned and the story turns to the dominions of the Devil 'donde el hombre viene a ser puro juguete sin voluntad ni razón, víctima de poderosas fuerzas telúricas y siderales, leño frágil lanzado a un torbellino sin fondo' [where man becomes a mere plaything without will or reason, a victim of powerful telluric as well as sideral forces, a piece of driftwood thrown into a bottomless whirlpool].[15] But that is not the whole story and magic is not merely an atavistic relapse into irrationality in a modernizing world and the concomitant decline of social systems, as Adorno has suggested (see 1.3).

A closer reading of the narrator's introduction to the novellas reveals some further rifts in Whitenack's argument. Laura introduces the tale as a warning against adultery by women of loose morals and an encouragement to men to forgive women even if they behave badly. She adds that men are hard-hearted and that the blame normally falls on women. When she starts her tale she warns that a woman in despair is likely to do anything if she does not get what she craves. But then she proceeds by saying: 'No le sucedió por esta parte a doña Inés la desdicha, porque su esposo hacía la estimación de ella que merecía su valor y hermosura' [This misfortune did not befall Doña Inés, however, because her husband valued her in accordance with her virtue and beauty] (*Desengaños*, p. 266). Brownlee sees this as an example of Zayas's project of polysemy in which the reader is put on the wrong foot.

However, the tale is not simply the reverse of what it purports to be about. Whitenack says that Inés marries against her will, but, to be more precise, she marries in order to escape from her wicked sister-in-law. Once married, her husband departs on an extended trip to Seville, during which she falls victim to the Moor's spell. When he returns, he is persuaded by the treacherous sister-in-law (*la traidora cuñada*) to wall up his innocent wife. According to Vollendorf (*Reclaiming*) the spatial confinement of Inés hyperbolizes the patriarchal impulse to confine women. Walled-up women were not uncommon in early modern Spain but immurement was rarely used as punishment; most of the 'emparedadas' [walled-up women] were urban female hermits who lived in tiny cells in the walls of cities or convents.[16] The evil sister-in-law is convinced that Inés faked the enchantment to cover up her love affair: 'decía que doña Inés debía de fingir el embelesamiento por quedar libre de culpa' [she said that Doña Inés had to be faking the enchantment to avoid blame] (*Desengaños*, pp. 281–82). In her study of women in Zayas, O'Brien sets out her idea that the author portrays a community based on gyn/affection as well as its obverse: the 'perfidious sisterhood' (O'Brien, *Women in the Prose*, p. 37). The evil sister-in-law is a prime example of a woman's lack of solidarity and her siding with patriarchy. This interpretation is made explicit by the narrator, who says of the 'traidora cuñada' that 'por mujer, pudiera tener piedad de ella' [being a woman, she should have taken pity on her] (*Desengaños*, p. 282). Gorfkle sees the sister-in-law as the classical oedipal rival and a terrifying mother figure, although she does not elaborate on the point.[17] A cynical reader of the tale might agree with the sister-in-law, though: Inés *could* have feigned the whole thing, even during the tests, because if there is no magic, then we are left with any alternative explanation, including a cynical one. But there is simply too much emphasis on the efficacy of the spell for this interpretation to be convincing. At the end of the story, Inés is put in a convent, beautiful but blind. Greer, not too convincingly, sees Inés's blindness as a 'synecdochic punishment: it is inflicted on the eyes of the woman whose beauty arouses desire in the eyes of others, envy in those who do not possess her, and a thirst to punish her in the flesh on the part of the cruel sister-in-law' (Greer, *Baroque Tales*, p. 275). I would say that Inés's tale is about evil powers, sexual frustration, female entrapment and abandonment as well as betrayal by those who are supposed to look after their loved ones. Zayas exploits not only the indeterminacy surrounding magic, giving just enough room for the cynic to disregard the veracity of the spell, but also the fear of the irrational, the notion that women are not in control of their bodies or their fate. The same point is made on numerous occasions when narrators and characters express the paralysing power of the stars (see 5.3).

3.5 Verisimilitude and Magic

In his study of love magic already referred to, Ruggiero tells the following story. One day when mass was celebrated in Feltre, in the north of the Veneto, a waxen statue pierced with needles was found underneath the altar. It had been placed there by a young woman who had been seduced by a local rake. He had made her several promises of marriage and she was pregnant with his child. At one stage during the courtship her father and another male member of the family burst into her room and discovered the two in bed. They forced the young man to promise he would marry the girl in question and made him give her a ring. This would have been a valid marriage by pre-Tridentine standards. After Trent, however, such marriages, not having been sanctioned by the Church, were no longer accepted. The father took his case to the authorities, but they were reluctant to take action. He then built his case on honour and claimed his family had been dishonoured. Meanwhile, the rake had fled to fight in Flanders. At that point the duped woman (*burlata*) contacted a woman called Lucrezia, who had the reputation of being a witch and who was nicknamed Circe. This go-between had been successful at bringing about marriages through her spells and she was the one who suggested having the waxen effigy made and placing it beneath the altar.

All the classic ingredients of many a novella and *comedia* are present in this account: the girl who is seduced and then abandoned, the rake who leaves her to fight in Flanders, the stain on the family honour. We also have an Italian *strega* (witch) called Lucrezia and nicknamed Circe, exactly as we have it in Zayas's novella 'El desengaño amando'. Another case Ruggiero cites is reminiscent of the spell in 'La inocencia castigada'. A courtesan named Isabella has used magic as a way of ensuring that her lover Milano would come to her. She would burn a holy lamp in front of a Tarot card depicting the Devil. She did this 'so that Milano would come to me, that was my intention, that he come' (Ruggiero, p. 97). Another woman, Elisabetta Giantis, describes a ritual that allowed her to conjure up a shadow version of herself, a true and literal inversion, who would go out and reverse her lover's reluctance:

> She [Betta] also taught me that I should undress fully nude both having bought and said [that I bought] a candle in the name of the Devil. Then [having lit the candle] I should turn my face to the shadow [created] and say 'I have undressed myself and you dress yourself' and also say 'good evening my shadow, my sister you go to the heart of so and so'. Then I took the candle from behind me and I said, 'I understand that one must pay the Devil'. (Ruggiero, pp. 122–23)

In her study, referred to in Chapter 2, Sánchez Ortega gives some Spanish examples of the same type of conjuration: 'Sombra, cabeça tenéis como yo, cuerpo tenéis como yo, yo te mando que ansí como tienes mi sombra verdadera que tú vayas a Fulano e lo traigas a mí' [Shadow, you have a head like me, you have a body like me, I send you just as you are my actual shadow to fetch so-and-so and bring him to me] (Sánchez Ortega, p. 79). Examples such as these should convince us that, at least for some people in early modern Europe, magic was real. This means that for a portion of Zayas's readers, the magic episodes described in 'La inocencia castigada' and 'El desengaño amando' had a ring of truth. The novellas have what we might call 'popular verisimilitude', even if the term 'popular' is fiendishly difficult to define and problematic in that it suggests that there is such a thing as 'the people', that they are a monolithic unit and that we can know what it was they thought, when in fact all we know about them has been mediated and comes to us through written records.[18] Nevertheless, inquisitorial records like those studied by Kamen, Tausiet, Ginzburg, Sánchez Ortega, Ruggiero and Martín Soto offer us at least a glimpse of the thoughts and beliefs of 'the people', and at times their voices do come through. In the case of Zayas's description of efficacious magic this 'popular verisimilitude' would reconcile what some scholars like Foa and Montesa have seen as a contradiction in her work: the claim to verisimilitude alongside the use of the supernatural.

We should not, however, be tempted to read too much into the insistence by the narrators that their stories are true; it is also just part of a genre convention. At the start of the second *sarao*, Lisis instructs her *desengañadoras* only to relate true stories. Nise returns to this stipulation at the start of the third tale:

> Lisis manda que sean casos verdaderos los que se digan, si acaso pareciere que los desengaños aquí referidos, y los que faltan, los habéis oído en otras partes, será haberle contado quien, como yo y las demás desengañadoras, lo supo por mayor, mas no con las circunstancias que aquí van hermoseados, y no sacado de una parte a otra, como hubo algún lego o envidioso que lo dijo de la primera parte de nuestro sarao. Diferente cosa es novelar sólo con la inventiva un caso que ni fue ni pudo ser (y ése no sirve de desengaño, sino de entretenimiento), a contar un caso verdadero, que no sólo sirva de entretener, sino de avisar. (*Desengaños*, pp. 199–200)

> [Lisis demands that all the stories we tell are true, and if it would appear you have already heard elsewhere the *desengaños* that have been told and are yet to be told, it must be because they were told by someone who, like me and the other *desengañadoras*, heard it first-hand, but not with the extra details that make these ones more pleasing, nor are they taken from various sources, like some uninformed or jealous person said was the case for the first part of our *Sarao*. It is one thing to tell a tale that never happened nor could ever happen based solely on the imagination (which could not serve as a *desengaño*, but only as amusement), and another to relate a true case that not only serves to entertain, but also to warn.]

Since sources have been found for almost all of Zayas's novellas, the insistence that her stories are based on actual events is nothing but empty rhetoric. That should not come as a surprise, since apart from Cervantes, who famously boasted that he invented his own plots, the novella tradition was all about reworking old tales to suit new tastes. In fact, Nise hints at Zayas's modus operandi: she adorns the stories she finds and has selected and reworks them in order to fit her pro-woman agenda:

to warn women of male perfidy. Her retelling of familiar tales — taken from Bandello, Boccaccio, Calderón, Cervantes, Masuccio, Timoneda and others — is also meant to evoke *admiratio* by the way it is achieved. This is where magic comes in; the sheer possibility of a preternatural intervention causes shivers to run down one's spine and at least part of the audience could indulge in a what-if fantasy. Zayas undoubtedly aimed to have as wide a readership as possible, both the elite (*culto*) and the 'people' (*vulgo*). For the *vulgo* audience, the magical episodes might have provided an exciting glimpse at a forbidden world (see Brownlee), whereas for the *culto* it was the way in which the story was told, with all its baroque complexities and contradictions, that caused admiration.

3.6 Seeds of Doubt: The Indeterminacy of the Preternatural

What we have seen so far is that the four stories that involve sorcery are either light-hearted or harrowing and magic is either efficacious or fraudulent. This leads to four possible combinations of variables: 'El castigo de la miseria' has comical elements and magic is a hoax; 'El desengaño amando y premio de la virtud' equally has comical elements, but magic is efficacious; 'La fuerza del amor' lacks comical elements and magic is a fraud; 'La inocencia castigada' is equally serious in tone but the spell is proved to be efficacious.

However, a closer analysis reveals that within the two tales that purport to show efficacious magic indeterminacy has nestled itself. As I have discussed, Zayas mentions Lucrecia's tricks and lies (*embustes*), while the story appears to bear out the reality of her spell. So, is the enchantment of Fernando an 'embuste' or not? Likewise, in 'La inocencia castigada', until he has seen Inés come to his bed, Diego, although happy to gaze upon the (nude) likeness of his beloved, is not so sure the Moor's enchantment will actually work: 'don Diego, aunque no muy seguro de que sería verdad lo que el moro le aseguraba, contentísimo cuando no por las esperanzas que tenía, por ver en la figura el natural retrato de su natural enemiga' [Don Diego, even though he was not really sure if what the Moor had promised him would come true, was nevertheless overjoyed, if not because of the hopes he entertained, then at least because he saw in the statue the very likeness of his natural enemy] (*Desengaños*, p. 276). The usual rhetorical stratagem used by Zayas is to give the reader options and leave it up to her or him to make a choice. As a result, even if the most likely scenario is usually indicated, we are still left with an alternative and thus a little seed of doubt is planted. We are told, for instance, that Fernando is attracted to Lucrecia *either* because he was tired of his wife's beauty and wanted something new, even if it was an ugly woman, *or* he was attracted by the prospect of having a lot of money to spend on games and gambling, *or else* he was attracted by her arts and spells (*artes y conjuros*), which is offered as the most likely case:

> Leyó don Fernando [la carta de Lucrecia], y como era vario de condición, y los tales tienen el remudar por aliño, porque cansados de gozar una hermosura, desean otra y tal vez apetecen una fealdad; que fuese esto o el interés de tener que gastar y jugar, o lo más cierto, que le inclinasen las artes y conjuros de

> Lucrecia, aceptó el partido que le hacía, acudiendo el mismo día a su casa. (*Novelas*, p. 381)
>
> [Don Fernando read Lucrecia's letter and since he was fickle — people like that are prone to spicing up things by changing them around, because when they are tired of enjoying one beauty, they desire another and may even be attracted by someone ugly; whether it was this, or the lure of having money to spend on games, or else, most likely, because he was won over by Lucrecia's arts and spells — he accepted her offer and went over to her house the very same day.]

In the same novella, Octavio's ghost appears *either* because the spell has worked, *or* because it was God's will, which is stated as the most likely cause and is later borne out by Octavio's own words:

> Tres [noches] serían pasadas cuando, o que las palabras del papel tuviesen la fuerza que el embustero estudiante había dicho, o que Dios, que es lo más cierto, quiso con esta ocasión ganar para sí a doña Juana haciendo instrumento al demonio y sus cosas para que fuese el mismo la causa de su conversión. (*Novelas*, p. 387)
>
> [Three nights or so had passed when either the words on the bit of paper had the power the deceitful student claimed it had, or that God, which is much more likely, wanted to use this opportunity to win over Doña Juana, making use of the Devil and his works in order that he, the Devil, would be the cause for her conversion.]

In 'La inocencia castigada' Inés, after she has been summoned by the Moor's spell, returns to her house without anyone noticing her, *either* because everyone happens to be sound asleep, *or* because they are also under a spell: 'Y llegando a [su casa], abrió, y volviendo a cerrar, sin haberla sentido nadie, o por estar vencidos del sueño, o porque participaban todos del encanto, se echó en su cama' [And arriving back home, she opened the door and shut it again behind her, without anyone noticing her — either because they were overcome by sleep, or because they were part of the spell — and threw herself on her bed] (*Desengaños*, p. 278).

This indeterminacy spills over into other areas, too. In 'El castigo de la miseria' Marcela tricks Marcos *either* because she wants to be rid of him *or* because she was a maid, implying all servants are untrustworthy:[19]

> Parecióle a Marcela ser don Marcos hombre poco pendencioso, y así se atrevió a decirle tales cosas, sin temor de lo que podía suceder; o ya lo hizo por salir de entre sus manos y no miró en más, o por ser criada, que era lo más cierto. (*Novelas*, p. 282)
>
> [Marcela reckoned Don Marcos was not the quarrelsome type, which is why she dared to tell him such things, not fearing what might happen; either doing it to get away from his clutches, not caring about the consequences, or because she was a maid, which is more likely.]

In the open grave near the roadside chapel Laura cannot reach the dead men's heads to extract their teeth, *either* because God prevents her from committing something so horrifying, *or* because she lacks the skills. In 'La inocencia castigada' God allows Inés to survive her six years of martyrdom *either* because he wanted to punish those who were guilty, *or because of her merit*. And Inés loses her eyesight *either* because she had been deprived of light, *or* because she had wept so much:

> En primer lugar, aunque tenía los ojos claros, estaba ciega, o de la oscuridad (porque es cosa asentada que si una persona estuviese mucho tiempo sin ver luz, cegaría), o fuese por esto, u [*sic*] de llorar, ella no tenía vista. (*Desengaños*, p. 287)

> [In the first place, even though her eyes were clear, she was blind, either because of the darkness (because it is well known that if a person is deprived of light for a long time, he or she will go blind), either it was because of that, or it was on account of her weeping that she lost her eyesight.]

The indeterminacy in Zayas goes much further than these examples. I have already referred to Brownlee's notion of polysemy and the idea that readers are wrong-footed and forced to reconsider their initial judgement. The fifth novella is a good example of this strategy. The *desengañadora* of that evening is Laura, a widow who says the following about her married life:

> Viví tan dulcemente engañada, el tiempo que fui amada y amé, de que me pudiese dar la amable condición de mi esposo causa para saber y especificar ahora desengaños; que no sé si acertaré a darlos a nadie; mas lo que por ciencia alcanzo, que de experiencia estoy muy ajena, me parece que hoy hay de todo, engañadas y engañados, y pocos o ningunos que acierten a desengañarse. (*Desengaños*, p. 262)

> [I lived so charmingly hoodwinked in the days when I loved and was loved that the kind nature of my husband hardly gave me cause to know anything about *desengaños* and share them with you today; I am not sure if I will succeed in offering a tale of disillusion to anyone, but from what knowledge I have — not having any personal experience — it seems to me that there are all sorts: deceived men as well as women, and few, if any, manage to see through the deceit.]

The happily married Laura seems an unlikely candidate to tell the harrowing tale of Inés's ordeal. But her mention of knowledge (*ciencia*) and experience (*experiencia*) is crucial, not just for this tale, but the whole collection. Lisis eventually becomes un-deceived (*desengañada*) through knowledge, having vicariously lived through the experiences of the ten preceding tales of disillusion (*desengaños*).

Returning to the case of Inés, that somehow a trace of an alternative interpretation lingers is evident in the discussion afterwards, where the discussants say that although she did not deserve to be tortured she would have deserved to die had she committed the sin of adultery:

> pues cuando doña Inés, de malicia, hubiera cometido el yerro que le obligó a tal castigo, no merecía más que una muerte breve, como se ha dado a otras que han pecado de malicia, y no darle tantas y tan dilatadas [muertes] como le dieron. (*Desengaños*, p. 289)

> [and even if Doña Inés, in her wickedness, had committed a crime for which they had to punish her, she only deserved a quick death, like those other women who have sinned out of wickedness, instead of making her die a thousand deaths, as they did.]

The nun Estefanía seems to imply that Inés did wrong when she exclaims: '¡Ay, divino Esposo mío! Y si vos, todas las veces que os ofendemos, nos castigais así, ¿qué fuera de nosotros?' [O, divine Husband of mine! If you punished us like this every time we offended you, what would become of us?] (*Desengaños*, p. 289). The tale of Inés's rape is introduced and commented upon as if she might have been guilty of adultery, and throughout there is ambiguity, even though the spell itself is tested and found to be effective. Surely there is no better example of the dizzying narrative twists and turns that are testimony to both Zayas's deep pessimism and her baroque mastery.

★ ★ ★ ★ ★

It is clear that Zayas uses magic in a variety of ways and this polyvalent use is an integral part of her project in which she plays complex games designed to elicit *admiratio*. Moreover, she taps into the contemporary epistemological uncertainty about the supernatural *sensu lato* by showing us real and efficacious forms of magic alongside impostures. In addition, the indeterminacy surrounding magic has spilled over to other aspects of her novellas. We have seen that all black magic was supposed to be based on a pact — tacit or explicit — with the Devil, and that Lucrecia is said to have the Devil on her side. What I have not discussed so far are actual manifestations of the Evil One himself, and when we look at those episodes, it becomes clear that not everything is what it seems and that the devil is often in the detail.

Notes to Chapter 3

1. Joaquín del Val, 'La novela española en el siglo XVII', in *Historia general de las literaturas hispánicas*, III (Barcelona: Barna, 1953), p. lix.
2. Masuccio Salernitano, *Il Novellino*, ed. by Alfredo Mauro (Bari: Laterza, 1940), p. 183.
3. I have not been able to find Pardo Bazan's *Biblioteca de la mujer* in the Biblioteca Nacional in Madrid or anywhere else and have taken the quotation from José Hesse's introduction to his edition of two novellas by Zayas (*La burlada Aminta y venganza del honor; El prevenido engañado*) and from Samuel Gili Gaya, 'Apogeo y desintegración de la novela picaresca', in *Historia general de las literaturas hispánicas*, III (Barcelona: Barna, 1953), pp. iii–xxv (p. xxi).
4. See Mercedes Maroto Camino, 'Spindles for Swords: The Re/Dis-Covery of María de Zayas's Presence', *Hispanic Review*, 62.4 (Autumn 1994), 519–36.
5. Zayas uses the Spanish name, Piedra Blanca. It was one of the *contados* of Naples, a network of surrounding villages with plots of arable land, orchards and villas. See Tommaso Astarita (ed.), *A Companion to Early Modern Naples* (Leiden: Brill, 2013). In the modern metropolitan Naples area there is still a Via Pietra Bianca. This is an example of a precise topographical reference that makes the author's stay in Naples more than likely (see 1.1).
6. See Rosilie Hernández Pecoraro, '"La fuerza del amor" or The Power of Self-Love: Zayas's Response to Cervantes's "La fuerza de la sangre"', *Hispanic Review*, 70.1 (Winter 2002), 39–57.
7. Henry Lea, *The Inquisition in the Spanish Dependencies* (London: Macmillan, 1908), p. 86.
8. Ingrid Matos-Nin, *Las novelas de María de Zayas, 1590–1650: lo sobrenatural y lo oculto en la literatura femenina española del siglo XVII* (Lewiston, NY: Edwin Mellen, 2010), p. 64.
9. Shakespeare, *Antony and Cleopatra*, Act II, scene 2.
10. See 1 Samuel 28. In the King James Bible, the woman is not called a witch, but a 'woman that hath a familiar spirit'. In the early modern period there was some controversy over whether

Saul actually saw Samuel's spirit. Martín del Río thought he had, but not on account of the spell. Reginald Scot, on the other hand, was convinced the woman was a charlatan and a ventriloquist.

11. Diana Álvarez Amell misreads the description of the statuette and takes the figurine to be headless, writing that as a result Inés has been represented by a 'falsa imagen fálica y acéfala' [a false phallic and acephalous image] and thus robbed of her autonomy. Diana Álvarez Amell, 'El objeto del cuerpo femenino en el "Quinto Desengaño" de María de Zayas', in *Actas Irvine-92 II Asociación Internacional de Hispanistas*, ed. by Juan Villegas (Irvine: University of California, 1994), p. 29.
12. She translates: 'no pareció más' as 'Don Diego was never seen again', when in fact it is the Moor who disappears. Don Diego is apprehended earlier on in the story and sent to prison: 'Con esto mandó el Corrigidor poner a don Diego en la cárcel a buen recaudo' [With this the magistrate had Don Diego taken into custody and put in jail] (*Desengaños*, p. 281).
13. See Matthew Stroud, 'Artistry and Irony in María de Zayas's *La inocencia castigada*', in *Zayas and Her Sisters*, II: *Essays on Novelas by 17th-Century Spanish Women* (New York: Global Publications Binghamton University, 2001), pp. 79–95.
14. Edward Friedman, 'Innocents Punished: The Narrative Models of María de Zayas', *Confluencia*, 20.1 (2004), 9–16 (p. 14).
15. Victorino Polo García, 'El romanticismo literario de Doña María de Zayas y Sotomayor', in *Murcia. Anales de la Universidad* (1967), 557–66 (p. 562).
16. See Anne Cruz, 'The Walled-In Woman in Medieval and Early Modern Spain', *Gender Matters: Discourses of Violence in Early Modern Literature and the Arts*, ed. by Mara R. Wade (Leiden: Brill, 2014), pp. 349–66.
17. See Laura Gorfkle, 'Seduction and Hysteria in María de Zayas's "Desengaños amorosos"', *Hispanófila*, 115 (1995), 11–28.
18. See Roger Chartier, *Forms and Meanings: Texts, Performances, and Audiences from Codex to Computer* (Philadelphia: University of Pennsylvania Press, 1995), especially Chapter 4.
19. At various points in Zayas servants are lambasted. At the end of the collection Lisis says: 'Porque los criados y criadas son animales caseros y enemigos no excusados, que los estamos regalando y gastando con ellos nuestra paciencia y hacienda, y al cabo, como el león, que harto el leonero de criarle y sustentarle, se vuelve contra él y le mata, así ellos, al cabo, matan a sus amos' [Because servants are domestic animals and inexcusable enemies, seeing as how we waste and give away our patience and our wealth, and in the end, just like the lion turns on the lion tamer who raised it and brought it up, and kills him — because that's what they do — in the end they kill their masters] (*Desengaños*, p. 508). In Calderón's play *El médico de su honra* Gutierre uses the same exact words: '¡Oh criados! | *aparte*: En efecto enemigos no excusados; | turbados de temor los dos se han puesto' [Oh servants! *To himself*: Inexcusable enemies, to be more precise; they both look worried with fear] (ll. 2435–37).

CHAPTER 4

Baroque Games with the Devil

> To do aught good never will be our task,
> But ever to do ill our sole delight.
> (Milton, *Paradise Lost*, 1.159–1.160)

The Devil is mentioned in nearly all of Zayas's novellas, although he only makes a physical appearance in three.[1] In the other instances the word 'demonio' is used to refer to hideousness, imps, evil in general and sinful thoughts, especially about suicide. In this, Zayas is far from unique and the malleability of the concept of the Devil is typical of her time. The concept of the Devil has a long history which has changed considerably over time. It is also unstable and has been called 'a loose assembly of images united by their negative relationship to God'.[2] His name 'Satan' derives from the Hebrew for 'adversary', while his cognomen 'Lucifer' (bearer of light) hints at his status as a fallen angel who became the Prince of Darkness. In his archdiabolical capacity he is also known as Beelzebub, often said to come from the Hebrew for 'lord of the flies' although more likely to be a corruption of the name of a Canaanite god or a derogatory Hebrew pun.[3] Early Christians rebranded pagan gods and spirits as demons and made the Devil their supreme commander, thus creating a mirror image of the celestial hierarchy. The Evil One was thought to dwell in the hearts of men, implanting evil suggestions in them and inciting them to heresy and apostasy. According to St Thomas Aquinas, the Devil could kindle wicked thoughts but not force individuals to sin. In popular literature and on stage he was often nothing more than a crafty but ultimately gullible trickster. In the atmosphere of confessional strife of the early modern period this aspect was overshadowed and the Devil ceased to be a laughing matter. Satan became an all-powerful lord, raging against his imminent defeat and promoting large-scale apostasy, leading to the execution of tens of thousands of women thought to be in league with him. At the same time, as a correlate to a more internalized style of devotion — usually associated with Protestantism but also affecting Catholicism, as is clear in St Ignatius de Loyola's *Spiritual Exercises* for example — the Devil became more exclusively associated with wicked thoughts, temptation and religious doubt. In the end, the belief faded away — more so in Catholic countries than in Protestant Northern Europe and the United States — and the Devil has fared less well than God in our modern age, despite the ubiquity of evil.[4]

4.1 Ugly Devils

Perhaps the least acceptable mention of the Devil in Zayas's work, certainly the most distasteful in our eyes, is the comparison between black people and the Devil. In 'El prevenido engañado' Fadrique follows Beatriz, with whom he is in love, to find her going to the stables where she speaks to an African young man with whom she has an affair. The young man, Antonio, is dying from sexual exhaustion and berates his mistress for her wanton behaviour. He is described as being as ugly as the Devil: 'Parecía en la edad de hasta veintiocho o treinta años, mas tan feo y abominable que no sé si fue la pasión o si era la verdad, le pareció que el demonio no podía serlo tanto' [He seemed to be no older than twenty-eight or thirty, but he was so ugly and repulsive — I don't know whether it was because of Don Fadrique's shock and rage or because he really looked like that — that it seemed to him that the Devil could not be more hideous] (*Novelas*, p. 309).

Pérez-Erdélyi sees this episode as an example of Zayas's 'novelística picaresca-cortesana'. In her study she contrasts Castillo Solórzano's women, who move up in the world and become 'aburguesada' [bourgeois] and 'acortesanada' [courtly], with some of Zayas's noblewomen, like Beatriz, who become 'apicarada' [picaresque].[5] The male-narrated story traces the unsuccessful attempts of the naïve Fadrique to find the perfect wife. One of them turns out to be having an affair with a black stable boy, another refuses to marry and makes him sleep in bed with her and her cousin, who pretends to be her husband, while yet another innocently cheats on him even though he made her wear a coat of armour at night.[6] It was one of the stories that was adapted by Scarron. Although the episode with the stable boy is often said to be taken from Marguerite de Navarre, a much more likely source is Masuccio's novella XXIV.[7] In Navarre, a nobleman finds the widow he is courting in the arms of a (presumably white) stable boy in a game park. In Masuccio, a man who has been rejected by the woman he loves follows her and sees his beloved sneak into a storehouse, where she meets a black muleteer. She shuts the door behind her, speaks coaxingly to him, lies back on the saddles and proceeds to: 'tirarse il orribilissimo moro adosso, il quale, non aspettando altri inviti, posto mano a' ferri, la' cominciò a la canina a martellare' [pull the horrible Moor on top of her, who, without waiting for further encouragement, got to work and began to hump her like a dog] (Masuccio, p. 223). This is much closer to Zayas than Navarre's tale, and much more scabrous than either.

A very baroque aspect of the story is the contrast between the whiteness of Beatriz — she is said to have 'blanquísimas manos' [very white hands] — and the blackness of Antonio: 'pareciendo en la hermosura ella un ángel y él un fiero demonio' [she, in her beauty, looked like an angel, whereas he looked like a fierce Devil] (*Novelas*, p. 309). The same contrast crops up in 'Tarde llega el desengaño' (also attributed to Marguerite de Navarre but probably based on a novella by Bandello: *Seconda Parte*, XII) in which Jaime has locked up his wife Elena in a kind of kennel following a false accusation by his black slave, whom he then dresses up in his wife's fineries and jewels, offering her the place of honour at his table. Like Beatriz, Elena has beautiful white hands in which she carries the skull of her murdered lover and from which

Jaime makes her drink: 'Traía en sus hermosas manos (que parecían copos de blanca nieve) una calavera' [She carried in her hands (which were like white snowflakes) a skull] (*Desengaños*, p. 237). A moment later, the black slave enters:

> La otra que por la puerta salió era una negra, tan tinta, que el azabache era blanco en su comparación, y sobre esto, tan fiera, que juzgó don Martín que si no era el demonio, que debía ser retrato suyo. (*Desengaños*, p. 237)

> [The other woman who came in through the door was black, so dark that jet was white in comparison, and in addition, so fierce-looking that Don Martín reckoned that if she were not the Devil herself, she was his spitting image.]

What is evident is the author's desire to shock the audience and to create a topsy-turvy world, a narrative chiaroscuro contrasting black and white, nobility and servility, good and evil, all the while complicating matters by making the stable boy Antonio the voice of morality, persuading his mistress to give up her vice and find a husband:

> ¿Qué me quieres, señora? ¡Déjame ya, por Dios! ¿Qué es esto, que aun estando yo acabando la vida me persigues? No basta que tu viciosa condición me tiene como estoy, sino que quieres que, cuando ya estoy en el fin de mi vida, acuda a cumplir tus viciosos apetitos. Cásate, señora, cásate, y déjame ya a mí, que ni te quiero ver ni comer lo que me das; morir quiero, pues ya no estoy para otra cosa. (*Novelas*, p. 310)

> [What do you want from me, my lady? Leave me alone, for the love of God! What is this? I'm at death's door and still you come after me? Is it not enough that I am in the state I'm in on account of your vice? Why do you want me, about to breathe my last, to satisfy your vicious appetites? Get married, my lady, get a husband and leave me be, because I don't want to see you, nor eat the food you bring me; I want to die, since that's all I'm good for now.]

With this, Zayas deftly adds another twist to the tableau: the devilishly hideous black servant Antonio is a virtuous victim, whereas the angelic, beautiful, noble white Beatriz is a depraved sexual predator.

4.2 Evil Inspirations

Apart from the epitome of ugliness, the Devil is often referred to as the generic source of evil. In 'Amar sólo por vencer', Esteban dresses up as Estefanía in order to court Laurela, making the narrator comment that thus 'el demonio teje sus telas' [the Devil weaves his webs] (*Desengaños*, p. 299). In 'Mal presagio casar lejos', Blanca finds her husband in bed with his page, engaged in 'tan torpes y abominables pecados que aun el demonio se avergüenza de verlos' [sins so vile and abominable that even the Devil would blush on seeing them] (*Desengaños*, p. 361). In some instances men are said to be as bad as or worse than demons, as in 'La fuerza del amor', when Laura, before setting out to the *humilladero*, rages about her abusive husband: 'eres hombre, cuyos engaños quitan el poder a los mismos demonios' [you are a man, and the deceit of your kind makes the very devils seem powerless] (*Novelas*, pp. 363–64). Even though Laura's rage can be construed as feminist, calling wicked men demons was not that unusual. Covarrubias's definition of 'demonio' reads: 'Al hombre malo y perverso suelen decir que es un demonio, por imitarle y tener su condición' [Evil and perverse men are often called devils, because they imitate him and have the same nature]. In Tirso de Molina's *El burlador de Sevilla* Don Juan is constantly given diabolical features: his body is glowing with fire and at one point he is referred to as the Devil incarnate.[8] But it is not only men who are accused of being diabolical. When Laura is about the relate the story of Inés, she refers to the Devil when she denounces women who avenge themselves on their husbands' infidelities by having affairs themselves: 'no puedo imaginar sino que el demonio las [sic] ha propuesto este modo de venganza de que usan las que lo usan' [I can only imagine that the Devil suggested this vengeance to those who carry it out] (*Desengaños*, p. 263).

Sometimes it is not clear whether the Devil is behind an action or whether it is God, as when in 'El traidor contra su sangre' Alonso, having killed his sister and beheaded his wife, flees to Genoa, where he is caught stealing silk stockings 'persuadido del demonio o que Dios lo permitió así' [persuaded by the Devil or because God permitted it] (*Desengaños*, p. 397). This is another example of Zayas's strategic narrative indeterminacy, as discussed at the end of the previous chapter (see 3.6).

There is no such lack of clarity when it comes to Isabel's rage when she has been raped by her best friend's brother in 'La esclava de su amante'. In her 'furor diabólico' [diabolical fury] she attempts to kill Manuel with his own sword. In 'La más infame venganza', Juan avenges the dishonour of his sister by dressing up as a woman and entering the house of the perpetrator to rape his young wife Camila at knife point. She realizes that resistance is useless: 'no tuvo fuerzas para defenderse, y si lo hiciera, estaba ya tan resuelto y vencido del demonio, que la matara' [she lacked the strength to defend herself, and even if she had, he was so determined and possessed by the Devil, that he would kill her] (*Desengaños*, p. 193). Like her attacker, her husband Carlos too is possessed by the Devil and decides to poison his innocent wife: 'vivió poco más de un año, al cabo del cual reinó en Carlos el demonio y la [sic] dio un veneno para matarla' [she lived little more than a year, at the end of which the Devil reigned in Carlos and he gave her poison in order to kill her] (*Desengaños*, p. 195).[9]

The Devil as the ultimate inspiration for evil is described most elaborately and vividly in the closing tale of the *desengaños*, 'Estragos que causa el vicio', where Dionís goes on a murdering rampage after he has been led to believe that his wife has committed adultery.[10] In some respects the story is reminiscent of Lope de Vega's *Los comendadores de Córdoba*, as Montesa amongst others has pointed out, but there are some crucial differences. First, Dionís is set up to believe his wife Magdalena has betrayed him, while in Lope's play the adultery is real. Second, Dionís is himself guilty of adultery with his wife's half-sister Florentina, while Lope's Veinticuatro is everything but an adulterer. In Zayas's tale the two women are raised together and when Dionís courts Magdalena, Florentina falls in love with him. After the wedding, she seduces him and for four years they have an affair.

Dionís promises to marry Florentina should Magdalena die. Florentina's servant then concocts a plan to make this happen, comparing her ruse to King David's sending Uriah the Hittite to a certain death so that he could marry Bathsheba.[11] She will arrange it so that it looks like Magdalena is cheating on her husband with the result that Dionís will kill her. The trap works, but things spin out of control and in his wrath Dionís puts everyone in the household to the sword. Florentina is the only one who manages to escape because a black slave stands between her and the raging Portuguese nobleman. She is found badly wounded in the street and taken in by the Spanish Gaspar, to whom she tells her story.

When she relates what happened, Florentina calls the maid who came up with the plan: 'la atrevida mujer, en quien pienso que hablaba y obraba el demonio' [the intrepid woman, in whom, I think, the Devil spoke and worked] (*Desengaños*, p. 494). When she puts the plan into action Florentina says that the maid carried out the 'oficio de demonio' [the Devil's work] (ibid.). Both of them are thus caught in Satan's web: 'todas seguíamos lo que el demonio nos inspiraba' [we all did what the Devil inspired us to do] (ibid.). In fact, the entire house seems possessed by the Evil One: 'el demonio que ya estaba señoreado de aquella casa' [the Devil, who had already taken possession of that house] (*Desengaños*, p. 496). When Dionís is about to kill the malevolent maid, she exclaims: 'La muerte merezco, y el infierno también' [I deserve to die, and to go to hell] (*Desengaños*, p. 498) and appears to have no faith whatsoever in the salvific power of confession. Instead, she commends her soul to the Devil: 'Recibe, infierno, el alma de la más mala mujer que crió el Cielo, y aun allá pienso que no hallará lugar' [Hell, receive the soul of the wickedest woman ever created by Heaven, and I don't think there will a place for me even there] (ibid.). When he thinks he has killed everyone, Dionís lets himself fall on his sword — just as Saul does in 1 Samuel 31 — and, like the maid, he commends his soul to the Devil: 'Se dejó caer sobre la espada, pasando la punta a las espaldas, llamando al demonio que le recibiese el alma' [He let himself fall onto his sword, making the point stick out of his back, calling on the Devil to receive his soul] (*Desengaños*, p. 499).

William Clamurro has argued that Dionís is a 'monstrous double', both an adulterer and an avenger, and therefore he must kill the one who has stained his honour — whether adultery was committed or not — as well as himself.[12] The honour code is taken to its logical, blood-splattered conclusion. What is more, both Dionís and the maid show a blasphemous disregard for the possibility of redemption. Both are possessed by Satan, and in the case of Dionís it is clear that the thought of suicide was suggested to him by the Devil ('insistido del demonio').

This association between self-murder and the Devil is made apparent in two other tales. In 'La inocencia castigada', when Inés finds herself immured and is standing in her own excrement, she is no longer plagued by lewd dreams or asking to be killed for having been wicked; instead she bitterly protests her innocence (see 3.4). In her worst moments she confesses to having suicidal thoughts: 'muchas veces me da imaginación de con mis propias manos hacer cuerda a mi garganta para acabarme; mas luego considero que es el demonio, y pido ayuda a Dios para librarme de él' [many times I have fantasized about using my own hands to strangle myself, but then I realize it is the Devil and ask God's help to rid myself of him] (*Desengaños*, p. 286). The Devil as the inspiration for suicidal thoughts also plays a role in 'El castigo de la miseria', which warrants a longer discussion.

4.3 The Devil Vanishes in 'El castigo de la miseria'

We have already encountered the fraudulent magician and his demon Calquimorro — in reality a cat with its tail on fire — in 'El castigo de la miseria' (see 3.1). Marcos engaged the magician's services because he wanted to find out what had happened to the money Isidora had stolen from him. After the sham ceremony, which scared him a great deal, he is taken to court and everyone has a good laugh about the prank that was played on him. Marcos is angry and wants to kill the false magus and then himself: 'estando Don Marcos tan corrido que quiso mil veces matar al encantador y luego hacer lo mismo de sí' [Don Marcos was so angry that he wanted to kill the enchanter a thousand times over and then do the same to himself] (*Novelas*, p. 287). He cannot bear the shame of his humiliation. To add insult to injury, when he comes home he finds a letter from Isidora in which she mocks him cruelly. This causes such a shock that he falls ill with a fever and dies a few days later. Isidora gets her come-uppance when she is robbed of the money she stole and ends her days begging on the streets of Madrid. In the first edition of the *Novelas*, however, Marcos does not die of a shock-induced fever, but he hangs himself. After receiving Isidora's letter he leaves the house. When he gets to a bridge he meets his marriage broker Gamarra who asks him where he is going. Gamarra then confesses he is about to hang himself because he has been found stealing from the Duke of Osuna. He offers Marcos some of his rope and together they go ahead and carry out their plan. A man lying asleep underneath the tree where they want to hang themselves overhears their conversation, but he only sees Marcos, who appears to be talking to himself or to someone invisible. He runs off to alert the authorities and when they arrive on the scene they find the lifeless body of Marcos dangling alongside an empty noose, 'por donde coligieron, junto con lo que el hombre decía que oía hablar y no ver quién, que era el demonio que, por desesperar a don Marcos, había venido con aquel engaño' [this, as well the man's testimony of having heard him speak to someone he couldn't see, made them conclude that it was the Devil who had come up with this trick to make Don Marcos despair] (*Novelas*, p. 290 note 56). In subsequent editions this passage was eliminated, although there are a few exceptions, such as the pirated edition printed in Barcelona in 1646. It is not immediately clear why Zayas chose to write the Devil out of her story. As Alicia Yllera pointed out in a paper dedicated to the two endings of the story, the novellas of the 1637 edition were 'de nuevo corretas, y enmendadas por su misma Autora' [corrected and amended by the author herself], so it is possible that Zayas herself was persuaded to alter the ending, possibly out of fear for censorship, as Sandra Foa appears to suggest: 'Given the Inquisitorial religious climate of the age we may therefore conjecture that, although the preliminaries to the two editions are identical, María de Zayas was persuaded to alter the *desenlace* of the second edition prior to its republication' (Foa, p. 78). Yllera, however, ends her article with the suggestion that 'la autora suprimiese este final por razones más literarias que morales, no deseando castigar tan duramente a su personaje' [the author suppressed this ending for reasons that were more literary than moral, not wishing to punish her character so harshly].[13] Current scholarly consensus agrees with this point of view. Greer, for instance, writes:

> Zayas's decision to excise the original ending of 'El castigo' should not be attributed to institutional, religious censorship, but to her own authorial recognition that removing the literal intervention of the Devil better centred don Marcos's guilt where she wishes to situate it — in the personal, freely assumed sin of overweening lust not for women but for wealth. (Greer, *Baroque Tales*, p. 249)

After all, Zayas had already been granted a *licencia* for the version in which the original ending appeared and compared to the alleged good deed by the Devil in 'El jardín engañoso', or other more scandalous episodes such as the homosexual scene in 'Mal presagio casar lejos' or the suggestion of inter-class and inter-race sex in 'El prevenido engañado' referred to above, the passage in question seems rather inoffensive; indeed, it can easily be read as instructive. As with Inés in 'La inocencia castigada' and Dionís in 'Estragos que causa el vicio' the urge to commit suicide is inspired — in the etymological sense of the word — by the Devil: it is the Evil One who whispers these thoughts into their ears and implants in them the idea — and Heaven's loss is the Devil's gain. Although as a suicide Marcos is damned, a dispensation is obtained to bury him in consecrated ground, an action censured by the narrator: 'ésta es la vanidad del mundo, honrar el cuerpo aunque el alma esté donde la de este miserable' [such is the vanity of this world, that they honour the body even if the soul is where this poor wretch's is] (*Novelas*, p. 290, footnote 56).

Like Greer, Olivares opines that Marcos ought to die because of his avarice and not after he has been cheated by the Devil, having already been cheated by Isidora. The same emphasis on morality comes through in Paul Scarron's French adaptation, analysed in detail by Serrano Poncela. In the French version Marcos travels to Barcelona where Isidore, Augustinet and Inez are about to board a ship. The miser, followed by Isidore and Augustinet, is thrown overboard together with a chest containing his valuables. Desperate to cling on to his treasure, Marcos drowns. Other differences are that the Frenchman leaves out references to latrines and *Amadís*, but he elaborates the scene in which Marcos discovers he has been deceived by Isidora, and Zayas's false magician becomes a Jewish usurer. In addition, he adds comments about Spain, comparing it negatively to France. His tale is more moralistic and the sympathy we might feel for Marcos in Zayas's novella disappears in Scarron's adaptation.[14]

Olivares further suggests that Zayas eliminated this negative reference to the Devil because she wants to present him in a good light. One of the good deeds he claims for the Devil is the conversion of Juana in 'El desengaño amando', although I have argued above that the situation is more complex than that, and it is God who uses the student's spell to save Juana's soul (see 3.3). The second good deed by the Devil supposedly occurs in 'El jardín engañoso'. The Spanish scholar writes: 'Con punzante ironía, Zayas tal vez quería representar al demonio con mayor sentido de bondad y "caballerosidad" que los mismos caballeros de su época' [With sharp irony Zayas may have wanted to show the Devil as being better and more 'gentlemanly' than the gentlemen of her period] (*Novelas*, p. 98). I cannot agree with this point of view, however, because while it is true that Zayas clearly relishes the opportunity to shock her readers and is a master at transgressive scenes full of unexpected points of view, I believe it is wrong to think that Zayas wants to paint a positive picture of the Devil. Instead, I contend that she subtly, baroquely, highlights his deceptive nature. We shall return to this matter in 4.5.

As for the reasons behind Zayas's decision to excise Marcos' suicide, I would say that the passage is simply superfluous to the plot. To begin with, Marcos has already had the thought of killing the fake magician and then himself when he left the judicial hearing. And when in the original ending he leaves his house after receiving Isidora's hurtful letter, he has already made up his mind to hang himself (see 3.1). The Devil just gave the last push by handing him a piece of rope, but before doing so, the Devil-as-Gamarra embarks on a long-winded story about a double crime that detracts from the main story — he gambled away the Duke of Osuna's money and then stole from him to make up for his losses. Although strictly speaking Zayas rewrites the ending, in fact, all she does is simply erase the episode, replacing the convoluted paragraph by one short sentence: 'en pocos días acabó los suyos miserablemente' [and within a few miserable days he was dead] (*Novelas*, pp. 288–89). In my mind, the only successful element of the elided passage, and therefore a loss, is the uncanny touch of the empty noose.

4.4 The Devil Bites the Dust in 'La perseguida triunfante'

The Devil makes a more permanent appearance in the longest of the novellas, a hagiographical tale called 'La perseguida triunfante'. It tells the story of Beatriz, an English noblewoman who marries Ladislao, the King of Hungary. Her brother-in-law Federico lusts after her and when her husband is away he attempts to seduce her. She refuses his advances and in order to prevent any further mishap she puts him in a golden cage where he is well looked after but cannot get to her. When the king's return is announced she lets Federico out. He wastes no time in telling his brother that Beatriz tried to seduce *him* and that when he refused, she put him in a cage. Without checking the story, Ladislao orders that his wife be taken to the woods and killed, Snow White style. She persuades her executioners to spare her life and they gouge out her eyes instead. No sooner have they left than a mysterious lady appears and restores Beatriz's eyes. After wandering around in the forest, she is taken in by a duke. Federico is on her trail when he meets 'un hombre vestido a modo de escolástico, de horrible rostro' [a man dressed like a scholar with a horrendous face] (*Desengaños*, p. 436). The stranger claims to be a magician who will help him on condition that he does not tell anyone, not even his confessor. It is, of course, the Devil himself, the übermagician. He gives Federico a magic ring with strange inscriptions, which he uses to gain entrance to the palace where Beatriz now lives in order to slip treasonous letters in her sleeve. The travelling doctor then announces himself at the duke's court with the message that a plot against his life has been hatched. The letters planted on Beatriz are found and she is taken to the place where she first met the duke. Federico is hot on her heels and when he catches up with her he tries to rape her, bragging blasphemously that 'aun el Cielo no es poderoso para librarte' [not even Heaven has to power to save you now] (*Desengaños*, p. 445), but a fierce lion suddenly appears and attacks him. Not much later, Beatriz is found by the German Emperor and his six-year-old son, who takes an immediate liking to her. The Emperor persuades her to come home with him and look after the boy. But disaster strikes again when Federico sneaks into the prince's bedroom and stabs him to death, leaving the blood-stained knife next to Beatriz, who is unceremoniously taken away to be beheaded. Her mysterious protectress appears once more to save her life. After that, she decides to live as a hermit. A number of years pass before the mysterious lady reveals herself to be the Mother of God, who tells her protégée to don male attire and heal the sick. Beatriz's fame as a healer spreads and she is summoned to come to the Hungarian court where Federico is gravely ill. When she is about to administer his medicine, she makes him confess his sins. Initially, he leaves out his treason, but when she insists that he risks losing not only his life but also his soul he confesses it all, much to his companion's displeasure. 'Más importa el alma y la vida' [One's life and soul are more important] (*Desengaños*, p. 464), Federico tells his master. The king weeps, but then Beatriz appears dressed in the same clothes she wore all those years ago when she was taken to the woods. The Devil realizes his game is up: '¡Venciste, María, venciste! ¡Ya conozco la sombra que amparaba a Beatriz, que hasta ahora estuve ciego!' [You've won, Mary, you've won! I now realize who the shadow that sheltered Beatriz was and see that I have been blind all this time!] (*Desengaños*, p. 465), whereupon he departs, leaving the obligatory thick — and presumably foul-smelling — plume of smoke behind. The king is eager to have Beatriz back as his wife, but she refuses, saying that she has found 'el Esposo celestial' [the celestial Husband]. Impressed, the king follows her example and abdicates to enter a monastery. He sends for Beatriz's sister who marries Federico and together they will reign over Hungary.

Scholars have given a variety of possible sources for the story. Langle de Paz claims that the heroine of the tale was modelled on Beatriz de Aragon (1457–1508), the daughter of Fernando I, King of Naples, who was Queen of Hungary. Others have suggested a connection with the Portuguese noblewoman Beatriz da Silva, the foundress of the order of the Immaculate Conception.[15] Edwin Place, in turn, suggests the tale is based on 'The Jewish Kazi and his pious wife', one of the stories in *One Thousand and One Nights* (see O'Brien, *Women in the Prose*). That may be an old version of the same type of legend but it is an unlikely direct source for Zayas's version. Enríquez Salamanca, Barbeito Carneiro and O'Brien have all suggested that 'La perseguida triunfante' is a retelling of the story of Genevieve of Brabant, who was likewise falsely accused of adultery.[16] The problem with that suggestion is that the earliest Spanish translation of the legend appears to be from 1726.[17] Matos-Nin (*Lo sobrenatural*) locates the origin of the tale in the fifth of the *Cantigas de Santa Maria*, which relates the story of Beatriz, the wife of a Roman emperor, who is nearly raped, first by her brother-in-law, then by the brother of a duke, who rescues her after the emperor decided to have her killed, and lastly by a Syrian sailor.[18] This story may in turn have been the basis for Timoneda's twenty-first *Patraña*, which Foa cites as the source of Zayas's *desengaño*. In his version, Geroncia, who is married to the King of England, first has to fight off her brother-in-law, then one of the would-be executioners and finally the brother of the Marquis of Denia, who has taken her in after she was almost killed. Elements of both versions are evident in Zayas's rendition. Timoneda's story mentions both England and Hungary and has Geroncia and her husband Marcelo abdicate in order to end their days in separate cloistered communities 'a do acabaron sus días muy sanctamente' [where they ended their days very saintly].[19] The subject matter of the fifth *Cantiga* does not follow Zayas's tale as closely as Timoneda, but Zayas does mention King Alfonso X 'el Sabio' — the supposed author of the *Cantigas de Santa Maria* — according to whom the thick forest of men's hearts is teeming with lions of cruelty, wolves of deceit, bears of malice and snakes of wrath.[20] As a self-avowed avid reader it is quite possible that Zayas was familiar with both the *Patrañuelo* and the *Cantigas*. What is interesting is that Zayas, as is her wont, has taken a relatively well-known story and complicated and elaborated it. Things becomes even more entangled when we read that Beatriz is said to have written down her own story before she died, and that the narrator Estefanía says she read the manuscript herself when she was in Italy with her parents, which is often taken to be an autobiographical interpolation by Zayas (see 1.1). Zayas's version is seven times as long as Timoneda's and a noteworthy addition is the Devil.

The miraculous restoration of the eyes seems to be original and occurs neither in Timoneda nor the *Cantigas*. The event fits well with the hagiographical subject material and a similar miracle occurs in Ribadeneyra's *Flos sanctorum*, where the Scottish St Brigid refuses to marry anyone else except her Celestial Lord. In order to ward off potential suitors she asks God to make her ugly, which He obligingly does by bursting her eye. Her father then allows her to enter a convent, but when she touches the altar, something wondrous happens: 'el ojo de la virgen quedó sano y su rostro tan hermoso comes antes' [the virgin's eye was made whole and her face as beautiful as before].[21] Ribadeneyra's collection of hagiographies was one of the most important of the early modern period in Spain and was first published in Madrid in 1599 — and reprinted in 1601, 1604, 1616, 1651 and 1675 — and it is more than likely that a voracious reader like Zayas was familiar with these tales.

In the scene where Federico gives his soul to the Devil there appears to be a confusion of traditional elements. In the classic Faustian scenario, a man thirsting for knowledge trades in his afterlife in paradise for fleeting earthly prowess by making a deal with Mephistopheles. And in Calderón's play *El mágico prodigioso* we have Cipriano, who yearns for wisdom and desires Justina, which leads him to strike a deal with the Devil, only to see through the latter's deceit in the end and become a martyr alongside his beloved. In Zayas it is the *Devil* who presents himself as a doctor with a love for learning, while Federico is reduced to a lust-ridden, vengeful man:

> Soy, para que no estés suspenso, un hombre que ha estudiado mucho todas las ciencias, y sé lo pasado y por venir, porque soy mágico, que es la facultad y ciencia de que más me precio, pues con ella alcanzo y sé cuánto pasa en el mundo. (*Desengaños*, p. 436)
>
> [I am, not to keep you in suspense, a man who has studied all the sciences and I know the past and the future, because I am a magician, which is the faculty and science I prize above all, because with magic I know everything that is going on in the world.]

There is never an explicit mention of a pact, but the text does say that Federico is 'embelesado' [spellbound] and that the ring with the secret marks has magic power: 'obrando en él la fuerza del encanto' [working a spell on him] (*Desengaños*, p. 438). The dangers to the soul of a diabolical pact are severely underplayed in this hagiographical tale and the Devil has been brought in, it seems, merely to highlight male perfidy. Federico becomes *all* men. He is not driven by a thirst for knowledge but by his relentless concupiscence. Even if he has not made an explicit pact, he is in league with the Devil by relying on black magic. And yet he never pays for his lustful crimes or for his diabolical alliance. It suffices for the Devil to acknowledge the Virgin's superiority and for Federico to admit to his guilt. In a warped way, his pernicious persistence pays off when he marries Beatriz's sister, who is 'no menos hermosa que su hermana' [no less beautiful than her sister] (*Desengaños*, p. 466) and ascends to the throne of Hungary.

The story is told by a nun who says that she has dedicated her whole life to her Heavenly husband who will never deceive her, but the novella is not about a husband's infidelity but rather about his rashness to believe slander and, more important, about male lasciviousness. As Estefanía reminds her audience, the aim of the novella is to offer a *desengaño*, humorously threatening the men that if they are not 'chastised' by her tale they are welcome to come to her convent where she will hand them over to a dozen of her fellow nuns, 'que será como echarlos a los leones' [which will be like throwing them to the lions] (*Desengaños*, p. 410). What is highlighted too is the protective, motherly presence and power of Mary, who is referred to as 'Madre de Dios' eight times in the novella, and a ninth time in connection with Beatriz in the frame narrative. In her Lacanian interpretation of Zayas's oeuvre Greer sees the tale as a progression from the house of the Father to the house of God, the convent: a feminine space outside of the Symbolic Order. This is why we never hear what goes on inside the cloistered space, since language and the Symbolic Order are inextricably linked, and what goes on outside of it cannot be expressed in words. On a moral level the story is much more pessimistic. Federico is not punished for his deal with the Devil and gets more or less all he could ever want. However, whether in the end his pact will come to haunt him and the Devil will claim his soul, we do not know. The same uncertainty with regards to salvation marks the next novella to be discussed, in which the Devil has the last laugh.

4.5 The Devil's Purported Magnanimity in 'El jardín engañoso'

The closing tale of the *Novelas* is 'El jardín engañoso', which takes place in Zaragoza where Jorge and his brother Federico court the two sisters Constanza and Teodosia. Constanza accepts Jorge's courtship, albeit reluctantly; Teodosia, however, loathes Federico and is secretly in love with Jorge. Out of spite she tells Jorge that Constanza does not love him but his brother. In a jealous rage Jorge kills Federico and flees. During his absence Constanza is courted by the impoverished nobleman Carlos who feigns a mortal illness to win her affection. The trick works and they are married. Then Jorge returns to town and starts courting Constanza with renewed vigour, but she refuses his advances. Her sister falls ill from envy and Constanza suggests that Jorge marry her; he rejects the proposal and becomes ever more adamant. In her exasperation and not without sarcasm Constanza exclaims that if he can produce a spring garden in the heart of winter she will give in to him. 'Éste es el precio de mi honra; manos a la labor, que a un amante tan fino como vos no hay nada imposible' [This is the price I put on my honour; now, get to work, since for a genteel lover like you, nothing is impossible] (*Novelas*, p. 527). Jorge is distraught, realizing Constanza has asked for the impossible. But then he meets a mysterious stranger who rebukes him for his 'lágrimas femeniles' [womanly tears] and offers his assistance. '¿Qué puedes tú hacer cuando aun al demonio es imposible?' [What can *you* do what even the Devil cannot accomplish?] (*Novelas*, p. 528) comes Jorge's reply, to which the strangers retorts: '¿Y si yo fuese el mismo que dices?' [What if I were the very same you mention?] (ibid.). Jorge asks him for his price, and the answer is as expected:

> Pues, mándame el alma — dijo el demonio — y hazme una cédula firmada de tu mano de que será mía cuando se aparte del cuerpo, y vuélvete seguro que antes que amanezca podrás cumplir a tu dama su imposible deseo. (*Novelas*, p. 528)
>
> ['Well, promise me your soul,' said the Devil, 'and sign this contract saying you will be mine when your soul leaves your body, and rest assured: before the sun goes up you will be able to fulfil your lady's impossible demand.']

Jorge signs away his soul without hesitation and the next morning he dresses up and confidently walks over to the garden that has miraculously sprung up in front of Constanza's house. When she sees him and the enchanted garden, she faints. When she comes to, she begs her husband to kill her rather than allow him to lose his honour. When Carlos understands what has been going on he offers to kill himself instead, thus allowing his wife to keep her word and Jorge to claim his unjust reward. Jorge witnesses this gallant display of self-sacrifice and absolves Constanza from her promise, after which he grabs his sword, ready to kill himself. He has lost his desire for Constanza and realizes that in addition he has forfeited his eternal salvation. At that point the Devil appears, waving the contract in the air. While one would expect him to rub his hands in glee, Zayas makes him do something extraordinary. The Devil literally shouts out ('y dando voces, les dijo'):

> No me habéis de vencer, aunque más hagáis, pues donde un marido, atropellando su gusto y queriendo perder la vida, se vence a sí mismo, dando licencia a su

> mujer para que cumpla lo que prometió; y un loco amante, obligado de esto, suelta la palabra que le cuesta no menos que el alma, como en esta cédula se ve me hace donación de ella, no he de hacer menos que ellos. Y así, para que el mundo se admire de que en mí pudo haber virtud, toma don Jorge. Ves ahí tu cédula; yo te suelto la obligación, que no quiero alma de quien tan bien se sabe vencer. (*Novelas*, p. 532)
>
> [You won't defeat me, whatever you do, because when a husband, riding roughshod over his desire and wishing to end his life, overcomes himself, giving his wife permission to fulfil her promise, and a mad lover, compelled by this act, forfeits the reward, which costs him no less than his salvation, as you can see in this contract here, which says that he has offered his soul to me, I refuse to be outdone. And so, in order that everyone be amazed that I can have virtue too, take this, Don Jorge, here is your contract back; I will not press my claim seeing as I don't want the soul of anyone who is able to conquer himself so well.]

Upon this, he disappears with the obligatory loud bang and fetid smell, and with him the magic garden. Jorge marries Teodosia and they live happily ever after. No one finds out that he has killed his brother until the story is written up by Teodosia after his death.

'El jardín engañoso' is an adaptation of a tale from Boccaccio's *Decameron* (day 10, story 5).²² The original story is set in the Friuli, where Dianora is courted by Ansaldo, who enlists the help of a local magician to create 'un giardino di gennaio bello como di maggio' [a garden in January as beautiful as one in May] (*Decameron*, p. 805). The next day, when she informs her husband of what happened, he tells her to keep her word and give herself to Ansaldo. Moved by his integrity, Ansaldo relinquishes his prize and the men become good friends. The magician dismantles the garden and leaves the region.

In the introduction to her translation, Patsy Boyers states that the tale is 'a prototypical masculine story' (Zayas, *Enchantments*, p. xxiii) which is subtly subverted by Zayas and concludes: 'This conscious pastiche technique of reworking recognizable motifs is fundamental to Zayas's feminization of Golden Age literature and to her resoundingly modern feminist message' (Zayas, *Enchantments*, p. xxiv). Although Zayas writes about women, from the perspective of women and in defence of women, to call her feminism 'resoundingly modern' goes too far. Nor is it clear what is so typically masculine about the story. Moreover, there is nothing remarkable about Zayas's procedure per se, which I would hesitate to call 'pastiche'. Zayas draws from a large well of stories that were reworked, copied, adapted and altered to suit the tastes of a nation, a period or an author. What is interesting about Zayas's project is that she turns fairly straightforward Renaissance models into complex baroque narratives, full of contradiction and false appearances.

Greer analyses the story as a reversal of the expulsion from Paradise and the garden as created by carnal desire and the Devil. O'Brien disagrees with Greer and sees the Devil's garden as a spectacular, artificial recreation of the Garden of Eden, but not its inversion.²³ But Greer's point goes beyond what the garden consists of and focuses on the narrative events that have been changed. Whereas in Genesis

Cain slays Abel *after* their parents have been expelled from the Garden of Eden, Jorge kills his brother *before* the Devil's creation of a false paradisiacal garden. And rather than ending his days like Cain, a marked and restless wanderer on the face of the earth, Jorge embarks on a happy, connubial life. Commenting on the supposed happy ending, Greer poses the question: 'Why would Zayas thus subvert her own subversion of the patriarchal narrative?' (Greer, *Baroque Tales*, p. 141) and suggests: 'Perhaps because her complicity in the ideological structure of that society made it possible for her to criticize its effect on women but not re-imagine it beyond the realm of theory and fantasy' (ibid.). I think this is an important insight, and it is one of the reasons Zayas cannot be called a fully fledged feminist according to Lerner's definition (see Introduction). Moreover, I think the ending is not the unqualified happy ending Greer seems to suggest it is.

Zayas has considerably complicated the story by doubling up the protagonists, giving Jorge a brother, whom he kills, and Constanza a sister, who betrays her and who is one of Zayas perfidious females, like Inés's sister-in-law in 'La inocencia castigada' and Florentina in 'Estragos que causa el vicio'. Like 'La perseguida triunfante' the story is said to have been written down by one of the protagonists, Teodosia. But if this is the case, then the transmission must have undergone serious mediation, since the story as told by Laura exposes all of Teodosia's flaws and takes a different perspective.[24] What is more, the story is the only one in the collection that does not claim to be verisimilar:

> No quiero, discreto auditorio, venderos por verdades averiguadas los sucesos de esta historia; si bien todos son de calidad que lo pudieran ser, matar un hermano a otro, ni ser una hermana traidora con su hermana, forzándolos al uno celos y al otro amor y envidia, no es caso nuevo. (*Novelas*, p. 512)

> [I don't want to sell you, my discerning audience, the events of this story as verified truths; even though they are such that they might well be, since for a brother to kill his brother or a sister to betray her sister — one being driven by jealousy, the other by love and envy — is nothing new.]

The aim of the story is to be exemplary, 'pues el decirla [la maravilla] yo no es más de para dar ejemplo y prevenir que se guarden de las ocasiones' [since if I tell the tale it is to hold up an example and give a warning to be wary of what may happen] (*Novelas*, p. 513). But what purports to be a tale of warning against jealousy and treason between brothers and sisters turns out very differently. This supposedly exemplary tale, adapted from Boccaccio, is transformed into a complex novella with an up-ended morality. Once again, the reader has been wrong-footed and the story is not what it appears to be.

This deception goes deeper than has hitherto been acknowledged by critics, and in my view almost everyone has been led up the garden path with regards to the Devil's purported good deed. Zayas replaces Boccaccio's magician with the Devil, but there is no narrative reason for this. She makes use of magicians and necromancers elsewhere, so why would she have recourse to the Devil here? Zayas's version has profound salvific implications for Jorge and for the message of the story as a whole. Let us return to the key scene of the story. When the Devil returns Jorge's contract he claims he has been impressed with the willingness of the two rivals to sacrifice themselves and says he does not want to be outshone. The audience of the frame narrative is duly blown away by this oxymoronic demonic good deed and at the end of the story, rather than discussing the morality of the fratricide, they debate who has been the most magnanimous: 'unos alegaban que el marido, y otros que el amante, y todos juntos que el demonio, por ser en él cosa nunca vista el hacer bien' [some argued that it was the husband, others that it was the lover, but then all agreed it was the Devil, because it was unheard of for him to do a good deed] (*Novelas*, p. 534).

Like the participants of the *sarao*, modern critics have not failed to comment on the Devil's supposed altruism. Vasileski writes that: 'María de Zayas hace que el mismo demonio tenga un momento de arrepentimiento y una acción noble en "El jardín engañoso", tal vez implicando que aún para la personificación del mal habrá oportunidad de salvación' [María de Zayas makes even the Devil have a moment of repentance and commit a noble act in 'El jardín engañoso', perhaps implying that even for the personification of evil there will be an opportunity for salvation] (Vasileski, p. 36). This demonic good deed is often seen as unique in Spanish literature, at least according to Krabbenhoft,[25] Brownlee and Paun de García, with the latter writing: 'muy consciente de esto, declara que su versión del pacto roto es original, nunca oído, ni leído antes, y me figuro después' [very conscious of this, she declares that her version of the broken pact has never been heard or read anywhere else before, nor afterwards, I imagine' (Paun de García, 'Magia y poder', p. 52). Williamsen claims the story can be read as a revisionist myth that challenges the fundamental opposition between good and evil.[26] O'Brien calls it a thought-provoking and theologically subversive case of injustice that Teodosia's marital happiness is due to an uncharacteristic volte-face of the Devil as it 'represents the ultimate baroque equivocation: the Devil unexpectedly supplants God as an agent of good' (O'Brien, 'Games in the Garden', p. 1016). Friedman is less extreme and calls the Devil's action a performance against type. Matos-Nin (*Lo sobrenatural*) asserts that Federico's soul has no worth for the Devil and that the latter mocks him for his inconsistency and failure to keep his word. She goes even further and suggests that the Devil, as a fallen angel, has honour: 'Para las personas de esta época, el diablo es el ángel caído que posee ciertos poderes inherentes a su creación divina y, como tal, también tiene honor' [For people of this period the Devil was a fallen angel who has certain traits inherent to his divine origin and, as such, he also has honour] (Matos-Nin, *Lo sobrenatural*, p. 43). This goes against all demonological treatises of the period, however, and reflects a poor understanding of the nature of Satan and must be discarded as an explanation of his behaviour.

My own reading of the ending is rather different. Let us review the facts. Laura announces the story to be about hatred between siblings. Teodosia lies to Jorge about her sister's affection and kills his brother. When he returns from exile he ends up striking a deal with the Devil to win over Constanza. When she asks her husband to kill her because she would rather that than lose her honour, Jorge makes up his mind to kill himself instead. Thus he is prepared to pile up one damnation upon the other by contemplating suicide and dying an unconfessed death having already signed away his soul in order to commit adultery with the woman for whom he has murdered his own brother. Ostensibly, this chain leading straight to eternal hellfire is broken by the Devil's unusual decision to tear up the contract. We are told that Jorge marries Teodosia, who, not unlike Federico in 'La perseguida triunfante', seems to be rewarded for her treachery by becoming the wife of the man she loved all along:

> Vivieron muchos años con hermosos hijos, sin que jamás se supiese que don Jorge hubiese sido el matador de Federico. Hasta que después de muerto don Jorge, Teodosia contó el caso como quien tan bien lo sabía. (*Novelas*, p. 534)
>
> [They lived many years and had beautiful children, without anyone ever finding out that Don Jorge was the one who had murdered Federico. Until, after the death of Don Jorge, Teodosia, being in full possession of the facts, told what had actually happened.]

And they lived happily ever after... Or so it would seem. But in fact Zayas is crucially silent about how Jorge dies — or Teodosia for that matter. Does he repent at death's door and commend his soul to God? Or has he forgotten all about his multiple sins and die unconfessed? The tale is open-ended as far as Jorge's salvation is concerned and, for all we know, the Devil has the last laugh when he drags his victim off to eternal damnation, having in addition hoodwinked a good deal of people by making them think he is capable of doing good. After all, why should anyone trust the Arch-Deceiver and Father of Lies? When Laura introduces her tale, not only does she indicate that she does not expect us to believe everything, she also points at 'otras secretas causas' [other secret causes] that would explain the Devil's seemingly incredible action:

> Ni lo hallo muy grande en que el demonio, por llevar cautivos a su temerosa y horrible prisión, con apariencias falsas dé al entender que gusta de hacer lo que los hombres desean. Lo que más es de admirar que haya en él ninguna obra buena, como en mi maravilla se verá. Mas para eso puede haber otras secretas causas que nosotros ignoramos. En esto no os obligo a creer más de lo que diere gusto. (*Novelas*, pp. 512–13)
>
> [Nor do I find it too much to believe that the Devil, in order to take people captive and drag them to his terrifying and horrible prison, uses false appearances to suggest that he likes to do what people want him to do. What is more amazing is that he should be able to do good, as you will see in my tale. But there may be secret causes that we don't know about. In this, I don't oblige you to believe more than you please.]

She puts her finger on it when she writes that the Devil uses false appearances to make people believe that he does their bidding, only to carry them off later to a place of weeping and gnashing of teeth. Rather than the oxymoron it is often taken to be, the supposed good deed is a deceptive act of subterfuge and double bluff on the Devil's part, not unlike what happens to Paulo in Tirso de Molina's *El condenado por desconfiado*, where a hermit is tricked by the Devil — appearing to him as an angel — into believing he has been damned, causing him to give up his saintly life and become a criminal. Zayas plays a magisterial game of contradictions here. In a story that is not supposed to be taken at face value, the purported aim is diverted and the end deceptive. We find ourselves lost in a narratively constructed maze where what you read is not what it seems (*lo que lees no es lo que es*).

The apparent fairy-tale endings of 'La perseguida triunfante' and 'El jardín engañoso' are deceptive. Federico and Jorge are tricked by the Devil and lulled into a false sense of security. And if they are not, the message is all the more devastating. At least if they fall into the Devil's snares, they will get what they deserve and at least there is justice, even if it is in the after-life. Should they get away with diabolical pacts and fratricide and see their perfidy rewarded, then there really is no justice in this world *or* the next, and no hope for anyone, especially women.

★ ★ ★ ★ ★

The Devil takes on various guises in Zayas's novellas. Distasteful but not unsurprising for the period are the references to black people as devils. The most interesting aspect in those stories is the baroque chiaroscuro, the opposition between black and white, good and evil, saintliness and sin, and above all the moral inversion of making Antonio the black stable boy a pious victim of his depraved white mistress. In addition we have also seen the Devil as the inspiration to do evil, often linked to suicide. A more traditional, personal Devil makes his appearance in three novellas, in two of them striking a deal with one of the protagonists. In both cases Zayas is silent about the eventual fate of the character in question. Rather than seeing this as an oversight, even less an oxymoronic good deed, I see this silence as strategic and an important aspect of the author's aim to introduce indeterminacy in her work. We are led up the garden path and Zayas plays a clever and baroque game with us.

So far I have discussed episodes containing magic and the Devil, but to fully understand the deployment of the supernatural *sensu lato* in the work of Zayas, we must now turn to other events, some of which clearly pertain to the order of miracles, while others are neither diabolical nor strictly speaking miraculous but supernatural all the same. And what we see in many of these episodes is that they are imbued with a sense of the fantastic, highlighting yet another important aspect of Zayas's novellas.

Notes to Chapter 4

1. The Devil is usually referred to as 'demonio' and sometimes as 'diablo'. Six out of ten *Novelas* mention him, and nine out of ten *Desengaños*.
2. Darren Oldridge, *The Devil in Tudor and Stuart England* (Stroud: History Press, 2000), p. 12.
3. See Manfred Lurker, *The Routledge Dictionary of Gods and Goddesses, Devils and Demons* (London: Routledge, 2004) for instance.
4. For more on the Devil, see Darren Oldridge, *The Devil: A Very Short Introduction* (Oxford: Oxford University Press, 2012); Robert Muchembled, *A History of the Devil from the Middle Ages to the Present*, trans. by Jean Birell (Cambridge: Polity Press, 2003); and Jeffrey Burton Russell's trilogy: *Satan: The Early Christian Tradition* (Ithaca, NY: Cornell University Press, 1981); *Lucifer: The Devil in the Middle Ages* (Ithaca, NY: Cornell University Press, 1984); and *Mephistopheles: The Devil in the Modern World* (Ithaca, NY: Cornell University Press, 1986). For a Spanish perspective, see Francisco Flores Arroyuelo, *El diablo en España* (Madrid: Alianza, 1985).

5. See Mireya Pérez-Erdélyi, *La pícara y la dama: la imagen de las mujeres en las novelas picaresco-cortesanas de María de Zayas y Sotomayor y Alonso de Castillo Solórzano* (Miami: Universal, 1979).
6. This episode can also be found in Sercambi's novella 'De transformatione nature' in which a womanizer called Renaldo marries a simpleton named Ginevra, whom he forces to wear a suit of armour and stand guard at their bedroom. When he is away, she innocently cheats on him with a young gallant. The tale was known in other variants too, but Zayas's version is remarkably close to Sercambi. See Donald McGrady, 'Were Sercambi's "Novelle" Known from the Middle Ages on? (Notes on Chaucer, Sacchetti, "Cent Nouvelles nouvelles", Pauli, Timoneda, Zayas)', *Italica*, 57.1 (Spring 1980), 3–18.
7. María Jesús Rubiera Mata has suggested that the episode with the black slave and a later episode in the same novella (about a man marrying a naïve young girl who proceeds to deceive him) are ultimately derived from Arabic sources via Italian and points to Sercambi and Boccaccio. Less convincing is her suggestion that Zayas might have had access to the original stories. See María Jesús Rubiera Mata, 'La narrativa de origen árabe en la literatura de Siglo de Oro: el caso de María de Zayas', in *La creatividad femenina en el mundo barroco hispánico: María de Zayas — Isabel Rebeca Correa — Sor Juan Inés de la Cruz*, ed. by Monika Bosse, Barbara Potthast and André Stoll, 2 vols (Kassel: Reichenberger, 1999), I, 335–49. She also links this episode to the eighth *patraña* by Timoneda in which Octavio walks in on his wife Brasilda who lies in the embrace of a servant, but the story and the details are too different to be a likely source.
8. At one point Don Pedro says about Don Juan: 'pienso que el demonio | en él tomó forma humana, | porque, vuelto en humo y polvo, | se arrojó por los balcones' [I think the Devil took human shape in him, since he turned into smoke and dust when he threw himself off the balcony] (*El burlador de Sevilla*, ll. 364–67).
9. From both quotations on this page it is clear that Zayas has a tendency to *laísmo*: using the feminine direct object pronoun "la" instead of the indirect object pronoun "le". This is still typical of informal speech in Madrid.
10. At the end of the *Sarao*, Lisis changes her mind about marrying Diego and, either sarcastically or as a slip of the tongue, calls him Dionís, the most murderous of all murdering husbands. See Mary Ellen Kohn, *Violence against Women in the Novels of María de Zayas y Sotomayor* (Ann Arbor, MI: UMI Dissertation Services, 1994).
11. See II Samuel 11. O'Brien (*Women in the Prose*) claims, not all too convincingly, that the girl is raised in status because she knows the Biblical story so well and sees it as a form of cross-class mobility.
12. See William Clamurro, 'Madness and Narrative Form in "Estragos que causa el vicio"', in *María de Zayas: The Dynamics of Discourse* (London: Associated University Presses, 1995), pp. 219–33.
13. Alicia Yllera, 'Las dos versiones del "Castigo de la miseria" de María de Zayas', in *Actas del XIII Congreso de la Asociación Internacional de Hispanistas* (Madrid: Castalia, 1998), pp. 827–36 (p. 835).
14. See Segundo Serrano Poncela, 'Casamientos engañosos (Doña María de Zayas, Scarron y un proceso de creación literaria)', *Bulletin Hispanique*, 64 (1962), 248–59.
15. See Teresa Langle de Paz, 'Beyond the Canon: New Documents on the Feminist Debate in Early Modern Spain', *Hispanic Review*, 70.3 (2002), 393–420; and Eavan O'Brien, 'Personalizing the Political'. See also Montesa.
16. See Barbeito Carneiro (*Mujeres y literatura del siglo de oro*); Cristina Enríquez de Salamanca, 'Irony, Parody and the Grotesque in a Baroque Novella: "Tarde llega el desengaño"', in *Maria de Zayas: The Dynamics of Discourse* (London: Associated University Presses, 1995), pp. 234–53; O'Brien, *Women in the Prose*; and Eavan O'Brien, 'Locating the Diary of Persecuted Innocence: María de Zayas's Adaptation of Hagiographic Historias', *Bulletin of Spanish Studies*, 87.3 (2010), 295–314.
17. See Magdalena Maurici Frades, 'Genoveva de Brabante: génesis del personaje y su lugar en la historia de la edición', *Bulletin hispanique*, 110.2 (2008), 573–600.
18. See the Oxford *Cantigas de Santa Maria* Database <http://csm.mml.ox.ac.uk/?p=home>.
19. Juan de Timoneda, *El patrañuelo*, ed. by Rafael de Ferreres (Madrid: Castalia, 1971), p. 208.
20. A similar reference is made in 'La inocencia castigada'. The source of the quotation has not been found. Grieve claims Alfonso X 'never said anything of the kind' (Grieve, p. 93), but that is probably too definitive.

21. Pedro de Ribadeneyra, *Vidas de santos: antología del Flos sanctorum*, ed. by Javier Azpeitia (Madrid: Lengua de Trapo, 2000), p. 142.
22. Brownlee (*Cultural Labyrinth*) adds that variations on the theme can be found in Boccaccio's *Filocolo*, Chaucer's *Franklin's Tale* and Boiardo's *Orlando Furioso*.
23. See Eavan O'Brien, 'Games in "The Garden of Deceit": A Seventeenth-Century Novella by María de Zayas y Sotomayor', *The Modern Language Review*, 104.4 (2009), 955–65.
24. See Edward Friedman, 'Constructing Romance: The Deceptive Idealism of María de Zayas's "El jardín engañoso"', in *Zayas and Her Sisters*, II: *Essays on Novelas by 17th-Century Spanish Women*, ed. by Gwyn Campbell and Judith Whitenack (New York: Global Publications Binghamton University, 2001), pp. 45–61.
25. See Kenneth Krabbenhoft, *Neoestoicismo y género popular* (Salamanca: Universidad de Salamanca, 2001).
26. See Amy Williamsen, 'Engendering Early Modern Discourse: Subjectivity and Syntactic Empathy in "Al fin se paga todo"', in *Zayas and Her Sisters*, II: *Essays on Novelas by 17th-Century Spanish Women* (New York: Global Publications Binghamton University, 2001), pp. 33–43.

CHAPTER 5

The Miraculous, the Fantastic and the Fatalistic

Confirmando esta propensión supersticiosa, doña María de Zayas cree ciegamente en los sueños fatídicos, en la influencia de las estrellas y sabiduría de los astrólogos, en el valor de los agüeros. (Amezúa, in Zayas, *Novelas* (1948), p. xxviii)

[Confirming this superstitious proclivity, Doña María de Zayas believes blindly in fateful dreams, the influence of the stars and the wisdom of astrologers, and in the veracity of omens.]

Apart from appearances of the Devil and episodes concerning magic and sorcery, Zayas's novellas contain a number of miracles. We have already seen how the Mother of God restores Beatriz's gouged-out eyes in 'La perseguida triunfante'. In two other novellas a dead person is resurrected: one a beautiful young bride after her ex-lover prays to the Crucifix, the other a hanged man who returns from the dead to help a would-be sinner. There are further elements that could be classed as supernatural, such as disembodied voices, premonitory dreams and pristine corpses. Throughout her oeuvre the author also shows a belief in the influence of the stars that harks back to the Renaissance episteme and the figure of the magus, although with Zayas the conviction that are our lives are ruled by the stars and good or bad fortune is deeply pessimistic and fatalistic. What is more, she appears to suggest that fate is more powerful than free will. These are the remaining aspects of the supernatural in the work of Zayas that need to be discussed if we are to get the full picture.

So far we have looked at the marvellous or preternatural and we have seen how it was in flux and marked by indeterminacy. But the miraculous was not immune to change either. Andrew Keitt's study of so-called holy men and women (*beatos* and *beatas*) in Madrid in the 1640s gives us a useful insight into the changing attitudes. Reading the inquisitorial records Keitt was struck by the abundance of words like *fingir* [to pretend], *embuste* [trick], *impostura* [imposture] and *embaucar* [to deceive]. The self-proclaimed saints were seen as imposters and frauds and described as scandalous in the etymological sense of the word: a stumbling block to faith. As a result they stood accused of 'haciendo invención del sagrado' [inventing the sacred] (Keitt, p. 2).

The miraculous was not ruled out but its domain was shrinking. Just as Salazar and Pedro de Valencia thought the Devil's work was possible in theory but unlikely in actual cases involving witchcraft and sorcery, miracles were thought to occur, but in some instances miraculous claims were rejected. Keitt writes that he began to see 'the preoccupation with imposture less as a confident assertion of Counter-Reformation disciplinary power and more as a symptom of profound conceptual turmoil and epistemological uncertainty' (Keitt, p. 7). We can see something similar in the writings of Huarte de San Juan, who advocated for a more naturalistic — as opposed to miraculous — interpretation of extraordinary events, adding that God no longer works miracles in our day and age:[1]

> Pero el vulgo de los hombres no sabe que las obras sobrenaturales y prodigiosas las hace Dios para mostrar a los que no lo saben que es omnipotente, y que usa de ellas por argumento para comprobar su doctrina, y que, faltando esta necesidad, nunca jamás las hace. Esto bien se deja entender considerando cómo ya no obra Dios aquellos hechos extraños del Testamento nuevo y viejo. (*Examen de ingenios*, p. 60)

> [But the common people do not know that God does supernatural and prodigious things to show his omnipotence to those who do not know Him, and that he uses his powers as an argument to prove his doctrine, and that, failing that necessity, he never ever performs them. This can be clearly seen when we consider how God no longer works those strange things we read about in the Old and New Testament.]

In the same passage Huarte de San Juan explains why he thinks that people are so keen to attribute things to God. He blames it on their impatience, arrogance, laziness and religious zeal. He also mentions that many people fake miracles in order to attract followers: 'Y por esta razón hemos visto muchos hombres fingir milagros en las casas y lugares de devoción; porque luego acuden las gentes a ellos y los tienen en gran veneración' [And for that reason we have seen many men fake miracles in houses and places of devotion; because the people flock to them forthwith and show them great veneration] (ibid.).

But not everyone shared Huarte de San Juan's preference for natural explanations of unusual events and miracles were widely reported. If we compare the reporting of miracles with that of magical activities we see a contrast. To get a flavour of the difference in treatment between the supernatural *sensu stricto* and the preternatural it is worth taking a brief look at the attitudes displayed in the *Avisos* by Pellicer and Barrionuevo.[2] These newsletters written in the 1640s and 1650s contain much material that would not be out of place in a modern newspaper, but in addition to discussing political events, natural disasters, heinous crimes and sundry rumours, they also report on preternatural events, evincing an ambivalent stance. In one of his letters Barrionuevo mocks a report concerning an exorcism that had taken place, and which resulted in a huge number of demons being cast out:

> A D. Francisco Guillen del Aguila, alcalde de Corte, que está endemoniado, como todos los de este pelaje, le han sacado del cuerpo 14 cuentos, 990.850 legiones de demonios, echando por la boca extraordinarias señales. Llamábase el general de todos Asrroel. Cada legion tenía un capitan, y se componía de

6.666 soldados. Mire Vm. cuál sería el bagaje, artillería y tren, y lo que cabe en el cuerpo de un alcalde. Y aún dicen que estaban holgados y muy á su placer.[3]

[14 million demons — 990,850 legions — were driven out of the body of Don Francisco Guillen del Aguila, a magistrate of the Court, who is possessed by the Devil like everyone of his ilk, ejecting them from his mouth with an extraordinary display. Their general was called Asrroel. Each legion consisted of 6,666 devils and had its own captain. Just imagine what the baggage train and artillery must have been, and all of that inside the body of a magistrate. And they even said they were comfortable and very well at ease.]

He adopts a similarly scornful tone when he talks about some women who were apprehended as witches, referring to their accoutrements as 'a thousand falsehoods':

El Marqués de Liche ha tornado á recaer, unos dicen de debilidad y flaqueza de estómago, y lo más cierto, de hechizos. Anoche prendieron tres damazas, ricas y de buena cara, por hechiceras. La Inquisicion las envió luego á Toledo. Halláronles mil embustes, manos de niños muertos, cabellos, dientes, cintas de atacar de hombres y otras mil cosas. (Barrionuevo, p. 98)

[The Marquis of Liche has suffered a relapse, some say because of a weakness of the stomach, or, most likely, because of an evil spell. Last night they arrested three ladies, rich and good-looking, for being witches. The Inquisition immediately sent them to Toledo. They found a thousand falsehoods: hands of dead children, hair, teeth, men's trouser strings, and a thousand other things.]

However, these proto-journalists were not always so sceptical. In a letter from 29 May 1656 Barrionuevo relates in all seriousness the account of a boy from Rome who could speak all languages. When his case was investigated they found a little whistle (*pitillo*) on the roof of his mouth. When they took it away, he had no more knowledge of what he had said and done. He claimed he had been given the whistle by a friar, who was nowhere to be found when they looked for him, leading to the assumption that it must have been the Devil. In the end the whistle was thrown on the fire where it crackled like a chestnut. On 5 July 1639 Pellicer writes that two men shot Don Diego de Pareja while he was praying to the Virgin; the bullet was stopped by 'una imagen de papel de Nuestra Señora de los Remedios que tenía en el pecho' [a paper image of Our Lady of the Remedies which he carried on his breast]. And almost a year later, on 4 June 1640, he relates the following miracle:

A este tiempo obró Nuestra Señora del Pilar un milagro portentoso, restituyendo la pierna a cierto mancebo de Casa Pellicer, que hacía cinco años se la cortaron de enfermedad, y no se halló señal de ella en la parte donde la enterraron.[4]

[At that time Our Lady of the Pillar worked an amazing miracle, restoring the leg of a certain boy of the Pellicer household, who had lost it five years previously when it was cut off due to an illness, and there was no trace of it where they had buried it.]

In brief, the preternatural is treated with caution, sometimes ridiculed, sometimes reported neutrally, whereas the supernatural *sensu stricto* appears to be treated seriously and taken at face value.

Something similar pertains to miracles described in Zayas. We do not get the ambiguity and ambivalence we have seen with regards to sorcery or the uncertainty vis-à-vis the eventual salvation of men who make diabolical pacts. There are no stories involving fake miracles or fraudulent miracle workers alongside actual miraculous events. When we read about a supernatural intervention we are presented with it as a fact. What differs is the tone and the context. One series of miracles is described in a hagiographical tale ('La perseguida triunfante'), while another miracle takes place in a reworking of an ancient tale ('El imposible vencido'). Both stories are rather conventional and the miracles are presented as something inspiring piety and wonder. A third miracle, by contrast, has a warped morality and takes place in a much eerier context ('El verdugo de su esposa'). This fantastic quality is also evident in a number of scenes that could be either marvellous or miraculous. Disembodied voices and premonitory dreams might be classified as genuine supernatural events, since it is strictly speaking impossible to hear someone's voice after death and only God knows the future. Alternatively, it is possible to see them as manifestations of the preternatural — the voices could be an illusion, the dreams a fancy planted by the Devil. At some level we need to choose which it was. In this way, Zayas, even if she does not cast doubt on the miraculous as such, introduces a different kind of dubiety and hesitation as well as strengthening her pessimistic view of the fate of women.

5.1 Zayas, Miracles and Hagiography: Between Tradition and Innovation

There has been considerable debate about whether or not Zayas subverts hagiographies. In a much-referred-to study Grieve posits that 'Zayas invests her novellas with the formal properties of hagiography while subverting the ideology of that Church-sanctioned genre' (Grieve, p. 86). In doing so she created 'a revisionist text that subverts hagiography's patriarchal discourse' (Grieve, p. 89). This view has been backed up by some, but considered an overstatement by others like O'Brien.[5] To assess this claim it is worth having a closer look at one of the most popular anthologies of saints' lives in early modern Spain. In our discussion of 'La perseguida triunfante' (see 4.4.) we have already come across Ribadeneyra's tremendously popular *Flos sanctorum*, which features the tale of the Scottish St Brigid, whose eyes are miraculously restored just like Beatriz's.[6] These hagiographies, however, not only show a predilection for the miraculous, but women are also warned against the fickle nature of men and encouraged to take the veil. In the story of the slaves Nereo and Arquileo and their mistress Domicila, the daughter of a Roman consul who is about to marry, we read the following:

> Los hombres [...] antes que se casen, suelen mostrarse muy humanos, afables y amorosos hasta el día de las bodas, pero cuando ya tienen a sus mujeres en sus casas, múdanse de tal suerte que parecen otros y trátanlas como quieren: no sólo con malas palabras, sino con peores obras. (Ribadeneyra, p. 38)

> [Men [...] before they marry usually show themselves to be very humane, affable and loving until the day of the wedding, but as soon as they have their women in their homes, they change so much they seem to be different people and treat them how they see fit: not only with bad language, but with worse deeds.]

This is exactly what happens in 'Mal presagio casar lejos', where Blanca is courted by a Flemish prince — we never find out his name — who appears to be a paragon of virtue and courteousness, until he marries her and takes her back to Flanders, where he begins to mistreat her and has an affair with a page. In Ribadeneyra's story Domicila is told by her Christian slaves:

> si se pudiesen pintar en un retablo todos los trabajos, dolores, cuidados, temores y miserias que pasa una triste mujer cuando se casa con un hombre desbaratado, ellos solos bastarían para desengañar a todas las mujeres y quitarles el deseo de casarse [...] Escoge, pues, oh Domicila, señora nuestra, cuál de los dos esposos quieres: o a Jesucristo, que siempre regala a su esposa y nunca muere, o a un hombre mortal, que por bueno que sea te ha de dejar. (Ribadeneyra, p. 39)

> [If we could paint a picture of the travails, pains, worries, fears and misery that a pitiable woman has to endure when she marries a foolish man, these alone would suffice to disabuse all women and take away their desire to marry [...] Choose, then, oh Domicila, which of the two husbands you want: either Jesus Christ, who only has things to give to his bride and who never dies, or a mortal man, who, however good he might be, will have to leave you.]

This exhortation is echoed in Zayas when various protagonists explain why they have accepted Christ as their Celestial Husband. In 'La más infame venganza' we can read: 'Octavia profesó, siendo la más dichosa, pues trocó por el verdadero Esposo el falso y traidor que la engañó y dejó burlada' [Octavia took the veil, being the happiest woman on earth, since she exchanged her false and treacherous husband who deceived and left her for the true Husband] (*Desengaños*, p. 195). At the end of 'La esclava de su amante' Isabel too decides to enter the convent: 'tengo elegido Amante que no me olvidará y Esposo que no me despreciará' [I have chosen a Lover who will not forget me and a Husband who will not despise me] (*Desengaños*, p. 167). And the narrator of 'La perseguida triunfante' says: '[M]e sacrifiqué desde muy niña a Esposo que jamás me ha engañado ni engañará' [since I was a young child I have sacrificed my life to a Husband who has never betrayed me and never will] (*Desengaños*, p. 409). Note also how Ribadeneyra uses the verb 'desengañar' in exactly the same sense as Zayas does: if the slaves could only show how atrocious married life can be, their mistress would be disabused (*desengañada*) of any false notions about marriage.

Ribadeneyra's collection is also full of examples of wanton cruelty suffered by innocent women at the hands of their fathers. The Irish St Dimpna is murdered by her father who lusts after her, while St Christina is stripped naked, flogged and cut to pieces, after which she picks up a piece of her flesh and offers it to her father. St Barbara's ordeal too is gruesome and horrific. Her father, looking on, licks his lips and begs to be allowed to kill her:

> Había estado presente a todo este doloroso espectáculo Dióscuro, su padre, relamiéndose como tigre en la sangre de su hija y, endurecido más con sus tormentos, pidió al juez que le dejase a él ser verdugo de su hija y darle por su mano la muerte (Oh corazón de padre, ¿dónde estás?) Fuele concedido. (Ribadeneyra, p. 107)

[Dioscorus, her father, had been present throughout this whole painful spectacle, licking his lips like a tiger at the sight of his daughter's blood, and, his heart hardened by her torment, he asked the judge if he could be his daughter's executioner and kill her with his own hands (Oh, father's heart, where are you?) His wish was granted.]

This passage exemplifies Marina Warner's observation that in 'Christian hagiography, the sadomasochistic content of the paeans to male and female martyrs is startling' and 'the particular focus on women's torn and broken flesh reveals the psychological obsession of the religion with sexual sin and the tortures that pile up one upon the other with pornographic repetitiousness'.[7]

In Zayas there are similar scenes of torture at the hand of male relatives, although they lack the hyperbolical gore of the *Flos sanctorum*. Roseleta in 'El verdugo de su esposa' is bled to death by her husband. The same fate befalls Blanca in 'Mal presagio casar lejos', with her friend María witnessing the entire scene through a keyhole in voyeuristic horror. In 'La más infame venganza' Camila is poisoned by her husband after having been raped by the brother of his ex-lover in an act of vengeance. 'El traidor contra su sangre' has Alonso first murder his sister and later decapitate his wife with a large knife (*un cuchillón grande*). After being repeatedly raped under a spell, Inés in 'La inocencia castigada' is immured by her husband, goaded on by her sister-in-law. In 'Amar sólo por vencer' Laurela, after she has been seduced by Esteban posing as Estefanía, is killed by her father who has a wall collapse onto her. And in 'Estragos que causa el vicio' Dionís puts his entire family to the sword after he has been led to believe his wife had an affair.

The hagiographical tales from the *Flos sanctorum* should be seen as an intertext rather than a genre that is subverted by Zayas. It is true that Ribadeneyra's collection is not aimed at denouncing the wrongs done to women, but in terms of tone, imagery and themes it is remarkably close to Zayas in some respects. The difference between his martyrs and Zayas's victims of uxoricide is that the latter live in the real world, the *hic et nunc*, instead of the legendary days of yore (see Enríquez de Salamanca). Furthermore, Rhodes (*Dressed to Kill*) identifies Zayas's women as secular martyrs through whose broken bodies the failings of an ignoble nobility are denounced in a kind of rallying call to change the evil at the heart of patriarchy. This denunciation through martyrdom is also discussed at length in the work of Vollendorf. If that is tantamount to subversion, then Grieve is correct, but to suggest that Zayas undermines this type of Church-sanctioned literature is to misread both her novellas and the original hagiographies.

A conventional miracle in 'El imposible vencido'

'El imposible vencido' tells the story of Rodrigo, who is betrothed to Leonor and who must leave her to join the Duke of Alba, who is fighting in Flanders. While he is there, he solves the mystery of a ghost that haunts a Spanish lady called Blanca — the spook turns out to be a spurned lover who walks around on stilts, dressed in a sheet and rattling chains. Meanwhile, Leonor's parents tell their daughter that Rodrigo has contracted marriage in Flanders and they marry her off to the rich Alonso. When Rodrigo returns to Spain and Leonor sees him, she literally drops dead and is buried. In his grief, Rodrigo bribes a verger to gain entrance to the crypt and opens her tomb. He embraces his departed beloved and prays to a crucifix to restore her to him. His prayer is heard and Leonor is resurrected, although she never loses the pallor of death. The event is hailed as a true miracle. After proclaiming the banns in accordance with Tridentine directives, Rodrigo marries Leonor. However, the newly-weds face a lawsuit by Alonso, which Rodrigo, after the intervention of a bishop, wins. And as far as we know, Rodrigo and Leonor live happily ever after.

In an insightful article Edwin Morby discusses Zayas's novella as one of the most complete versions of the *difunta pleiteada* topos: the litigation over a deceased woman.[8] He refers to work done by María Goyri de Menéndez Pidal, who analysed a number of *romances* and *comedias* on the theme — including *La difunta pleiteada*, attributed to Lope de Vega — as well as various French and Italian sources, including Bandello's novella XLI and the fourth story of the tenth day of the *Decameron*. The basic ingredients of the story are the following. A young woman is desired by many and gives her word to one of her suitors. Her father wants to marry her to another, richer, young man. The suitor leaves his beloved to go on a business trip far away. During his absence, the young woman is married to the party of her parents' choosing, but she dies (or appears to die) on her wedding day. Her suitor returns from his trip, bribes his way into the vault where she is buried and tries to kill himself out of grief, but his hand is stayed by the Virgin, who resuscitates the (seemingly) dead bride. They marry, but when her first husband recognizes her he files a lawsuit, which he loses.

There are a few notable differences between this ur-version and Zayas's novella, the most interesting — or puzzling, given the prominence of Marian interventions in other tales and her supposed attachment to the Virgin of the Immaculate Conception (see 1.1) — is that the miracle is not performed by the Mother of God but by the power of the Crucifix. One possible explanation could be that the narrator is male and that Zayas 'reserves' her Marian interventions for female-narrated tales. Zayas also insists more than other sources that Leonor is truly dead, as opposed to merely appearing to be so, which is what happens in Bandello's version. The theme of the young girl appearing to be dead and buried, with her lover subsequently coming to her tomb and killing himself in despair, is of course very old and is known in many variations, perhaps the scene of Romeo's suicide in *Romeo and Juliet* being the most famous of all. Shakespeare did not invent the plot and the story probably ultimately goes back to a version of Ovid's Pyramus and

Thisbe.[9] In that light it is no coincidence that the narrator of 'El imposible vencido' starts his story by telling his audience that the two lovers are born under the star of Pyramus and Thisbe. In addition, Rodrigo does not commit suicide, which would be un-Christian, but prefers to have himself killed in battle: 'si no me quito la vida, es porque soy cristiano; mas yo iré donde me la quiten los enemigos para que te acompañe en muerte quien te adoró en vida' [if I don't take my own life, it is because I am a Christian; but I shall go to where my enemies will take it from me, so that he who adored you in life may accompany you in death] (*Novelas*, p. 475). In the frame narrative Lisis's betrothed Diego does the same at the end of the *sarao* when Lisis announces that she will not marry him:

> Don Diego, descontento, con bascas de muerte, sin despedirse de nadie, se salió de la sala; dicen que fue a servir al rey en la guerra de Cataluña, donde murió, porque él mismo se ponía en los mayores peligros. (*Desengaños*, p. 510)

> [Don Diego, distraught and mortally afflicted, left the room without saying goodbye to anyone; they say he went to serve the king in the war in Catalonia, where he died, because he put himself in the greatest of dangers.]

As discussed, for most of Zayas's novellas it is possible to suggest one or more sources, a testament to her wide reading. 'El imposible vencido' as well as 'La burlada Aminta y venganza del honor' and 'Tarde llega el desengaño' share elements of their plot with novellas by Bandello. If Zayas spent her late teenage years and early twenties in Naples, it would be reasonable to assume she could read Italian (see 1.1). However, as Morby suggests, Zayas also includes elements from Spanish romances and there are echoes too of the legend of the lovers of Teruel, about whom Zayas's friend Pérez de Montalbán wrote a *comedia*. As it is impossible to ascertain exactly which sources Zayas used, we should focus on what Zayas does with the tales that inspired her. She always adds her own material and in the process usually complicates the narrative, as she does with her adaptation of Boccaccio's 'El jardín engañoso' (see 4.5). In 'El imposible vencido', not only does she elaborate the lawsuit, which Morby finds more convincing than the one in Lope's play, but she also fleshes out the episode abroad. Sandra Foa claims that Zayas changes the story to fit her feminist agenda. While that is arguably the case with other stories — even if a baroque tendency to render her stories more complex so they end up riven by internal contradictions is at least as prevalent — it is not clear how precisely this story has become more feminist as a result of Zayas's additions.

Rodrigo's adventures in Flanders are a prelude and counterpoint to the later events in Salamanca. Blanca is in love with Rodrigo, but he tricks her into marrying Beltrán, who is desperately in love with Blanca. She promises to marry Beltrán in front of a witness, thinking he is Rodrigo, 'quedando con esto, según las costumbres de Flandes, tan confirmado el matrimonio como si estuvieran casados' [and so, according to Flemish customs, they entered into matrimony just as if they had actually married] (*Novelas*, p. 466). In other words, theirs is a marriage according to pre-Tridentine rites. Leonor and Rodrigo, on the other hand, rigorously and explicitly apply the procedures stipulated by the Council of Trent, like proclaiming the banns of marriage: 'para su casamiento, demás de haberse aconsejado con teólogos y letrados, habían procedido todas las solemnidades que se requieren, como lo manda el santo Concilio de Trento' [for their marriage, in addition to having consulted theologians and lawyers, they followed all the requisite rites, as ordained by the Holy Council of Trent] (*Novelas*, p. 481).

Then there is the episode of the fake phantom, which provides a contrast not only to the miracle of Leonor's resurrection in the second half but equally to Octavio's real ghost (see 3.3). In Greer's view this resurrection is a male fantasy where ideal love overcomes parental authority, civil and ecclesiastical institutions, and even death itself. While the novella certainly suggests that love conquers all, albeit with a little divine help, it is not clear why this should be a particularly male fantasy, nor do I think that Greer's statement that 'in part or in whole, in a variety of ways, in one manner or another, every male-narrated story turns back on its narrator or narrative model to expose the psychic origins of male (mis)treatment — verbal and physical — of the women the men love and fear' (Greer, *Baroque Tales*, p. 198) applies to this male-narrated novella.

The lover pretending to be a ghost falls into the category of comical episodes containing bogus magic, like the sham magic ceremony in 'El castigo de la miseria' (see 3.1). A similar story is told by Castillo Solórzano in 'La fantasma de Valencia'. In that novella Rodrigo, who is in love with Luisa, resorts to dressing up as a phantom and roams around in an abandoned house adjacent to his beloved's, leading to speculations that the owner has come back to haunt it. He wears a white sheet and drags chains to scare everyone. In the fear and confusion thus created, he sneaks into Luisa's room to woo her.

In short, in 'El imposible vencido' Flanders is the locus of false appearances, old-fashioned marriage rites and fake phantoms, whereas Spain is associated with Tridentine rigour and the miraculous. This contrast fits Zayas's overall xenophobic agenda and projects fraudulence onto foreigners. In other tales there are numerous references to the egregious nature of strangers, the best example being the title and premise of the novella 'Mal presagio casar lejos', a tale about the misfortune that befalls three sisters who marry foreign men (for a discussion, see O'Brien, 'Personalizing the Political').

An eerie miracle in 'El verdugo de su esposa'

A further miracle occurs in 'El verdugo de su esposa', which tells the story of Juan and Pedro, two Spaniards who live in Palermo and are known by all — 'por antonomasia', Cervantes might have added — as 'los dos amigos' [the two friends]. After having an affair with a local woman called Angelina, Pedro marries Roseleta, but this does not stop from him regularly inviting his best friend Juan over to his house. The inevitable happens and Juan falls in love with his best friend's wife. Roseleta resists his advances, however, and when she has had enough, she tells her husband about it, showing him a love letter by Juan's hand. Stung by jealousy, Pedro arranges for his wife to promise to meet her would-be lover at a country estate so he can catch him in flagrante delicto. On the way to the tryst, Juan hears the Angelus being rung and perfunctorily recites an Ave Maria. Promptly, he arrives at a gallows where three bodies are hanging. One of the hanged men addresses him and offers to go to the meeting in his stead. Juan accepts and follows him at a little distance and sees how Pedro storms out of the house, kills the hanged man and throws him down a well. When this is done, the undead man comes back to Juan to explain the miracle:

> Y mira lo que los cristianos pecadores debemos a la Virgen María, Madre de Dios y Señora nuestra, que con venir, como venías, a ofender a su precioso Hijo y a Ella, se obligó de aquella Avemaría que le rezaste, cuando, saliendo de la ciudad, tocaron a la oración [...] me mandó viniese de la manera que has visto, para que tomando a los ojos de don Pedro y sus criados tu forma, lleven creído que te dejan muerto y sepultado en aquel pozo, y tú tendrás lugar de arrepentirte y enmendarte. (*Desengaños*, p. 217)

> [And see what we Christian sinners owe to the Virgin Mary, the Mother of God and Our Lady, because coming as you did to offend her precious Son and Her, she felt obliged on account of the Ave Maria you prayed to her when they rang the bells as you were leaving the city [...] to send me in the way you have seen, taking your shape in the eyes of Don Pedro and his servants, making them think they have left you dead and buried in that well, while you will have the opportunity to repent and make amends.]

Shocked and contrite, Juan leaves the scene and enters a monastery — one of the few men in Zayas to do so. Pedro's love for his wife turns to hatred. He cannot stand the sight of her and moves in with his former lover Angelina, who subsequently sets him up against his wife, proving herself to be a true member of the 'perfidious sisterhood' (see O'Brien, *Women in the prose*). Eventually he ends up killing Roseleta by removing a bandage around her throat so that she bleeds to death.

There can be little doubt about Zayas's sources for this novella. On the one hand it has clear echoes of Cervantes's 'El curioso impertinente', while on the other, Roseleta's death is a reference to Mencía's fate in Calderón's *El médico de su honra*.[10] The story is preceded by 'La más infame venganza' in which Camila is courted by another Juan but decides *not* to tell her husband about it. When he finds out anyway, he wreaks his revenge by poisoning her. She does not die immediately; instead her body swells up to monstrous proportions and turns an ugly hue. Eventually a heavenly voice speaks and she gives up her ghost. The two stories form a neat pair of opposites. In the first story the woman is killed because she does not tell her husband she is being pursued by another man. In the second, the woman dies after she tells her husband his best friend is making advances. This juxtaposition is not only a clear example of Zayas's message that women are doomed unless serious changes are made to society and have little recourse except to seek refuge in a convent, it also shows how Zayas uses a baroque aesthetics by putting two irreconcilable solutions side by side. The female protagonists face a paradox, described by Gracián as a 'monstruo de la verdad' [freak of truth].[11] Zayas makes an explicit reference to this strategy when she has the *desengañadora* explain in the middle of her story:

> En el discurso de este desengaño veréis, señoras, cómo a las que nacieron desgraciadas nada les quita de que no lo sean hasta el fin; pues si Camila murió por no haber notificado a su esposo las pretensiones de don Juan, Roseleta, por

> avisar al suyo de los atrevimientos y desvelos de su amante, no está fuera de padecer lo mismo, porque en la estimación de los hombres el mismo lugar tiene la que habla como la que calla. (*Desengaños*, pp. 211–12)

> [In the course of this *desengaño* you will see, ladies, how those who were born to misfortune cannot escape their fate, which will follow them until the very end; so if Camila died for not having told her husband about Don Juan's advances, Roseleta will suffer the same fate for having warned *hers* of the temerity and effort of her would-be lover, because in the opinion of men women who speak out get the same treatment as those who keep quiet.]

There is a serious moral issue at stake here. Juan betrays his best friend's trust by trying to seduce his wife and yet he is saved by the Virgin because he happens to have mumbled an Ave Maria when he heard the church bells ring. There is no sign of any real devotion and he has no second thoughts about his adulterous rendezvous; instead, he impertinently asks the Virgin to forgive the sin he is about to commit: 'pidiendo a la Virgen María, nuestra purísima Señora, que no mirando la ofensa que iba a hacerle, le librase del peligro y le alcanzase perdón de su precioso Hijo' [asking the Virgin Mary, our most pure Lady, that she ignore the offence he was about to give her and deliver him from danger and obtain forgiveness from her precious Son] (*Desengaños*, p. 213). It is not until he has seen what happens to the hanged man that he repents and decides to enter a monastery. The Virgin is most merciful and saves a sinner even when he has not (yet) shown contrition. This may seem surprising, but in her study of the Marian cult Marina Warner states that this attitude is typical of the Mother of God:

> the more raffish the Virgin's supplicant, the better she likes him. The miracles' heroes are liars, thieves, adulterers, and fornicators, footloose students, pregnant nuns, unruly and lazy clerics, and eloping monks. On the single condition that they sing her praises, usually by reciting the *Ave Maria*, and show due respect for the miracle of the Incarnation wrought in her, they can do no wrong. Her justice is her own: whatever his conduct, anyone pledged to her protection is her liegeman and she his responsible suzerain. (Warner, p. 325)

But while it may not be so unusual for Mary to save a raffish and rakish sinner, even if he shows no regret and only perfunctorily offers her a prayer, the mercy shown to Juan stands in shrill contrast to the fate of Roseleta, who is abandoned by her husband in favour of his ex-lover and thereafter murdered by him. We can understand that the world is evil and that men mistreat and kill innocent women, but why would the Virgin come to the aid of a would-be sinner and not save a wretched woman? The only answer Zayas has to offer is to say that she was born under an unlucky star (see 5.3), or the old cliché that God moves in mysterious ways his wonders to perform: 'a Dios no se puede preguntar por qué hace esos milagros, supuesto que sus secretos son incomprensibles, y así, a unos libra y a otros deja padecer' [one cannot ask God why he performs these miracles, since his secrets are unfathomable, and so he will save some and let others suffer] (*Desengaños*, p. 223).

Apart from the moral ambiguity of the story, there is another salient aspect worth scrutiny. As we have seen, on his way to his secret meeting with Roseleta, Juan is addressed by a hanged man. This is how the passage reads:

> Al llegar don Juan casi enfrente del funesto madero, oyó una voz que dijo: '¡Don Juan!', que como se oyó nombrar, miró a todas partes, y no viendo persona ninguna, porque aunque ya había cerrado la noche hacía luna, aunque algo turbia, pasó adelante, pareciéndole que se había engañado; y a pocos más pasos oyó otra vez la misma voz, que volvió a decir: '¡Don Juan!' Volvió, espantado, a todas partes, y no viendo persona ninguna, santiguándose, volvió a seguir su camino; y llegando ya enfrente de la horca, oyó tercera vez la misma voz, que dijo: '¡Ah, don Juan!' (*Desengaños*, p. 213)

> [When Don Juan had almost reached that dismal gibbet, he heard a voice saying: 'Don Juan!' and when he heard his name called out, he looked around, but didn't see anyone, because although night had fallen, the moon shone in the sky, albeit wanly; he rode on, thinking he had been mistaken, but after a few steps he heard the same voice again, repeating: 'Don Juan!' Scared stiff, he looked around, but he didn't see anyone, whereupon he made the sign of the cross and continued on his way; and when he passed in front of the gallows, he heard the same voice exclaiming for the third time: 'Ah, Don Juan!']

There ensues a discussion between the hanged man and the would-be adulterer. The hanged man explains he was innocent of his crime and confessed his sins, which is why he was saved. Critics who have written about the scene all appear to suggest that the hanged man is resurrected in order to speak to Juan and save him. Greer talks about his 'twice-dead body' when he is thrown in the well (Greer, *Baroque Tales*, p. 263), while Brownlee writes that God has 'revived a man from the dead' so that Juan 'can elude the assassins' (Brownlee, *Cultural Labyrinth*, p. 117) and Rhodes mentions the 'miraculously resuscitated body of the thief who saves Juan's life' (Rhodes, *Dressed to Kill*, p. 112). Boyer ('Towards a Baroque Reading') and Ursula Jung also refer to a resurrected hanged man.[12] Closer inspection reveals that in reality something else miraculous has happened. When he has caught Juan's attention, the not-yet-dead hanged man asks Juan to cut him down, whereupon Juan asks him: '¿Pues estás vivo?' [Are you alive, then?] (*Desengaños*, p. 214), to which the hanged man replies: 'Pues si no lo estuviera [...] ¿qué necesidad tenía de pedirte que me quitases?' [If I weren't [...] why would I need to ask you to cut me down?] (ibid.). Juan then wants to know how come he is still alive. But the hanged man does not give a detailed explanation; he merely says that nothing is impossible for God and then refers to a miracle worked by Santo Domingo de la Calzada, who made a roasted cockerel and hen come back to life and sing a song to save an innocent man who had been hanged. This reference gives us a clue as to what might have happened. The story of Santo Domingo de la Calzada is told, amongst others, by Jaume Roig in his (misogynist) book *Espill* or *Llibre de les Dones*, where a hanged man, who was executed on his way to Santiago de Compostela, is miraculously held up by St James:

> The next Wednesday as I was leaving town, I happened on bitter company, just for me, I'm sure. Following milestones, plains, mountains and low places and crossing rivers, I went on to visit the Holy Corpse of La Calzada, a walled city. A foul and despicable innkeeper with whorish inclinations had staying at that time in her inn a band of pilgrims, old and young. One of them caught her fancy and she asked him to give her pleasure; he declined. The vile [innkeeper]

put a cup in his baggage and when he went on his way she 'discovered' it missing. She had him hung for the theft. The other pilgrims in his group went on to Compostela and fulfilled their vow. On the way back, they went by just to see him hanging there, a little way off the great road. He was alive! He said: 'Get me down from here! The Blessed St James has held me up.' The dastardly plot was exposed and was given further confirmation, for the pilgrims ran and put their case before the presiding judge. As he was responding to their complaint, right before their eyes, two cooked birds miraculously came back to life and began to crow loudly, both the hen and the cockerel. The condemned innkeeper was hanged without further ado.[13]

The first miracle in this novella is therefore not a resurrection from the dead, but being held aloft by an invisible force and so escape death. However, the hanged man does reappear after he has been shot by Pedro and his men and thrown down a well, so it seems he is resurrected at this point to pass on a message of redemption to Juan, presumably to die a second time straight after he has fulfilled this purpose, just as happens at the end of Calderón's *La devoción de la cruz*, when the raffish but ultimately contrite Eusebio comes back from the dead, takes confession and dies a second death. After the return of the hanged man, Juan admits that: 'La cosa más rara y milagrosa que se ha visto es ésta' [This is the strangest and most miraculous thing that was ever seen] (*Desengaños*, p. 214). He wonders whether it is a dream or a spell, but the hanged man assures him: 'No sueñas, ni estás encantado' [You are neither dreaming nor under a spell] (*Desengaños*, p. 217). A last, uncanny touch is that on his way back to the city Juan passes the gallows again and: 'como llegó enfrente de la horca, miró hacia allá y vio en ella los tres hombres como antes estaban' [as he was passing in front of the gallows, he looked up and saw three men hanging there, like before] (*Desengaños*, p. 218).

Unlike the straightforward miracles related in 'El imposible vencido' and 'La perseguida triunfante' there seems to be something else going on. The desire to write a shocking and thrilling story is apparent. The secret tryst, the moon shining wanly in the sky, the bodies swaying on the gallows, the creepy voice calling out three times, all this seems designed to cause a frisson, as indeed happens to Juan himself: 'Embelesado estaba don Juan oyéndole con mil asustadas palpitaciones que el corazón le daba, que le hacía temblar el cuerpo sin poder aquietarle' [Don Juan listened to him spellbound, his frightened heart giving him a thousand palpitations and making his body shake uncontrollably] (*Desengaños*, p. 216). Zayas's intention is not — or at least not merely — to shore up belief in Church-sanctioned miracles and give a pious account of a wonder wrought by Mary to give succour to those who venerate her, as she does in 'La perseguida triunfante', but to turn the miraculous into something eerie.

5.2 The Fantastic in Zayas

In a famous study Tzvetan Todorov discusses the fantastic, which he considers to be an in-between category, a suspension of judgement.[14] Something out of the ordinary happens, something fantastic, and at the end of the story the reader —

though not necessarily the character — needs to decide whether the event was supernatural or not. If it was, the work belongs to the marvellous, and if not, to the uncanny. Thus the fantastic may evaporate at any moment and yet there is no reason to see the fantastic as an evanescent genre. Todorov posits two subgenres: the fantastic-uncanny and the fantastic-marvellous. In the first, the supernatural receives a rational explanation at the end. In the second, we learn it was a miracle. There is also the pure uncanny, in which extraordinary, shocking, singular, unexpected or disturbing events provoke a similar reaction to the one provoked by the fantastic. Horror, says Todorov, belongs to the pure uncanny. The term uncanny is a clever and apposite translation of Freud's notion of 'unheimish', which he defined as 'that species of the frightening that goes back to what was once well known and had long been familiar' and now arouses uneasy, fearful horror.[15] In his study on the phenomenon, Nicholas Royle defined the uncanny as something closer to Todorov's fantastic, seeing it as ghostly genre 'concerned with the strange, weird and mysterious, with a flickering sense (but not conviction) of something supernatural' and involving 'feelings of uncertainty, in particular regarding the reality of who one is and what is being experienced', although he later also mentions the 'commingling of the familiar and the unfamiliar' and the notion of liminality.[16] Examples of the uncanny he gives include corpses, the return of the dead and things that are strangely beautiful. The uncanny 'is essentially to do with hesitation and uncertainty' (Royle, p. 19).

In Zayas there are a few episodes that have the hallmarks of the fantastic. As we have seen, she plays with indeterminacy in her magical stories, where the reader must make up her or his mind whether or not the spell cast by Lucrecia (see 3.3) or the Moorish necromancer (see 3.4) is real, regardless of the narrative insistence that Fernando and Inés were actually enchanted. Depending on one's beliefs, these stories are either fantastic-uncanny or fantastic-marvellous, since either the spell is fake and there is a rational explanation for the episode — Lucrecia uses her charms and enchants Fernando with her looks, Inés merely pretends she was under a spell to explain her illicit affair, as her sister-in-law suggests — or there are preternatural forces at play. Since Todorov uses the term 'marvellous' to refer to the supernatural *sensu lato*, I propose a third category: the fantastic-miraculous, to which the episode of the hanged man belongs.

Other examples of the fantastic in Zayas are premonitory dreams, pristine cadavers, disembodied voices and the sudden appearance of an inexplicable light shining on a corpse. All of these fall outside of our ordinary experience of the world, but whether they are the work of a preternatural agent or pure miracles is not clear. These events could be fantastic-uncanny, fantastic-marvellous or fantastic-miraculous. A disembodied voice could have a rational explanation (it is imagined or in fact not a disembodied voice at all but, say, someone talking through a tube); it could also be the Devil's handiwork or a divine intervention. In this way Zayas introduces hesitation and uncertainty into the miraculous as well as the marvellous. As we have seen, with regards to magic the ambivalence is clear: sometimes magic is real, sometimes it is not. In her stories about the Devil, the lack of certainty lies in the unknown outcome. Are those who strike a deal with the Evil One saved

The Miraculous, the Fantastic and the Fatalistic

in the end or are they damned? Should we believe the Devil's generosity or doubt it? In her fantastic-miraculous tales we are confronted with something strange and extraordinary. We do not know how to categorize the event. Is the hanged man calling out to Juan real? Does Juan imagine it? It is a trick? Is it a miracle? Sometimes we are given an explanation — always a miraculous one in Zayas — but sometimes we are given no explanation at all. In either case, the objective is to make the reader's hair stand on end.

Disembodied voices and Gothic foreshadowings

I have already briefly mentioned 'La más infame venganza' in which Camila is poisoned by her husband and her body swells up to monstrous proportions as a result (see 5.1).[17] Camila lies in agony for many months until finally a mysterious voice calls out to announce her death:

> De esta suerte vivió seis meses, al cabo de los cuales, estando sola en su cama, oyó una voz que decía: 'Camila, ya es llegada tu hora.' Dio gracias a Dios porque la quería sacar de tan penosa vida; recibió sus sacramentos, y otro día en la noche murió, para vivir eternamente. (*Desengaños*, p. 195)
>
> [In this way she lived for six months, at the end of which, lying alone in her bed, she heard a voice, saying: 'Camila, your time has come.' She gave thanks to God for taking her away from such a wretched life; she received the last rites and the next night she died, to enjoy everlasting life.]

The scene could come straight out of a classic hagiography: the tortured woman, her patient suffering, the voice from heaven announcing her death, the comforting thought of everlasting bliss after this vale of tears. Camila is in a sense a latter-day martyr immolated on the altar of patriarchy.

Another, altogether more ominous, disembodied voice is heard in 'Estragos que causa el vicio', which centres on Gaspar, a young Spanish nobleman who has followed Philip III to Lisbon and who is courting four Portuguese sisters. One night, having been given a key to the back door of their house, he enters the basement and hears a voice moaning piteously. He searches everywhere to ascertain the provenance of these laments and eventually finds a hook sticking out of some loose sand on the floor. As he pulls on the hook, he lifts up the head of a dead man. He later returns with some monks from a nearby monastery and starts digging by the light of a lantern held up by one of the sisters. This experience dissuades the young wooer (*galán*) from courting the four sisters any further, the wondrous event being interpreted as a warning from God. But not long afterwards he falls in love with Florentina, who already has an affair with her sister's husband. One evening he walks down her street and finds her bathing in a pool of her own blood, after which she tells him how her sister's husband murdered the entire household and then committed suicide.

The scene in the basement is a far cry from Camila's saintly suffering and the divine voice calling her to the heavenly bosom, even if Gaspar interprets the episode as a warning from God, which he then proceeds to ignore. The dark basement, the eerie laments, the description of Gaspar groping around and finding a dead man's head on an iron hook, the monks digging up the corpse of a mysterious young man by the light of a lantern held aloft by one of the lascivious sisters, all this reads like an episode from Walpole's *The Castle of Otranto*. The scene is reminiscent of Laura's visit to the roadside chapel in the middle of the night and that of the hanged man calling out to Don Juan in 'El verdugo de su esposa'. If the disembodied voice is used in a quasi-hagiographical fashion in 'La más infame venganza', here it smacks of the fantastic and looks ahead to Gothic literature.

A number of critics have commented on this proto-Gothic aspect of Zayas's work. Welles, for example, writes that her novellas 'prefigure the effects sought in the gothic novel of the late eighteenth century' (Welles, p. 304). And according to Goytisolo her tales 'contienen, en efecto, numerosos episodios que anticipan el mundo novelesco de Walter Scott, Eugène Sue o Victor Hugo, con ahorcados, resurrecciones y criptas góticas' [contain, in effect, numerous episodes that anticipate the novelistic world of Walter Scott, Eugène Sue or Victor Hugo, with hanged men, resurrections and Gothic crypts] (Goytisolo, p. 105). Elizabeth Rhodes goes a little further and claims that, although Spain's participation in the Gothic was minimal, as its experience of the Enlightenment was vexed:

> the Gothic aesthetic itself may have had its origin in the agonizing demise of Europe's greatest Catholic state. Seventeenth-century Iberia provided the Gothic imagination with more than the literary lexicon of a power-hungry, perverse Inquisition, death-trap convents, sex-driven monks, malicious nuns, and an arrogant aristocracy. (Rhodes, *Dressed to Kill*, p. 170)

This is all too evident if we read Matthew Lewis's *The Monk*, for example, which contains all of the above ingredients as well as incest and a diabolical pact. Rhodes furthermore points out that the rarely acknowledged source of Walpole's *Mysterious Mother*, also containing incest, is Pérez de Montalbán's *La mayor confusión*. Another episode in Zayas that looks ahead to Romantic literature is the telepathic warning which Laura's brother receives when she is stumbling around in the pitch dark surrounded by rotting corpses (see 3.2). This supernatural form of communication also happens, to give but one famous example, at the end of *Jane Eyre*, where the eponymous heroine is sitting next to a dying candle, with beams of moonlight streaming into the room, when she receives a telepathic summons by Mr Rochester, making her flesh quiver on her bones.[18]

Premonitory dreams

In the early modern period much store was set by dreams, although it was acknowledged that they came in various types. A popular treatise on dreams was one by the second-century physician Artemidorus, in which it is clear that some dreams were seen as displacements long before Freud (see Greer, *Baroque Tales*). Del Río too discusses dreams in the context of divination. 'Certain dreams accurately foretell an event. Some make no prediction or make one which is illusory. Therefore one may legitimately take note of some, but not of others' (Del Río, p. 174). Ciruelo says dreams can have three causes: natural, moral and theological.

Humours influence dreams too — bile makes you dream of fire, black bile about death, phlegm about 'cosas claras de agua o de babas' [clear watery things or saliva] (Ciruelo, p. 129). These humours in turn can be influenced by external factors like changes in the air. Morally caused dreams come about if someone has occupied his or her mind with one thing all day — we would call them day-residue dreams. Theological or supernatural causes for dreams are revelations from God, who stirs man's imagination and represents what he wants to show us. These never contain any vain images and only happen rarely and when the stakes are high. In general, however, says Ciruelo, not too much attention should be paid to dreams:

> Y todo buen cristiano debe apartar de sí este cuidado de pensar en los sueños, porque como ellos puedan venir por muchas y diversas causas, la gente simple no acierta a saber por cuál causa vienen y el diablo, como es sutil, presto podría engañar a los que se dan de esta vanidad. (Ciruelo, p. 132)

> [And all good Christians have to steer clear of this preoccupation of thinking about dreams, because they can come about for many and diverse reasons, and simple-minded people cannot know where they came from and the Devil, in his slyness, can easily fool those who are taken in by this vanity.]

Not everyone heeded Ciruelo's warning and there were famous cases of political visionaries such as Lucrecia de León, some of whose dreams have received Freudian explanations. Richard Kagan, for example, calls Lucrecia's dream-substitution of her father by the king 'an almost textbook case of Oedipal displacement'.[19] Most of her dreams revolve around Philip II, who is seen as the symbol of everything that was wrong with the country: a corrupt Church, oppressive taxes, a lack of justice, and a weak national defence. Lucrecia predicted the defeat of the Armada and foretold the death of the king and that of his heir apparent. She was arrested in 1590, tried by the Inquisition and eventually sentenced in 1595. She received one hundred lashes, was locked up in a religious house for two years and banished from Madrid.

The opening tale of Zayas's collection, 'Aventurarse perdiendo', is riddled with references to fate, fortune and the influence of the stars (to which we shall turn in 5.3), and at two crucial moments in the story the heroine has a premonitory dream, one announcing who her husband will be, the other presaging his death. In the story we are told how Fabio chances upon a young lad singing his woes on the flanks of Montserrat. The lad turns out to be a girl called Jacinta, who proceeds to tell him her story. She lived happily in Baeza until one night she had a fateful dream:

> Diez y seis años tenía yo cuando una noche estando durmiendo, soñaba que iba por un bosque amenísimo, en cuya espesura hallé un hombre tan galán que me pareció — ¡ay de mí, y cómo hice despierta experiencia de ello! — no haberle visto en mi vida tal. Traía cubierta el rostro con el cabo de un ferreruelo leonado, con pasamanos y alamares de plata. Paréme a mirarle, agradaba del talle y deseosa de ver si el rostro confirmaba con él. Con un atrevimiento airoso, llegué a quitarle el rebozo, y apenas lo hice cuando, sacando una daga, me dio un golpe tan cruel por el corazón que me obligó el dolor a dar voces. (*Novelas*, p. 180)

[One night when I was sixteen I dreamt I was walking in a delightful forest, in the midst of which I found a man so elegant that he seemed to be — oh, how I experienced the truth of this once I'd woken up! — the most handsome man I had ever seen. He hid his face behind a slip of his tawny cape, decorated with silver buckles and clasps. I stopped to look at him, and since I liked the way he looked, I wanted to see if his face was as handsome as I thought. With a bold and graceful gesture I uncovered his face, and no sooner had I done so than he drew a dagger and stabbed me so cruelly in my heart that I screamed in agony.]

Not long after that, the brother of one of her friends, who had been fighting in Flanders, returns to Baeza. She sees him from her balcony and knows it is the man from her dream. They court and, predictably, she gives herself 'body and soul' to Félix, for that is his name, after he gave her his word to marry her, rejecting a rich, young widow for her sake. The spurned widow writes a letter to Jacinta's father telling him about his loss of honour and a duel between Félix and Jacinta's brother ensues, in which the latter is killed. Félix flees to Flanders, 'refugio de delincuentes y seguro de desdichados' [refuge for delinquents and safe haven for the unfortunate] (*Novelas*, p. 193) from where he regularly writes to his beloved. Jacinta's father, however, intercepts Félix's epistles, substituting them with a fake letter announcing his death, whereupon she takes the veil. In a dramatic turn of events, Félix returns to Spain, locates Jacinta, who lets him sleep with her in her convent cell, and promises again he will marry her, even proposing to travel to Rome to get a papal dispensation. Jacinta joins him and together they visit the Eternal City and are given permission to marry. On the way back, however, Félix receives a summons to fight, and honour demands that he leave his betrothed and they go their separate ways. Once back in Spain, Jacinta has another premonitory dream:

> Más habían pasado de cuatro meses que pasaba esta vida, cuando una noche, que parece que el sueño se había apoderado más de mí que otras (porque como la fortuna me dio a don Félix en sueños, quiso quitármele de la misma suerte), soñaba que recibía una carta suya, y una caja que a la cuenta parecía traer algunas joyas, y en yéndola a abrir hallé dentro la cabeza de mi esposo. (*Novelas*, p. 200)

> [More than four months of this life passed when one night it seemed that I had fallen into a heavier sleep than on other nights (since Fortune had given Félix to me in a dream, she wanted to take him from me in the same way) and I dreamt that I received a letter from him as well as a chest that appeared to contain jewels, but when I went to open it, I found it contained the head of my husband.]

Not long afterwards, the dream is confirmed when she hears the news that Félix has drowned. She mourns him, but, calling herself the phoenix of love (*fénix de amor*) she soon falls for a typical rogue and philanderer called Celio, who has no intention whatever of marrying her. When he leaves for Salamanca, she wants to follow him, but she is betrayed by a gentleman who promised he would accompany her to Salamanca but takes her to Barcelona instead, robbing her of all her possessions. She dresses up as a boy and makes for Montserrat, where Fabio finds her. Fabio turns out to be one of Celio's friends who wants to marry Jacinta. If she does not want to do that, she should take the veil. But Jacinta declares she is not ready to forget Celio, nor is she willing to become a nun and accept Christ as her Celestial husband, even though she knows full well what the rewards would be.

In her extensive study of Zayas, Greer touches upon the dream sequence and likens the stabbing in the heart to Teresa of Ávila's well-known vision. She says that Zayas's audience would have recognized the dream as the expression of a submerged sexual wish (like us), but would have equally linked it to a premonition of the advent of her lover (unlike us). Furthermore, she analyses Jacinta's dream as a displacement in which she sees *herself* as the masked male stranger whom she would like to be in order to be deserving of her father's love and calls it 'an imaginary duplication of herself as both male and female, both subject and object of desire' (Greer, *Baroque Tales*, p. 118). Greer links this to the mention of hermaphrodites elsewhere in Zayas, which she sees as confirming Jacinta's cross-gender identification. Uta Felten has suggested that Jacinta, in desiring to unveil the masked stranger, commits 'concupiscentia occulorum'.[20] Roca Franquesa ('Aventurarse perdiendo') claims the novella is based on José de Camerino's 'El casamiento desdichado' but adds that Zayas has made it a tale full of psychological value, saying her style reminds us of Romanticism and anticipates Freud and Jung. Part of this perceived psychological value no doubt resides in Jacinta's two dreams, particularly the first. Similar comments are made by various other critics.[21] In this context we should not forget that Freud did not pluck the notion of the unconscious out of thin air; throughout the period preceding his work on dreams and the subconscious we can see the same ideas being developed and described in literature and the arts, which is why Todorov states that psychoanalysis dispensed with the need for the fantastic. What we see in the fantastic is the dramatization of the same notions and suspicions, with the reader acting as a psychoanalyst.[22]

In Zayas's novella the two dreams are first and foremost effective pieces of storytelling. The handsome masked stranger in the middle of the forest, the dagger plunged into the heart, the certainty of meeting the man of the dream — all this makes for an exciting read. The author disregards Ciruelo's injunction against taking dreams seriously and we cannot be certain about the origin of their content. They are unlikely to be what Ciruelo calls a theological dream. It could be a moral (day-residue) dream, but the dream and its outcome seem too serious for that. Alternatively the Devil might have inspired the dream to bring Jacinta to ruin, although there are no indications anywhere that this pertains. Instead, the story is replete with references to fate and it is suggested that Fortune herself gave Felix to Jacinta in a dream. In other words, there seems to be another supernatural order at work: the inexorable influence of the stars (see 5.3).

Incorrupt cadavers

Zayas's eighth *desengaño*, 'El traidor contra su sangre', contains a number of fantastic events. The story begins in Jaén, where Don Pedro, a rich and cruel nobleman, lives with his son Alonso and daughter Mencía — as so often in Zayas the mother is absent.[23] Pedro wants his son to inherit his entire fortune and plans to put Mencía in a convent against her wishes. She is courted by the dashing and wealthy Enrique, who does not stand a chance because his grandparents are rumoured to have been mere labourers and Pedro is adamant he will not mix his blood with someone of low birth: 'teniendo por afrenta que la sangre de don Enrique se mezclase con la suya' [considering it an affront if Don Enrique's blood were to mix with his] (*Desengaños*, p. 379). But Enrique finds favour with Mencía and encourages her to escape the 'eterno cautiverio de la religión' [eternal captivity of religion] (*Desengaños*, p. 373), assuring her that her beauty is all the dowry he needs. Without being noticed he speaks to Mencía through a grille every day. Before he fell in love with Mencía, however, he courted a girl by the name of Clavela, and when she finds out what is keeping him from seeing her, she decides to avenge herself by telling Alonso that his sister is being courted by Enrique. Alonso and his father plot to murder Mencía and her lover. Pedro absents himself from town and Alonso catches his sister writing a letter to her lover. He locks her up, calls a priest and forces him to hear her confession as he is about to kill her. The priest tries to dissuade him, but to no avail; he hears Mencía's confession with tears streaming down his face, after which Alonso stabs his sister multiple times. Nine hours later Enrique arrives at the accustomed meeting place when something portentous happens:

> llegó a la reja y pasó y tocó en ella, y apenas puso en ella la mano, cuando las puertas se abrieron con grandísimo estruendo y alborotado con él, miró por ver que en el pequeño retrete había gran claridad, no de hachas, ni de bujías, sino de luz que sólo alumbraba en la parte de adentro, sin que tocase a la de afuera. Y más admirado que antes, miró a ver de qué salía la luz, y vio al resplandor de ella a la hermosa dama tendida en el estrado, mal compuesta, bañada en sangre, que con estar muerta desde mediodía, corría entonces de las heridas, como si se la acabaran de dar, y junto a ella un lago del sangriento humor. (*Desengaños*, p. 382)

> [he arrived at the grille and tapped on it, and no sooner had he touched it than the doors flew open with a tremendous crash, and he saw that the little room was lit up brightly, not by torches or candles, but by a light that shone from within and did not leave the room. And even more astonished than before, he went to see where the light was coming from and by its radiance he saw the beautiful lady lying down on a dais, dishevelled and bathing in blood, which, even though she had been dead since noon, was still streaming from her wounds as if they had just been inflicted, and next to her there was a lake of the sanguine humour.]

Enrique is shocked and his body is shaking, but his terror is even greater when he hears Mencía's voice telling him she has already been dead for nine hours and warning him to make his escape as his life is in grave danger. The moment she finishes speaking the doors are slammed shut. Out in the street, Alonso and an accomplice, who have not heard a thing, ambush Enrique and stab him more than twenty times, leaving him for dead. By the intervention of the Most Holy Mother of God, though, he gets better and enters a monastery, where he has a beautiful tomb built for his beloved. When her body is brought there over a year later, many people claim that her wounds are still bleeding and that she is as beautiful as the day she was murdered:

> habiendo muchos testigos que se hallaron a verle pasar, que, con haber pasado un año que duró la obra, estaban las heridas corriendo sangre como el mismo día que la mataron, y ella tan hermosa, que parecía no haber tenido jurisdicción la muerte en su hermosura. (*Desengaños*, p. 385)
>
> [there were many witnesses who saw her being carried past and, although the building work had lasted a year, blood was still flowing out of her wounds like on the day when she was killed, and she was so beautiful that it seemed death had no jurisdiction over her beauty.]

Alonso is sentenced *in absentia* to be beheaded but flees to Naples, where he strikes up a friendship with a 'wild priest' (*prevete salvaje*) named Marco Antonio (see 1.1), who has something devilish about him and sets Alonso up to do horrible things. Alonso falls in love with the beautiful young Ana and marries her. They seem happy for a while and have a son, but eventually he begins to have regrets. Goaded on by Marco Antonio, he decides to kill her by cutting off her head with a large knife. The friends bury her head in a cave in the port and dump her body in a well. They flee to Genoa but are captured as they are trying to steal a pair of silk stockings, having been inspired by the Devil (see 4.2). When they are sentenced to death — Alonso will be beheaded, Marco Antonio hanged — Alonso says that two months previously he had dreamt that his sister was threatening him with a knife. He is executed and when the news of his death reaches his father during a card game, the latter continues to shuffle the deck and comments: 'Más quiero tener un hijo degollado que mal casado' [I'd rather see my son beheaded than unsuitably married] (*Desengaños*, p. 398). But fate soon catches up with him and he dies a few months later, leaving all his wealth to his grandson.

It is clear that Zayas knew Calderón's *El médico de su honra*, as three of the protagonists have the same names and roles: the father/king Pedro, the lover Enrique and the innocent sacrificial victim Mencía. Both Mencías — like Blanca in 'Mal presagio' — are allowed to confess their sins to a priest before they are murdered, and both die in pools of their own blood. But where Calderón can be said to criticize the honour code by showing what happens when it is taken to the extreme, Zayas is ultimately more interested in female victimhood, although the title of the novella also refers to another important theme, namely the obsession with pure bloodlines.[24]

Like 'Aventurarse perdiendo' this novella mentions the influence of fate a fair few times, although it is not as important a leitmotiv as it is in Jacinta's *historia calamitatum*. Likewise, there is a premonitory dream in which Alonso sees the sister he has killed brandishing a knife, a reference to both his impending death and the two women he murdered with a knife.

The fantastic-miraculous scene in which Enrique comes to the grille and the doors fly open with a crashing noise, after which he sees his beloved bathed in a mysterious light, is one of Zayas's more successful scenes in which she skilfully mixes hagiographic imagery with a sense of eerie contemporality. The hesitation that marks the fantastic is made evident when Enrique comes round after he has been stabbed and asks the magistrate to go to Pedro's house to see if what he had seen was 'la verdad o alguna ilusión fantástica' [the truth or some fantastic illusion] (*Novelas*, p. 384).

Zayas's tales share with hagiographical accounts the incorruptibility of dead bodies. In her excellent study on the female body in Zayas, Rhodes discusses how Inés ('La inocencia castigada'), Beatriz ('La perseguida triunfante'), Blanca ('Mal presagio casar lejos'), Roseleta ('El verdugo de su esposa'), Elena ('Tarde llega el desengaño'), Magdalena ('Estragos que causa el vicio') and Mencía ('El traidor contra su sangre') all radiate and become beautiful in death. The thrust of Rhodes's work is to argue that Zayas uses the wrongs heaped on women to highlight societal failings and she sees these radiant corpses as symbols: 'By trespassing the threshold that rightly separates life and death, these undead corpses point to the behavioural boundary wrongly crossed by the living and are cautionary voices from heaven' (Rhodes, *Dressed to Kill*, p. 112). According to the critic, the point is not that dead women are the most beautiful, but that God marks the body of the wrongly tormented woman with what the world esteems most: beauty. Post-mortem loveliness is a form of poetic justice; their physical appeal does not speak about God's gain, but of humanity's loss. But:

> although the final beauty of Zayas's dying and dead women is supernatural, it does not follow the pattern of hagiography. Martyred saints in early modern hagiographies may die in blazes of light and pools of flowing blood, but they are not stunningly beautiful in death. (Rhodes, *Dressed to Kill*, pp. 113–15)

That is not quite true, however, as there are hagiographical stories where a martyr's body becomes pristine and beautiful in death. The Dutch St Liduvina, for example, was ugly and suffered horribly throughout her life. First she breaks her leg skating, then she develops a huge abscess from which worms crawl, after which her right arms rots away, but when she dies, her body becomes beautiful: 'Su cuerpo, que en vida estaba feo y lleno de llagas, quedó entero y hermosísimo, y el rostro con tan rara belleza que ningún pintor le pudiera formar tan gracioso' [Her body, which, when she was alive, had been ugly and covered in sores, was made whole and very beautiful, and her face had such a rare beauty that no painter could have made it look prettier] (Ribadeneyra, p. 187).

A few good men

The two hapless lovers, Enrique from 'El traidor contra su sangre' and Felix from 'Aventurarse perdiendo', have something in common that, as far as I am aware, has not been remarked upon by Zayan scholars: they are essentially good men. As discussed, one of the key ideas in Eavan O'Brien's study of Zayas's work is the notion of gyn/affection, which she contrasts with the 'perfidious sisterhood'. Opposing female friendship and solidarity we have women who side with patriarchy and bring other women down. Examples are the sister-in-law in 'La inocencia castigada', who causes Inés to be immured, and Theodosia in 'El jardín engañoso', whose malicious rumours lead to the death of Federico at the hand of his brother Jorge, with whom she is in love. They have their counterpart in a small number of male characters who are genuinely good, thus completing the four possible combinations of evil/innocent and male/female. In the novellas we have plenty of evil men and innocent women; they are offset by a handful of perfidious women and a few good men.

As we have seen, Félix really loves Jacinta. When he has the chance to marry a beautiful, rich widow, he rejects her. This contrasts with other men in Zayas, who do not hesitate to marry for money. After fleeing to Flanders, he refuses to forget about Jacinta and when he returns to Spain, he renews his promise to marry her and together the lovers travel to Rome. It is on their way back that he receives a summons to join his unit, after which he tragically drowns. Enrique, too, truly loves Mencía and suffers the same fate as many of Zayas's heroines when he is nearly killed by her jealous brother. Like many of the women in the novellas who take the veil, he enters a monastery, where he has a magnificent tomb built for Mencía. Both Enrique and Félix court other women before they meet their real love and are betrayed by them. They are powerless when it comes to saving the women they love. The latter, for their part, decide to hand over their honour to their suitors and sleep with them in the expectation they will be wed soon, Mencía doing so in defiance of her father's wishes.

There are two further minor male characters who do not conform to type. The first is Martín in 'La burlada Aminta' who meets the eponymous heroine after she has been duped by Jacinto and his bisexual lover Flora (see 1.1). He offers to marry her and accompanies her to Madrid where she seeks out Jacinto and his lover and murders them, taking the law into her own hands. Afterwards, they change their names and live together as a couple in Madrid. The story is not only a tale of revenge, but of female empowerment. Aminta subscribes to the honour code and feels the need to avenge herself and does not want or need a male relative to do this for her.[25] Martín too defies the code by accepting a woman he knows has already given away her prized virginity to a scoundrel. A further 'good man' is the Marquis Don Sancho in 'El desengaño amando'. He is in love with Clara and willing to wait for her while she travels to Seville to track down her husband, Fernando, who has eloped with the witch Lucrecia (see 3.3). After her return and her husband's death, Clara marries her suitor and they live happily ever after. 'Doña Clara vivió muchos años con su don Sancho, de quien tuvo hermosos hijos que sucedieron en el estado de su padre, siendo por la virtud la más querida y regalada que se puede imaginar, porque de esta suerte premia el cielo la virtud' [Doña Clara lived many years with her Don Sancho, with whom she has beautiful children who inherited their father's estate, being on account of her virtue more loved and spoiled than you can imagine, because this is how the heavens reward virtue] (*Novelas*, p. 408).

5.3 Written in the Stars: Astrology and the Subordination of Free Will

In his prologue, Amezúa remarks upon the author's frequent use of the supernatural and marvellous, including her belief in astrology, blaming it on her female credulity. Montesa (*Texto y contexto*) too comments on Zayas's copious references to stars and fate. However, the profound implications of her stance on astrology, especially in relation to free will, have, as far as I can tell, not been analysed.

In her discussion of 'La inocencia castigada' Judith Whitenack refers to the notion of free will, coming close to suggesting that Inés could not have been subjected to the Moor's enchantment had she, deep down, wanted to resist it. This is a problematic reading, but the notion that free will trumps enchantment is affirmed in other works of the period. Don Quixote, for instance, says:

> Aunque bien sé que no hay hechizos en el mundo que puedan mover y forzar la voluntad, como algunos simples piensan, que es libre nuestro albedrío y no hay yerba ni encanto que le fuerce: lo que suelen hacer algunas mujercillas simples y algunos embusteros bellacos es algunas misturas y venenos, con que vuelven locos a los hombres, dando a entender que tienen fuerza hacer querer bien, siendo, como digo, cosa imposible forzar la voluntad.[26]

> [I know, of course, that there are no spells in the world that can control a person's will, as some simple people believe; for our free will is sovereign, and there is no herb or enchantment that can control it. What some silly strumpets and deceitful rogues do is to make certain poisonous mixtures that they use to turn men mad, claiming that they have the power to make them fall in love, whereas it is, as I have just said, impossible to coerce the will.][27]

In seventeenth-century Spain there raged a theological debate about free will.[28] This debate is known as the *De auxiliis* controversy, which, according to Henry Sullivan in his influential book on Tirso de Molina, is sometimes dismissed as 'an incomprehensible quibble' but in fact constituted 'a crucial moment in the history of ideas and in the development of human freedom'.[29] On one side of the debate there was the Dominican Domingo Báñez and his Mercedarian ally Francisco Zumel, who held that God foresees, predestines and causes man's free will to perform good deeds that will bring about his redemption and who distinguished between sufficient grace, granted to everyone, and efficacious grace, leading to actual individual salvation, and who further believed that humans could be condemned by 'negative antecedent reprobation', that is, the fact that God has not prevented the sins of a particular individual — in other words, God's omniscience takes precedence over man's free will. On the other side of the debate there was Luis Molina, a Jesuit professor at Coimbra, who believed in the doctrine of 'simultaneous concourse' according to which God's cooperation is only employed after a sin has been committed and that although God foresees everything, including conditional future contingent events, his prescience does not predetermine our acts. This interpretation of free will 'erects a wall of safety around human liberty emphasizing the importance of man's personal efforts, the value of earned merits and his determination in the success or failure of grace' (Sullivan, p. 34).

The debate was not restricted to the faculties of theology but reached a wide audience through its inclusion in plays of the period. The contribution of playwrights like Calderón de la Barca and Tirso de Molina was to staunchly defend free will — and their genius, to turn abstract theology into moving drama. No one is condemned a priori and there is no such thing as unmovable fate. In Calderón's *La vida es sueño* the prophecy that Segismundo was destined to cause civil war and vanquish and humiliate his father Basilio may come true, but the latter's imprudent desire to outwit destiny by locking up his son eventually turns him into an instrument of fate as Segismundo transforms from being a half-beast, subjected to violent passions, to a paragon of virtue and magnanimity. The stars do not lie (although astrologers can) but fate cannot coerce our free will — we have a choice in how we deal with adversity — and it is possible to reverse its effects: 'porque el hado más esquivo, | la inclinación más violenta, | el planeta más impío, | sólo el albedrío inclinan, | no fuerzan el albedrío' [because the most elusive fate, the most violent inclination, the most impious planet, only incline our will and do not force it] (ll. 787–91).[30] Likewise, in Calderón's *Las cadenas del demonio* the Devil is forced to admit that 'tiene el pecador | en su albedrío tal vez | más ancha la permisión que yo' [the sinner with his free will has perhaps more freedom to act than I] (Calderón, *Las cadenas del demonio*, p. 233). And in his play *La devoción de la cruz* the siblings Eusebio and Julia, who have both committed a litany of sins, repent and are saved. At one point Julia reminds her father that 'el hado impío | no fuerza el libre albedrío' [impious fate does not force our free will] (ll. 588–89). At the end of the play a miracle takes place to allow Eusebio, who has died unconfessed, to be redeemed (see 5.1).

Tirso de Molina's *El condenado por desconfiado* is more pessimistic and the hermit Paulo is allowed to be cruelly deceived by the Devil, who convinces him that he has been condemned by negative antecedent reprobation. It used to be thought that Tirso de Molina was a follower of Molina and that his pseudonym was a homage to the Jesuit theologian, but Sullivan convincingly argues that Tirso was in fact a follower of his fellow Mercedarian Zumel, who proposed a less rigid interpretation of Báñez's stance of free will. In *El condenado por desconfiado*, Paulo's undoing is doubting God's infinite mercy and not using his free will to ask for forgiveness, even when he thinks it is too late — because it never is. When the Good Shepherd comes on stage, looking for his lost sheep, he says: 'Diole Dios libre albedrío | y fragilidad le dio | al cuerpo y al alma; luego | dio potestad con acción | de pedir misericordia, | que a ninguno le negó' [God gave him free will and frailty of the body and the soul; and then he gave him the power to act and ask forgiveness, which he has never refused anyone] (ll. 1541–46). These plays are gripping drama, while at the same time expressing a profoundly optimistic faith in free will and God's boundless compassion.

In Zayas this optimism is replaced by a deep pessimism. One of the narrators comes close to blasphemy when she claims that free will cannot overcome fate. Having heard the stories of two women who were murdered by their husbands, one for not telling him that she was being courted by another man and the other for telling him that she *was*, she exclaims:

> Y cierto, que aunque se dice que el libre albedrío no está sujeto a las estrellas, pues aprovechándonos de la razón las podemos vencer, que soy de parecer que si nacimos sujetos a desdichas, es imposible apartarnos de ellas. (*Desengaños*, p. 228)
>
> [And for sure, even though they say that free will is not subjected to the stars — since by using our reason we can overcome their influence — I am of the opinion that if we are born to misfortune, it is impossible to avoid their influence.]

A similar, albeit slightly less fatalistic, remark is made in 'El traidor contra su sangre', where the narrator states:

> aunque se dice que el sabio es dueño de las estrellas, líbrenos Dios de las que inclinan a desgracias, que aunque más se tema y se aparten de ellas, es necesaria mucha atención para que no ejecuten su poder. (*Desengaños*, p. 374)
>
> [even though they say that a wise man is not subjected to the stars, may God deliver us from those that predispose to misfortune, because no matter how much one might fear or endeavour to avoid them, one has to be extremely careful not to let them exert their power.]

And in the first line of the opening tale of the *Sarao* the narrator tells us that 'para ser una mujer desdichada, cuando su estrella la inclina a serlo, no bastan ejemplos ni escarmientos' [if a woman is unfortunate, her star being thus inclined, neither exemplary tales nor moral lessons are of any use] (*Novelas*, p. 173), which is highly ironic given that the collection is entitled *Novelas amorosas y ejemplares* and the whole point of the stories is to 'dar ejemplo y prevenir' [offer examples and warnings] (*Novelas*, p. 513).

Throughout the tales there are many more references to the malign influence of the stars and the ineluctability of fortune and fate. The word 'fortuna' [fortune] is used about fifty times in the *Sarao*, often personified and once referred to as 'cruel enemiga del descanso, que jamás hace cosa a gusto del deseo' [cruel enemy of repose, who never does anything to please our desires] (*Desengaños*, p. 232). When Laura is at the roadside chapel (see 3.2), she cries out:

> No sé para qué el cielo me crió hermosa, noble y rica, si todo había de tener tan poco valor contra la desdicha, sin que tantos dotes de naturaleza y fortuna me quitasen la mala estrella en que nací. (*Novelas*, p. 363)
>
> [I don't know why Heaven made me beautiful, noble and rich, if all of this was going to be of little use against misfortune — all those gifts that nature and fortune bestowed upon me cannot liberate me from the evil star under which I was born.]

Further references to fate can be found in 'El imposible vencido', a tale about two star-crossed lovers that starts with the statement that 'los dos amantes habían nacido en la estrella de Píramo y Tisbe' [the two lovers were born under the star of Pyramus and Thisbe] (*Novelas*, p. 447).

Of all the novellas, 'Mal presagio casar lejos' has the largest number of bad omens and references to misfortune, as the title would lead us to expect. The tale relates what happens to Blanca and her sisters, all of whom marry foreigners and all of whom end badly. At the beginning of the story we learn that 'no les pudo prevenir el librarlas de la desdichada estrella en que nacieron [...] a la una y a la otra siguió su mala fortuna' [this could not prevent them from escaping the unfortunate star under which they were born [...] each of them being followed by their bad luck] (*Desengaños*, p. 338). And later on there are references to 'la adversa estrella con que había nacido' [the adverse star under which she was born] (*Desengaños*, p. 348) and 'su fatal desdicha y la estrella rigurosa de su nacimiento' [her fatal misfortune and the harsh star of her birth] (*Desengaños*, p. 360).

Astrology and the belief in the influence of the stars were part of the Neoplatonic world-view that was being eroded in the seventeenth century. In his treatise from 1538 Ciruelo still held that:

> los cielos y estrellas, alterando el aire y la tierra, también alteran a los hombres y a los otros seres vivos que moran en la tierra [...] Y el verdadero filósofo que conoce las virtudes y propiedades de las estrellas, podrá por ellas conocer los efectos sobredichos en los elementos y en los hombres [...] Y esta astrología es lícita y verdadera ciencia como la filosofía natural o la medicina. (Ciruelo, pp. 119–20)
>
> [the sky and the stars, through changing the air and the earth also change men and other living creatures that dwell on earth [...] And the true philosopher who knows the virtues and properties of the stars will be able to know through them the aforementioned effects they will have on people [...] And this astrology is lawful and a true science, just like natural philosophy or medicine.]

This attitude had changed by the time Zayas's contemporary Pellicer called astrology a 'useless ability and madness' in a letter from 11 March 1642:

> Murió el padre Andrés de León, de los Clérigos Menores, grande matemático y astrólogo, y por esta habilidad tan inútil muy consultado en la Corte de todos los que creen en los delirios de la Astrología. (Pellicer, p. 160)
>
> [Father Andrés de León, a minor-order priest, has died; he was a great mathematician and astrologer, and for that useless ability much sought after at Court by all those who believe in the madness of Astrology.]

Astrology was taught at the University of Salamanca, although in 1582 the Supreme Court took action to end this, presumably because it conflicted with the question of free will.[31] For a long time astrology was held in high esteem and pervaded various aspects of scientific thought, but in the course of the seventeenth century it lost its central role and ossified into an obsolete system of belief, which survives to this day in the form of star signs and horoscopes (see Thomas). Adorno has claimed that the decline of social systems causes paranoia and the search for irrational causes such as astrology and the occult, which, in his view, explains the witch-hunts of the early modern period.[32]

What Zayas does is recycle this Neoplatonic belief to fit her profoundly fatalistic agenda, but without reinserting herself into a bygone episteme, as has been suggested by Uta Felten. Zayas is deeply pessimistic about the position of women within society and their power of self-determination; she acknowledges there is free will, but sees it as powerless against the crushing wheel of fortune. If there is one subversive element hidden away in Zayas's prose, then this is it.

* * * * *

In her novellas Zayas deploys the full panoply of the supernatural *sensu lato*. She evinces a deep-rooted pessimism by denying free will when confronted with the influence of the stars. And alongside fake and frighteningly real magic and diabolical trickery, she recounts miraculous stories, some of which are infused with a sense of the fantastic, thus introducing a different kind of hesitation in her novellas. This is equally the case for events such as disembodied voices and premonitory dreams, which appear to anticipate the Gothic, although we should not forget this genre was a reaction to a very different set of circumstances. She uses the uncertainty surrounding the supernatural to symptomize irrational fears and express her profound pessimism. Rather than being ahead of their time, her novellas are eminently baroque: baroque in their fascination with the morbid and macabre, baroque in their convoluted prose and rambling sentences full of twists and turns and the occasional anacoluthon, and baroque in the contradictory positions taken up and defended, resulting in a game of false appearances and a labyrinthine narrative structure. In a sublime paradox Zayas attempts to make her readers see through deceit by deploying a highly deceitful strategy; she can be said to a play a game of *desengañar engañando* [to disabuse by deceiving]. Her stories are part pulp fiction, part clever composition; they are titillating tales that are highly critical of her society without being revolutionary (she does not have a forward-looking alternative vision). She aims to shock her readers out of their complacency, while at the same time resigning herself to the impassive tyranny of fate and fortune.

Notes to Chapter 5

1. This was also the view of mainstream Protestantism, even though Calvin mentions Protestant miracles in the context of a dispute that miracles per se cannot authenticate the Catholics' claim to be the true Church. See Euan Cameron, *Enchanted Europe: Superstition, Reason & Religion, 1250–1750* (Oxford: Oxford University Press, 2010), especially chapter 13. See also Stuart Clark, *Thinking with Demons*, chapter 17. Reginald Scot calls one of his chapters (book VIII, chapter 1) 'That miracles are ceased' and writes that 'in times past, it pleased God, extraordinarilie to shew miracles amongest his people, for the strengthening of their faith' (Reginald Scot, *The Discoverie of Witchcraft* (London: John Rodker, 1930; facsimile repr. New York: Dover, 1970), p. 89).
2. See Sander Berg, '"No es cosa de burlas": *mira* and *miracula* in Barrionuevo, Pellicer and Zayas', in *Studies on the Supernatural*, ed. by Stephen Hart (Cambridge: Cambridge Scholars Publishing, 2017), 91–106.
3. Jerónimo de Barrionuevo, *Avisos*, 1 (1654–1656) (Madrid: Imprenta y Fundición de M. Telio, 1892), p. xxvii.
4. José de Pellicer, *Avisos históricos* (Madrid: Taurus, 1965), p. 81.
5. Hernández Pecoraro argues that Zayas foregrounds hagiography in order to subvert it. Brownlee and O'Brien disagree with Grieve. O'Brien writes: 'Grieve overstates the subversive quality of Zayas's hagiographic discourse. Only through the wider effects of Beatriz's overt rejection of marriage can this denouement be considered in any way subversive' (O'Brien, 'Locating', p. 313).
6. Ribadeneyra's *Flos sanctorum*, also known as *Vidas de santos*, which was first published in Madrid in 1599 and reprinted in 1601, 1604, 1616, 1651 and 1675. Throughout the early modern period it remained the most important collection of hagiographies in Spain, until it was replaced by *Año cristiano*, a Spanish translation of a French original written by the Jesuit Croisset and first

published in 1753. These anthologies of descriptions of the lives of saints go back to the *Acta Martyrum*. See Javier Azpeitia's introduction to the *Vidas de santos*.
7. Marina Warner, *Alone of All Her Sex: The Myth and the Cult of the Virgin Mary* (New York: Vintage Books, 1976), p. 71.
8. See Edwin Morby. See also Nigel Glendinning, 'The Traditional Story of "La difunta pleiteada", Cadalso's *Noches lúgubres*, and the Romantics', *Bulletin of Hispanic Studies*, 38.3 (1961), 206–15.
9. *Romeo and Juliet* was probably based on Arthur Brookes's English rendition of Pierre Boaisteau's French adaptation of an Italian novella by Bandello, who may have taken the story from Da Porta, who in turn was inspired by Masuccio Salernitano's *Il Novellino*, which contained an updated — Italianized — version of Ovid's *Pyramus and Thisbe*, which was itself probably inspired by an even older story. See Arthur J. Roberts, 'The Sources of Romeo and Juliet', *Modern Language Notes*, 17.2 (1902), 41–44. There are also scholars who suspect that Shakespeare read Painter's *The Palace of Pleasure*, a collection of novellas based on Bandello, Boccaccio and others. Some scholars believe Shakespeare read all three Italian sources as well as the English ones. See Amanda Mabillard, 'Sources for Romeo and Juliet', *Shakespeare Online* (2009). This implies that Shakespeare could read Italian, which is claimed by at least one critic. See Naseeb Shaheen, 'Shakespeare's Knowledge of Italian', *Shakespeare Survey*, 47 (1994), 161–69.
10. Blanca in 'Mal presagio casar lejos' is also bled to death by her husband and dies 'desangrada, como Séneca' [bled dry, like Seneca] (*Desengaños*, p. 364).
11. Baltasar Gracián, *Arte de ingenio. Tratado de la agudeza*, ed. by Arturo del Hoyo (Madrid: Aguilar, 1960), p. 1178. He adds: 'Unir a fuerza de discurso dos contradictorios extremos, extremo arguye de sutileza' [To unite two contradictory extremes by the power of discourse is an extreme proof of subtlety].
12. See Ursula Jung, '¿La honra manchada? La reescritura de *El médico de su honra* en los *Desengaños amorosos* de María de Zayas', in *Escenas de transgresión: María de Zayas en su contexto literario-cultural* (Madrid: Iberoamericana, 2009), pp. 159–76.
13. Jaume Roig, *Spill* <http://www.spanport.ucla.edu/santiago/roigsant.html> [accessed 23 August 2016]. The online text reads '[t]he vile *baggage* put a cup in his baggage'. I have amended this obvious error. The resurrected cockerel and hen were probably included in the story because of the mention of La Calzada. Santo Domingo de la Calzada was not the first to resurrect roasted fowl. In Lope de Vega's *San Nicolás de Tolentino* the eponymous vegetarian saint is offered a roast partridge. He makes the sign of the cross and the animal gets up and flies away. The touch of the cup hidden in the baggage is of course straight from Genesis 44, where Joseph tests his brothers' loyalty to Benjamin by having a silver cup put in the latter's baggage and then accusing him of theft.
14. See Tzvetan Todorov, *The Fantastic: A Structural Approach to a Literary Genre* (Ithaca, NY: Cornell University Press, 1970).
15. Sigmund Freud, *The Uncanny*, trans. by D. McLintock (London: Penguin Books, 2003), p. 124. For a discussion on the English translation of the term and its relation to its antonym 'canny', see Maria Tatar, 'The Houses of Fiction: Towards a Definition of the Uncanny', *Comparative Literature Studies*, 33.2 (Spring 1981), 167–82.
16. Nicholas Royle, *The Uncanny* (Manchester: Manchester University Press, 2003), p. 1.
17. Stacey Parker Aronson claims that Camila, just like Inés in 'La inocencia castigada', is metamorphosed into a monster for having transgressed the gender code. Stacey Parker Aronson, 'Monstrous Metamorphoses and Rape in María de Zayas', *Revista Canadiense de Estudios Hispánicos*, 29.3 (2005), 525–47.
18. Charlotte Brontë, *Jane Eyre* (Toronto: Bantam Books, 1981), p. 401.
19. Richard Kagan, *Lucrecia's Dreams: Politics and Prophecy in Sixteenth-Century Spain* (Berkeley: University of California Press, 1992), p. 2.
20. See Uta Felten, 'En torno a la escoptofilia femenina en María de Zayas', in *Escenas de transgresión: María de Zayas en su contexto literario-cultural*, ed. by Irene Albers and Uta Felten (Madrid: Iberoamericana, 2009), pp. 65–73.
21. Goytisolo states that the dream appears to come straight out of Freud. Barbeito Carneiro calls the dreams Freudian anticipations, while Montesa claims that they would be the delight

of psychoanalysts. Paun de García ('Magia y poder') sees Inés's lascivious dreams as having Freudian implications, while Cardaillac Hermosilla writes about the Freudian intuition of María de Zayas. Uta Felten interprets the dream as reflecting the changing epistemology — Jacinta reads the world according to the out-dated episteme of analogy. She claims that Zayas subversively re-establishes an obsolete episteme.

22. See for example Nigel Smith, 'Gautier, Freud, and the Fantastic: Psychoanalysis *avant la lettre?*', in *Functions of the Fantastic: Selected Essays from the Thirteenth International Conference of the Fantastic in Arts*, ed. by Joseph Sanders (Santa Barbara, CA: Greenwood Publishing Group, 1995), pp. 67–75.
23. Greer (*Baroque Tales*) says that of the forty-seven female protagonists only thirteen have living mothers.
24. It used to be believed that Calderón supported the intransigent honour code as exemplified by plays such as *El médico de su honra*, *El pintor de su honra*, *El alcalde de Zalamea* and *A secreto agravio, secreta venganza*. For a discussion on the topic, see Manuel Delgado's introduction to *La devoción de la cruz* (Madrid: Cátedra, 2000). Not all critics share these insights, though. Amy Williamsen ('Challenging the Code'), for example, claims that Calderón's staunch support of the honour code may explain his lack of universal appeal.
25. Hipólita does the same in 'Al fin se paga todo' when she murders her brother-in-law who has tricked her into sleeping with him by sneaking into her bed when her husband was out of the house in the middle of the night because he, the brother-in-law, had let the horses loose.
26. Miguel de Cervantes, *Don Quijote de la Mancha*, ed. by Fransciso Rico (Barcelona: Galaxia Gutenberg, 2004), pp. 262–63. Something similar is said in his novella 'El licenciado de vidriera', where Tomás is given a poison to force his will: 'Y así, aconsejada de una morisca, en un membrillo toledano dio a Tomás unos destos que llaman hechizos, creyendo que le daba cosa que le forzase la voluntad a quererla: como si hubiese en el mundo yerbas, encantos ni palabras suficientes a forzar el libre albedrío' [And so, on the advice of a Morisca, she gave Tomás a potion in a Toledan quince that was supposed to 'enchant' him, thinking she was giving him something that would force his will to love her: as if there were in this world herbs, spells or words that could by themselves force free will] (*Novelas ejemplares*, II, 52).
27. Miguel de Cervantes, *Don Quixote*, trans. by John Rutherford (London: Penguin, 2003), p. 180.
28. Not just in Spain; in the Netherlands the Calvinist Balthasar Bekker published *De betoverde wereld* [The Enchanted World] (1691) in which he writes: 'so weet ik door de Reden wel so veel, als dat des Menschen Wille nooit gedwongen word' [through Reason I know enough to know that the will of man cannot be forced] and 'oversulx en magh de Duivel sich niet laten voorstaan, dat hy heeft den will van dien Mensche, welke hy tot ondertekeninge van 't verdrag gedwongen heeft' [and moreover, the Devil cannot claim to have the will of the man whom he has forced to sign the pact] (Balthasar Bekker, *De betoverde wereld* (Amsterdam: Daniel van Dalen, 1691), II, 14).
29. Henry W. Sullivan, *Tirso de Molina & The Drama of the Counter Reformation* (Amsterdam: Rodopi, 1976), p. 30. Sullivan describes the debate on free will as a drama played out in three acts. The first act was the debate that pitted the Protestants Luther, Melanchthon, Zwingli and Calvin against Erasmus and the Catholic theologians. The second act took place in Spain and consisted of a heated debate between Jesuits and Dominicans (the *De auxiliis* controversy). The third and final act was played out in France between Jesuits and Jansenists.
30. For a discussion, see Paul Lewis-Smith, *Calderón de la Barca: La vida es sueño* (London: Grant & Cutler, 1998).
31. See Charles Williams, *Witchcraft* (New York: Meridian Books, 1959).
32. For a more detailed discussion, see Chapter 2. The most elaborate study on the phenomenon, which puts Adorno's view in perspective, is Stuart Clark's *Thinking with Demons*.

CONCLUSION

> El tremendismo, la violencia, la crueldad, que con tanta frecuencia se manifiestan en las obras de arte del Barroco, vienen de la raíz de esa concepción pesimista del hombre y del mundo que hemos expuesto y a su vez la refuerzan. El gusto por la truculencia sangrienta se observa en muchas obras francesas, italianas, españolas [...] es un dato común peculiar de la situación histórica del Barroco en toda Europa. (Maravall, p. 335)
>
> [The shocking, stark realism, the violence and the cruelty that manifest themselves so frequently in baroque art stem from this pessimistic view of man and the world as we have shown, and at the same time reinforce it. The taste for bloody gruesomeness can be seen in many French, Italian and Spanish works [...] it is a common feature of the historical period of the baroque in the whole of Europe.]

In the preceding chapters we have seen how Zayas describes a wide variety of supernatural events, often introducing an element of indeterminacy or hesitation. We have read accounts of fake magicians, fraudulent witches, actual sorcerers, diabolical spring gardens, Marian miracles, but also of disembodied voices, incorrupt corpses and an undead hanged man. Some stories are clearly designed to be amusing, whereas others aim to thrill, titillate, shock or make us feel sorry for the protagonist. Her fantastic episodes, especially, cannot be separated from her desire to create sensationalist stories. In addition to the vast array of supernatural elements in the novellas we have fathers murdering their daughters, husbands and brothers slaughtering their wives and sisters, a murder seen through a keyhole, women dressing as men, men dressed as women, a man making love to his page and cruelly mocking his wife when she walks in on them, a woman lusting after other women and a noblewoman who uses an African stable boy as her sex slave until he dies from exhaustion. To fully appreciate Zayas as a baroque writer and understand the way in which the supernatural in all its forms fits into her oeuvre, we need to put her into a wider literary context.[1]

The 'novella craze'

Much has been said about the huge output of *comedias* in Spain's Golden Age — McKendrick estimates the total number at 10,000[2] — but less about the equally staggering number of novellas that were printed in the same period, especially in the seventeenth century. Romero Díaz claims that in the course of the 1600s fifty-eight original collections of novellas were published, plus sixty-five re-editions and five anthologies. She has linked this enthusiasm for the *novela cortesana* to the urban transformation that took place at that time.³

The novella tradition has its roots in the Middle Ages when oral tales were collected by authors like Boccaccio, Sercambi, Chaucer and the author of the *Cent nouvelles nouvelles*. These were transformed into *novelas cortesanas* in the Renaissance by writers like Bandello, Masuccio, Marguerite de Navarre and Timoneda. Many of the early novellas in Spain were modelled on or translated from Italian sources. In artistic terms, the genre probably reached its zenith with Cervantes as the novellas that follow lack the originality and wit of the *Novelas ejemplares*, although we should probably consider the author of Don Quixote as a case apart, since he consciously placed himself outside of the tradition by boasting that the stories were all his own invention. If Cervantes's novellas are playful, subtly critical and wonderfully aware of the plurality of discourse, the next generation of writers — Salas Barbadillo, Castillo de Solórzano, Pérez de Montalbán and Carvajal among them — either produced humdrum, run-of-the-mill novellas or else seemed bent on overwhelming their readers with outlandish stories. The genre's popularity declined after 1665, although many collections, including Zayas's, were reprinted well into the eighteenth century. To get an idea of what these stories were like, let us briefly turn to summaries found in Joaquin del Val's overview of the seventeenth-century novella in Spain. There we find Salas Barbadillo's *El necio bien afortunado* (1621), a funny picaresque novel with scenes of false witchcraft. Del Val also mentions the *Historias peregrinas y ejemplares* (1623) by Céspedes y Meneses, which are full of:

> amor y celos, voces misteriosas y espantables apariciones, como en *La constante cordobesa* en la que don Diego ve surgir de un sepulcro al padre de la mujer que ama, y el fantasma le amenaza para que renuncie a su hija. (Del Val, 'La novela española', p. lvii)

> [love and jealousy, mysterious voices and frightening apparitions, like in *La constante cordobesa*, in which Don Diego sees the father of the woman he loves coming out of his grave and his ghost threatening him to stop wooing his daughter.]

The same scholar discusses the work of Enríquez de Zúñiga, who imitated Cervantes's *Persiles* and wrote elaborate novels full of kidnappings, wanderings, and so on. In Suárez de Mendoza's *Eustorgio y Clorilene* (1629) a courtier enters a crypt and there follows a two-page description of the corpse of the protagonist's grandmother. Barrionuevo y Moya wrote *Soledad entretenida en que se da noticia de la historia de Ambrosio Calisandro* (1638), which brims with fights with Moors, mysterious caves, necromancers, anchorites, bandits and much more. Despite their shared taste for the sensational, Del Val calls Zayas, 'una figura excepcional en el conjunto de novelistas de esta época' [an exceptional figure in the collection of novelists from this period] (Del Val, p. lix).

Staying closer to Zayas's circle of friends, we should not fail to mention the work of Castillo Solórzano and Pérez de Montalbán, both prolific novella writers, with the latter having a:

> tendencia a lo terrorífico y desorbitado, por lo que debemos considerarlo un

verdadero prerromántico. [...] Sin vacilar puede afirmarse que son las más obscenas de su tiempo, y doña María de Zayas que ha sido considerada, desde lo afirmó Ticknor, como la novelista española más atrevida, nunca llegó a escribir una monstruosidad comparable a *La mayor confusión*. (Del Val, p. lvi)

[tendency to the horrific and exorbitant, on account of which we ought to consider him a true pre-Romantic. [...] Without hesitation we can state that his novellas are the most obscene of his time and that Doña María de Zayas, who has been considered, ever since Ticknor, Spain's most daring novelist, never wrote anything as monstrous as *La mayor confusión*.]

A brief look across the borders, moreover, makes us realize that the taste for the shocking, the horrific and the titillating was part of a wider trend in the seventeenth century. In France François de Rosset (1570–1619) and Jean-Pierre Camus (1584–1652) published hundreds of *histoires tragiques* that deal with similar themes and were very popular. Rosset wrote tales featuring incest, homosexuality, a priest accused of witchcraft, and a dalliance between a nun and a lieutenant who turns out to be the Devil. Camus was the prolific author of tales in which he describes 'terrifying, catastrophic, dramatic or horrible situations' and tells 'bloodcurdling or monstrous anecdotes' showing 'pleasure in approaching the forbidden, with an obvious voyeurism in the case of juicy details' (Muchembled, p. 134). These authors were influenced by the emerging popular press in France, the *canards*, which dealt with marvels, calamities, celestial phenomena and crimes that were described in gory detail (see Muchembled).[4] Likewise, some plays in Jacobean England are equally known for their gruesome details, including instances of incest. Not only do we have Walpole's *The Mysterious Mother*, but there is also Ford's *'Tis Pity She's a Whore* (1632), which portrays a love affair between a brother and his sister, with the former eventually ripping out the latter's heart and carrying it around on stage on the point of his dagger.

It would appear, then, that in the seventeenth century there was an insatiable demand across Western Europe for an ever more sensationalist repertoire of novellas and gruesome stories. Zayas's oeuvre was written in the middle of the novella craze and like the work of her contemporaries her tales are marked by sensationalism, of which the supernatural is part and parcel.

★ ★ ★ ★ ★

There cannot be many centuries in European history that are not marked by great changes and upheavals. The seventeenth century is no exception. Especially in the 1640s, when Zayas wrote her *Desengaños amorosos*, Spain faced rebellions and uprisings on many fronts. The Dutch Revolt had been ongoing since 1568 and would result in the humiliating Treaty of Westphalia in 1648, when Spain acknowledged the independence of the Republic of United Provinces. The Portuguese rose up in 1640 and finally regained their independence in 1668. Catalonia (1640–1659) and Naples (1647–1648) also rebelled against the Crown, although these uprisings were eventually unsuccessful. And after decades of dominance on the battlefields of Europe, the Spanish *tercios* were defeated by the French at Rocroi in 1643. The

Spanish empire seemed to be teetering on the brink and this led to a fair degree of soul-searching and finger-pointing. Like many of her contemporaries, Zayas is deeply distrustful of foreigners and heaps caustic comments on the serving classes. She blames the failings of the nation on the lack of virility of men and projects the national and societal chaos on the domestic scene — hence the uxoricidal episodes. The 'war of the sexes' that is waged in the novellas is in part a symptom of everything that was perceived to be wrong with the nation.

Apart from political upheavals, the seventeenth century also saw a shift in epistemology. The worldview that accepted magic and astrology as perfectly plausible explanations of phenomena was slowly being eroded. That many people still believed in witchcraft is clear when we look at studies done by Ruggiero, Sánchez Ortega and Martín Soto, although many of those who took recourse to magic evinced a pragmatic attitude and sometimes admitted it was all just make-belief. All the while, the most learned men of the country could not make up their minds whether or not witches actually flew to their sabbaths. Despite its bleak reputation, the Inquisition took a lenient view, both with regards to Satanic witchcraft, which the Holy Office thought was almost impossible to prove in individual cases, and to other magical practices, which were simply seen as fraudulent. The supernatural was subdivided into two distinct orders: the preternatural — the domain of the Devil — and the supernatural *sensu stricto*, or the miraculous. In this period, the sense-of-the-impossible was shifting and both orders shrank while their borders were more strictly policed. Miracles were in danger of being seen as social, legal and religious constructs, while the beliefs surrounding magic generated considerable uncertainty.

In Zayas we see the resulting indeterminacy clearly in her episodes dealing with sorcery, which is sometimes described as real, sometimes as a prank, now comical, then harrowing. Moreover, this uncertainty infects other elements of her stories and she often offers her readers a number of options as to the possible causes of a given event, indicating the most likely scenario, but leaving open alternative explanations, thus planting seeds of doubt. She equally plays a baroque game of deception when she makes the Devil claim he is capable of doing good, fooling the protagonists of the story, the characters in the frame narrative and modern scholars alike, thus providing a stark reminder of the Devil's subterfuge. What is more, she seems to suggest that either there is justice in the afterlife and the Devil has the last laugh, or there is no justice in this life *or* the next, especially not for women. Her other descriptions of the Devil are more straightforward, conventional and unremarkable. He is a quasi-comical figure who disappears in plumes of sulphuric smoke when he has been vanquished by the Virgin, or a trickster facilitating the suicide of a hapless miser. The Devil takes a more abstract form when he possesses people, driving them to do evil. This is at the same time a very old notion and also typical of the gradual interiorization of evil. Sometimes the Devil is merely the epitome of ugliness, even if in one story Zayas manages to turns things on their head by turning a black stable boy into a suffering saint. The indeterminacy and baroque games change to a profound pessimism when Zayas ascribes powers to the stars that, going against the prevailing theology, trump free will. This does not mean she still inhabits the

Neoplatonic world of Renaissance magi like Paracelsus, but rather that she uses astrology to express her fatalistic conviction that some people, especially innocent women, will suffer injustice, however ill-deserved, and that there is nothing anyone can do.

Like her stories involving the Devil, Zayas is rather conventional when it comes to miracles. The indeterminacy surrounding the preternatural episodes is absent, as one would expect, and we are not offered conflicting views of the miraculous, nor are we given alternative options, leaving room for doubt. One Marian episode, however, acquires a different flavour and becomes imbued with a sense of the fantastic when the would-be adulterer is addressed by a hanged man, swaying from the gallows by the wan light of the moon. Other episodes, including disembodied voices, the undead and premonitory dreams, share the same quality. Just as her belief in the power of the stars gives voice to her fatalism, these episodes express a deep unease that is evoked by the inexplicable. Todorov explained the fantastic as something that is in-between; at the end of the story the reader must make up her or his mind whether the event is supernatural or if there is a rational explanation. He differentiates between the fantastic-uncanny and the fantastic-marvellous. Bearing in mind the early modern tripartite division of orders, I have suggested a third possibility: the fantastic-miraculous. In the case of premonitory dreams, disembodied voices, incorrupt cadavers and inexplicable light Zayas never explains the uncanny aspect and thereby creates a sense of narrative uncertainty; it is up to the reader to decide whether the event has a natural, a preternatural or a miraculous explanation. This uncertainty is what links her supernatural, preternatural and fantastic episodes, and together they shape the experience of reading Zayas's novellas just as much as the feminist and transgressive passages.

The supernatural *sensu lato* in Zayas is a barometer of the shifting attitudes in the seventeenth century, but it is also deployed in an attempt to shock and thrill her audience. In that respect the scenes of voodoo rape, wily witches and egregious sorceresses are on a par with Zayas's descriptions of sodomy, lesbian lust, sibling and wife-murder, and racy interracial sex that pepper her collection. With these sensationalist elements she sought to attract the *vulgo*, while with the clever baroque composition she aimed to please the *culto*. For the former, the greatest appeal of her work would have been the 'pulp fiction' aspect of her tales of gore, superstition and irrational fear.[5] For the latter, the playful juxtaposition of opposing possibilities, the contrast between real miracles and efficacious magic on the one hand, and fake phantoms and fraudulent sorcerers on the other, would have been the main attraction. That is also clearly how the authorities saw her novellas, since she received her licence to print (*licencia*) without any problems — as far as we can tell, at least — and her stories were seen as well-crafted and not containing anything that ran counter to the Catholic faith. This way Zayas cast her net as wide as she was able to in order to spread her pro-woman message. In addition, her sheer audacity and gift for telling baroque, complex stories was proof that women, despite their humoral dispositions and supposed innate inferiority, *were* able to produce artful literature with a wide appeal.

Ever since her reappraisal in the dying decades of the last century, Zayas has been lauded for her transgressive prose, but to properly assess how unique she is in this respect much more research would have to be done into the novelistic output of contemporaries like Castillo Solórzano and Pérez de Montalbán. In addition, a comparative study could be made between her novellas and the French *histoires tragiques* by Camus and Rosset. Or else a firmer link could be established between the Jacobean theatre and the Spanish *comedias* and novellas. Her plots may be unoriginal, but then again that was the hallmark of the genre. Boccaccio, Bandello, Sercambi, Masuccio, Timoneda, Lope de Vega, Carvajal, Marguerite de Navarre, Chaucer and even Shakespeare were not out to write original plots; instead they rewrote existing tales to suit new audiences. Incidentally, in this process it becomes clear that good literature has little or nothing to do with a good plot. There is a world of difference between Bandello's and Shakespeare's rendition of the story of the star-crossed lovers from rival families in Verona, with Rojas Zorrilla's *Los bandos de Verona* somewhere in between the two, even though all three essentially tell the same story. Few are the novellas by Zayas for which at least one possible source has not been found; her typical modus operandi is to complicate a given story or combine elements from various sources. The result is often an elaborate tale that is full of paradox and opposition. In the process she laces her tales with the miraculous, the marvellous and the fantastic, giving voice to irrational fear, anger, frustration and fatalism, while at the same time (unconsciously, no doubt) cashing in on the indeterminacy surrounding the supernatural caused by an eroding episteme. Like a true alchemist, she creates out of her recycled plots a series of novellas that are, for all their predictability, occasional clichés and rambling syntax, an exciting read.

Notes to the Conclusion

1. Romero Díaz has made a similar point: '¿cómo entender la significación e implicación cultural de este género en el Barroco si sólo se estudian mujeres de forma aislada?' [how can we understand the cultural meaning and implication of this genre of the baroque if we only study women in isolation?' (Romero Díaz, *Nueva nobleza, nueva novela: reescribiendo la cultura urbana del barroco* (Newark, DE: Juan de la Cuesta, 2002), p. 14).
2. Melveena McKendrick, *Theatre in Spain, 1490–1700* (Cambridge: Cambridge University Press, 1989).
3. See Romero Díaz, *Nueva nobleza*.
4. The same has been said about Zayas and the *relaciones de sucesos*. See Appendix.
5. If we see Lisis as Zayas's alter ego (and there are good reasons to do so), she says she deliberately uses a plain style so that the educated and uneducated can understand her. Just before she is about to relate the last story of the collection, Lisis says the following: 'Y yo, como no traigo propósito de canonizarme por bien entendida, sino por buena desengañadora, es lo cierto que, ni en lo hablado, ni en lo que hablaré, he buscado razones retóricas, ni cultas; porque, de más de ser un lenguaje que con el extremo posible aborrezco, querría que me entendiesen todos, el culto, y el lego; porque como todos están ya declarados por enemigos de las mujeres, contra todos he publicado la guerra. Y así he procurado hablar en el idioma que mi natural me enseña y deprendí de mis padres; que lo demás es una sofistería en que han dado los escritores por diferenciarse de los demás, y dicen a veces cosas que ellos mismos no las entienden; cómo las entenderán los demás sino en diciendo, como algunas veces me ha sucedido a mí, que cansado el sentido por

saber qué quiere decir y no sacando fruto de mi fatiga, digo: "muy bueno debe ser, pues yo no lo entiendo"' [And you can be sure that, seeing as I have no desire to earn a reputation as a witty and intelligent writer but rather as a good *desengañadora*, in all I have said and will say I have not striven to be rhetorical or sophisticated; because, in addition to that being a language I find abhorrent to the extreme, I want to be understood by everyone, both the educated and the uneducated; because, since all have shown themselves to be the enemy of women, I have declared war on everyone. And so I have attempted to speak in a way that comes naturally to me and which I learned from my parents; since all the rest is sophistry that writers engage in to be different from the others, and they say that sometimes they write things they do not even understand themselves; how can anyone understand what they write except by saying, as has happened to me on occasion, when, having tired out my brain trying to figure out what is being said and not seeing my effort rewarded, I say: 'it has got to be good, since I do not understand it'?] (*Desengaños*, pp. 469–70).

APPENDIX

Zayas and the *relaciones de sucesos*

> Como doña María se vio desamparada de este público, agudizó en sus novelas la nota de lo novelesco; quiso cazar el público popular que busca interés, drama, aventura en la novela. Las *Novelas amorosas* son la obra verdaderamente literaria, fina, artista, de doña María; a partir de este volumen, todo lo que viene es de folletín popular. (Azorín, *Los clásicos redivivos*, p. 72)

> [Seeing as Doña María saw she had fallen out of favour with her audience, she began to emphasize the melodramatic tone of her work; she wanted to court the popular readership, who look for excitement, drama and adventure in a novella. The *Novelas amorosas* are Doña María's truly literary, refined and artistic work, all that follows is but pulp fiction.]

Just as has been suggested for François de Rosset and Jean-Pierre Camus and their sensationalist *histoires tragiques*, a number of scholars have suggested that Zayas was influenced by the then-emerging popular press. Stephanie Merrim, for example, writes:

> Zayas courts and astonishes her public in a manner reminiscent of the broadsides on Catalina de Erauso, with their tabloid aesthetic. Zayas's tales include cases of witchcraft, prophetic dreams, miracles, supernatural apparitions, miscegenation, and homosexuality. The most extreme violence enters her text under the aegis of inspiring *admiratio* and cementing the texts' didactic message. (Merrim, p. 74)

Henry Ettinghausen too suggests that Zayas may have been influenced by the news she read.[1] Marina Brownlee, who refers to work done by Ettinghausen, calls Zayas an:

> accomplished marketing strategist who manages to captivate readers with notably divergent alliances — conservative and radical, sentimental and sadistic — eluding censorship while cashing in on the 'tabloid' craze that gripped Spain in the seventeenth century. (Brownlee, 'Genealogies', p. 192)

The 'tabloids' and 'broadsides' referred to are the *relaciones de sucesos*: news pamphlets printed on two or four folios which were bought in bulk by middlemen and blind pedlars, who subsequently sold them on the streets and at fairs. Thematically they dealt with a wide variety of subjects, ranging from serious news items about war or royal visits to stories about comets, egregious murders, unlikely love stories written in verse or detailed descriptions of the witches' sabbath, as is the case for the *Relación de Logroño* (see 2.4). They survive in 'daunting profusion' (Ettinghausen, 'The News in Spain', p. 1) and were probably read out by semi-literate readers to a miscellaneous group of hearers, literate and illiterate alike, thus creating a fascinating mix of oral and print culture. The same applies to the *Avisos*, whose authors clearly expected their news letter to be read out loud. At one point, Barrionuevo for example writes: 'Digo esto, por los que *escucharen* o leyeren mis cartas' [I say this for those who might *hear* or read my letters] (Barrionuevo, *Avisos*, 3 October 1656 — emphasis added). Like the *relaciones*, the *Avisos* are full of stories about royal visits, military victories, heinous murders and rape, topped off with a large helping of xenophobia. Pellicer, who wrote his newsletters in the tumultuous 1640s, for instance, reports a story about a foreign soldier who steals large sums of money and then runs off with a nun three times over, each time involving a different nun and a different soldier.[2]

Apart from suggesting a general influence of the *relaciones de sucesos* on Zayas, Ettinghausen, Merrim and Brownlee do not offer concrete examples and it would be an impossible challenge to find a specific *relación* that could be shown to be the sole source of a novella by Zayas. We have seen that for almost all of her tales it is possible to suggest a literary source, either Italian or Spanish.[3] At the same time, the compilers of the *relaciones de sucesos* were hardly aspiring to write new and original stories. Instead, what we see are old stories rebranded as the latest news. Especially in the case of the *relaciones* in verse it is clear that we are dealing with recycled stories aimed at the popular market, a kind of seventeenth-century *Reader's Digest* in which a thirty-page *novela cortesana* is condensed to two or four sides of doggerel. While Zayas may well have read *relaciones*, the relationship between her novellas and these news pamphlets is at the very least a two-way street. In fact, it is far more likely that some *relaciones* were based on novellas by Zayas rather than the other way round. Often the plots of the 'news' stories had been doing the rounds for a few centuries and can be traced back to Italian collections by Boccaccio, Bandello, Masuccio and others. However, these are unlikely to be the direct sources for the Spanish *relaciones de sucesos*. Given the wide availability and great popularity of Zayas's novellas in precisely the period in which the *relaciones* were written, they must be considered plausible sources.

With only a modest amount of research it has been possible to find *relaciones* that share some or much of their plot with novellas by Zayas. One *relación* I found tells the story of a duped woman called Antonia who dresses up as a man, takes a sword and a shield and murders the man who betrayed her, after which she becomes a nun:

> Nueva relacion, y curioso romance, en que se declara un caso que sucediò en la Ciudad de Lisboa cõ un Cavallero llamado Don Pedro de Roxas. Declarase lo que passò con una dama, que se llamava Doña Antonia, a quien èl burlò cautelosamente. Y tambien se refiere la bizarrìa con que la Dama tomò la venganza desta ofensa por su propia mano.[4]
>
> [New relation, and curious romance, in which a case is presented that took place in the City of Lisbon concerning a Gentleman named Don Pedro de Roxas. It will be revealed what happened to a lady, whose name is Doña Antonia, whom he slyly duped. Also revealed will be the strange way in which the Lady avenged this offence by her own hands.]

This story is reminiscent of 'La burlada Aminta', which tells the story of a duped woman avenging herself by stabbing her ex-lover with a knife, but there are not enough details to speak of direct influence.[5]

Another *relación* I came across relates the story of Casandra, who is kidnapped by Turks and taken to Constantinople. She eventually returns and acts as a judge in the case of her own abduction.

> De don Rodulfo, y la hermosa Casandra: nueua relacion y curioso romance, en que se da cuenta, y declara los amores de una señora de la ciudad de Ungria y como fue juez de su propia causa.[6]

> [Of Don Rodulfo, and the beautiful Casandra: new relation and curious romance, in which account is given and the story told of the love of a lady from the city of Ungria and how she was a judge at her own trial.]

These events correspond neatly to Zayas's novella 'El juez de su causa' in which Estela ends up in Tunis and then escapes by dressing as a man and fighting for Charles V, after which she returns to her native Valencia to judge the case of her own disappearance. Her tale shares some elements with Lope de Vega's *Las fortunas de Diana*, although not the captivity by the infidels. Pérez de Montalbán too wrote a play called *El juez de su causa*, published in 1647, but written in 1619 (see chapter 1, note 30). The second half of the fifteenth *patraña* by Timoneda tells a similar story, which is essentially the same as Boccaccio's ninth story of the second day. In short, it was a well-known story. Returning to the *relación*, there is no hard evidence that it was based directly on Zayas's novella, but it is a credible contender and a more likely source than the older versions.

Then there is the story of a woman forced to drink from the skull of her lover, killed by her husband. This tale is sometimes said to be taken from Marguerite de Navarre's *Heptaméron*, although I have suggested that Zayas probably could not read French and that Bandello is a much more likely source (see 1.1 and 4.1). In 1722 this story, with a few minor alterations, was printed in Lisbon, claiming to be a recent story. The front page reads as follows:

> Nveva relacion, y cvrioso romance, en que se refiere, y da cuenta de las aflicciones que passo una señora, natural de la ciudad de Ostia, en Italia, por averle una Negra, inducida del Demonio, levantado un testimonio, diziendole a su Señor, que su esposa cometia adulterio con un primo suyo sacerdote, por lo qual combido el marido de dicha Señora a comer a su casa al Sacerdote, al qual mato y se le saco la calavera, y con ella le daba de beber a su muger. Con todo lo demas que se vera el curioso Lector. Sucedio este presente año de 1722.[7]

> [New relation and curious romance in which the story is told of the afflictions suffered by a lady from the city of Ostia, in Italy, on account of a Black Woman, who, inspired by the Devil, gave false testimony, telling her Master that his wife was committing adultery with a cousin who was a priest, after which the husband of said Lady invited the Priest to dinner, killed him and kept his skull, from which he gave his wife to drink. This and more the curious Reader will read. It happened this very year, 1722.]

This time we have a little more to go on. The *relación* is unlikely to have been taken directly from Bandello and shares a few key elements with Zayas that are absent in the Italian version: the servant who informed on her lady is black and she has been inspired by the Devil. What is lacking in both Zayas and Bandello is the fact that the woman cheated on her husband with her cousin, a priest.

An example of a *relación de sucesos* that shares too much with one of Zayas's tales to be coincidental is a short account in verse of the brothers Fadrique and Joseph who fall in love with the sisters Constanza and Theodosia. Fadrique loves Constanza, but she has already given her heart away to Joseph. In a rage Fadrique murders his brother, hides his body in a well and flees to Italy. After fourteen years he returns to court Constanza, who in the meantime has married a certain Carlos. He strikes a deal with the Devil to create a garden to win over Constanza:

> Jardin engañoso: nueua relacion, y curioso romance en que se refieren los amores de don Fadrique de Alvara, don Joseph de Alvara, doña Constanza, y doña Theodosia. Dase cuenta, como Don Fadrique dio muerte á su hermano, y lo echó en un pozo, y le entregó la alma al Demonio, por gozar de Doña Constanza; y como casó con Doña Theodosia.[8]
>
> [Deceitful garden: new relation, and curious romance in which the loves of Don Fadrique de Alvara, Don Joseph of Alvara, Doña Constanza, and Doña Theodosia are related. Account will be given of how Don Fadrique killed his brother, threw him in a well and gave his soul to the Devil in order to gain the favours of Doña Constanza; and how he married Doña Theodosia.]

We have seen that Zayas probably adapted 'El jardín engañoso' from Boccaccio but doubled up the protagonists and substituted the Devil for a magician (see 4.5). In this *relación* we have exactly the same plot and some of the same names as in Zayas: the sisters Constanza and Theodosia as well as the husband Carlos. Moreover, the *romance* is called *Jardín Engañoso*, exactly like Zayas's novella, which must be seen as a very likely source.

In sum, Zayas may have been inspired by *relaciones de sucesos*, although it is probably more accurate to say that the sensationalism espoused in the news pamphlets corresponds to a wider desire for shocking stories that was shared by pamphleteers and seventeenth-century novella writers alike. A brief glance at just a few *relaciones* suggests that the influence flows in the other direction too and it is very likely that some of them were based on well-known novellas, thus in a way carrying on the novella tradition of adapting the same old stories for a new audience. Given the popularity in print of Zayas's novellas and the fact that a number of *relaciones* seem to follow her plots quite closely, I would conjecture that her work is a plausible source for some of these news pamphlets. What started as collections of oral folk tales in the Middle Ages became literary works of varying quality in the Renaissance and baroque, only to end up as pulp fiction sold by blind pedlars and read out to semi-literate audiences. *Sic transit gloria mundi*.

Notes to the Appendix

1. See Henry Ettinghausen, 'The News in Spain: *Relaciones de sucesos* in the Reigns of Philip III and IV', *European History Quarterly*, 14 (1984), 1–20; 'Sexo y violencia: noticias sensacionalistas en la prensa española del siglo XVII', *Edad de Oro*, 12 (1993), 95–107; 'The Illustrated Spanish News: Text and Image in the Seventeenth-Century Press', in *Art and Literature in Spain, 1600–1800: Studies in Honour of Nigel Glendinning*, ed. by Charles Davies and Paul Julian Smith (London: Tamesis, 1993), pp. 117–33.
2. In this respect these stories have something in common with urban myths: they are only ever reported with the source being just out of reach (it always happened to a friend of a friend), they are predominantly oral and they tap into common fears.
3. As far as I am aware, there has not been an attempt to give a complete overview of Zayas's sources since Place's monograph from 1923 and this is therefore long overdue. In this study a number of new suggestions have been made.
4. See <http://bv2.gva.es/es/catalogo_imagenes/grupo.cmd?path=1008045> [accessed 6 January 2019].
5. A similar, but much bloodier, version is told by Bandello (*Prima parte*, novella XLII). The duped Violante abducts her ex-lover and cuts off his tongue and his finger tips and gouges out his eyes before stabbing him three times in the heart. She is caught, confesses everything and, although her pluck and courage are greatly admired, she is beheaded.
6. See <https://www.bidiso.es/CBDRS/ediciones/BDRS0001229/3476> [accessed 6 January 2019].
7. See <https://www.bidiso.es/CBDRS/ediciones/BDRS0001566/1686/ejemplar/1488> [accessed 6 January 2019].
8. See <http://bv2.gva.es/es/catalogo_imagenes/grupo.cmd?path=1007793> [accessed 6 January 2019].

BIBLIOGRAPHY

Adán Roca, María Amparo, *La influencia italiana en Doña María de Zayas y Sotomayor* (Valencia: Universitat de València, 1998)

Adorno, Theodor, *The Stars Down To Earth and Other Essays on the Irrational in Culture* (London: Routledge, 1994)

Alarcón, Juan Ruiz de, *El anticristo* (Barcelona: Linkgua, 2012)

—— *El dueño de las estrellas* (Barcelona: Red, 2016) Kindle ebook

—— *La prueba de las promesas* (Barcelona: Linkgua, 2007)

—— *Quien mal anda en mal acaba* (Barcelona: Linkgua, 2012)

Alberola, Eva Lara, 'Hechiceras y brujas: algunos encantos cervantinos', *Anales Cervantinos*, 40 (2008), 145–79

Albers, Irene and Uta Felten (eds), *Escenas de transgresión: María de Zayas en su contexto literario-cultural* (Madrid: Iberoamericana, 2009)

Alborg, Juan Luis, 'La novela corta: Zayas, Céspedes, Lozano', in *Historia de la literatura española*, II (Madrid: Gredos, 1970), pp. 498–504

Alcalde, Pilar, 'Autoría y autoridad en Ana Caro: la mujer dramaturga y su personaje en "Valor, agravio y mujer"', *Confluencia*, 19.2 (2004), 177–87

Almond, Philip, *England's First Demonologist: Reginald Scot and 'The Discovery of Witchcraft'* (London: I. B. Tauris, 2011)

Alfonso X, el Sabio, The Oxford *Cantigas de Santa Maria* Database <http://csm.mml.ox.ac.uk/index.php?p=poemdata_view&rec=5> [accessed 26 December 2018]

Alonso Palomar, Pilar, 'La presencia de la magia en la literatura española de los Siglos de Oro: breves apuntes', in *Homenaje al Profesor Emilio Alarcos García en el centenario de su nacimiento, 1895–1995* (Valladolid: Universidad de Valladolid, 1998), pp. 181–92

Álvarez y Baeza, José Antonio, 'María de Zayas y Sotomayor (Doña)', in *Hijos de Madrid ilustres en santidad, dignidades, armas, ciencias y artes*, 4 vols (Madrid: Cano, 1791; repr. Madrid: Atlas, 1973), IV, 48–49

Álvarez Amell, Diana, 'El objeto del cuerpo femenino en el "Quinto Desengaño" de María de Zayas', *Actas Irvine-92 II Asociación Internacional de Hispanistas*, ed. by Juan Villegas (Irvine: University of California, 1994), pp. 25–33

Ankarloo, Bengt, and Gustav Henningsen, *Early Modern Witchcraft* (Oxford: Clarendon Press, 1990)

Anonymous, *The Hundred Tales (Les Cent Nouvelles Nouvelles)*, trans. by Rossell Hope Robbins (New York: Bonanza Books, 1960)

—— *De don Rodulfo, y la hermosa Casandra: nueua relacion y curioso romance, en que se da cuenta, y declara los amores de una señora de la ciudad de Ungria y como fue juez de su propia causa* (Madrid: Andrés de Sotos, n.d.) <https://www.bidiso.es/CBDRS/ediciones/BDRS0001229/3476> [accessed 6 January 2019]

—— *Jardin engañoso: nueua relacion, y curioso romance en que se refieren los amores de don Fadrique de Alvara, don Joseph de Alvara, doña Constanza, y doña Theodosia. Dase cuenta, como Don Fadrique dio muerte á su hermano, y lo echó en un pozo, y le entregó la alma al Demonio, por gozar de Doña Constanza; y como casó con Doña Theodosia* (Madrid: Andrés de Sotos, n.d.) <http://bv2.gva.es/es/catalogo_imagenes/grupo.cmd?path=1007793> [accessed 6 January 2019]

—— *Nueva relacion, y curioso romance, en que se declara un caso que sucediò en la Ciudad de Lisboa cõ un Cavallero llamado Don Pedro de Roxas. Declarase lo que passò con una dama, que se llamava Doña Antonia, a quien èl burlò cautelosamente. Y tambien se refiere la bizarrìa con que la Dama tomò la venganza desta ofensa por su propia mano* (Valencia: Cosme Granja, n.d.) <http://bv2.gva.es/es/catalogo_imagenes/grupo.cmd?path=1008045> [accessed 6 January 2019]

—— *Nveva relacion, y curioso romance, en que se refiere, y da cuenta de las aflicciones que passo una señora, natural de la ciudad de Ostia, en Italia, por averle una Negra, inducida del Demonio, levantado un testimonio, diziendo a su Señor, que su esposa cometia adultorio con un primo suyo sacerdote* (Seville: Francisco de Leefdael, 1722) <https://www.bidiso.es/CBDRS/ediciones/BDRS0001566/1686/ejemplar/1488> [accessed 6 January 2019]

ARENAL, ELECTRA, 'Vida y teatro conventual: Sor Marcela de San Félix', in *La creatividad femenina en el mundo barroco hispánico. María de Zayas — Isabel Rebeca Correa — Sor Juana Inés de la Cruz*, ed. by Monika Bosse, Barbara Potthast and André Stoll, 2 vols (Kassel: Reichenberger, 1999), I, 209–19

ARTEMIDORUS, DALDIANUS, *The Interpretation of Dreams* (London: J. Bew, 1786; repr. Eighteenth Century Collections Online Print Edition, n.d.)

ASTARITA, TOMMASO (ed.), *A Companion to Early Modern Naples* (Leiden: Brill, 2013)

AVENDAÑO, NADIA, 'La violencia masculina en los "Desengaños amorosos" de María de Zayas', *The South Carolina Modern Language Review*, 5 (2006), 38–53

AZORÍN, *Los clásicos redivivos* (Madrid: Espasa Calpe, 1958)

BAILEY, MICHAEL, 'Witchcraft and Reform in the Late Middle Ages', in *The Witchcraft Reader*, ed. by Darren Oldridge, 2nd edn (London: Routledge, 2008), pp. 37–52; first published in *Battling Demons* (Pennsylvania State University, 2003)

BALLESTEROS, JOSÉ, 'El imperio desde el centro: la interpretación de María de Zayas del tema del indiano en Cervantes', *Romance Quarterly*, 53.2 (2006), 113–29

BANDELLO, MATTEO, *Le Novelle del Bandello* (Milan: Mondadori, 1942) <http://www.letteraturaitaliana.net/pdf/Volume_4/t77.pdf> [accessed 5 January 2019]

—— *The Novels of Matteo Bandello* (General Books LLC, 2009)

—— *Twelve Stories Selected and done into English with a Memoir of the Author by Percy Pinkterton* (London: John C. Nimmo, 1895) <https://archive.org/details/cu31924102029083/page/n9> [accessed 5 January 2019]

BARANDA, NIEVES, '"Por ser de mano femenil la rima": de la mujer escritora a sus lectores', *Bulletin Hispanique*, 100.2 (1998), 449–73

BARBEITO CARNEIRO, ISABEL, *Mujeres del Madrid Barroco: voces testimoniales* (Madrid: Horas, 1978)

—— *Mujeres y literatura del siglo de oro: espacios profanos y espacios conventuales* (Madrid: Safekat, 2007)

BARBERO, TERESA, 'María de Zayas y Sotomayor o la picaresca cortesana', *Estafeta literaria*, 527 (Nov 1973), 24–25

BARRIONUEVO, JERÓNIMO DE, *Avisos*, I (1654–1658) (Madrid: M. Telio, 1892; facsimile repr. by IGCtesting.com, n.d.)

BARSTOW, ANNE LLEWELLYN, *Witchcraze: A New History of the European Witch Hunts* (London: HarperCollins, 1994)

BAYLISS, ROBERT, 'Feminism and María de Zayas's Exemplary Comedy *La traición en la amistad*', *Hispanic Review*, 76.1 (2008), 1–17

BEHRINGER, WOLFGANG, 'Weather, Hunger and Fear: Origins of the European Witch-Hunt in Climate, Society and Mentality', in *The Witchcraft Reader*, ed. by Darren Oldridge, 2nd edn (London: Routledge, 2008), pp. 74–85; first pub. in *German History*, 13 (1995)

BEKKER, BALTHASAR, *De betoverde wereld* (Amsterdam: Daniel van Dalen, 1691) <http://www.dbnl.org/tekst/bekk001beto01_01/colofon.php> [accessed 14 December 2018]

BERG, SANDER, '"No es cosa de burlas": *mira* and *miracula* in Barrionuevo, Pellicer and Zayas', in *Studies on the Supernatural*, ed. by Stephen Hart (Cambridge: Cambridge Scholars Publishing, 2017), 91–106

BETRÁN MOYA, JOSÉ LUIS, 'El mundo mágico de Julio Caro Baroja', *Historia Social*, 55 (2006), 79–111

BLANQUÉ, ANDREA, 'María de Zayas o la versión de "las noveleras"', *Nueva Revista de Filología Hispánica*, 39.2 (1991), 921–50

BOCCACCIO, GIOVANNI, *Decameron* (Turin: Einaudi, 1956) <http://www.letteraturaitaliana.net/pdf/Volume_2/t318.pdf> [accessed 26 December 2018]

—— *The Decameron*, trans. by G. H. McWilliam (London: Penguin, 1972)

BOSSE, MONIKA, 'El sarao de María de Zayas y Sotomayor: una razón (feminina) de contar el amor', in *La creatividad femenina en el mundo barroco: María de Zayas — Isabel Rebeca Correa — Sor Juana Inés de la Cruz*, ed. by Monika Bosse, Barbara Potthast and André Stoll, 2 vols (Kassel: Reichenberger, 1999), I, 239–99

BOSSE, MONIKA, BARBARA POTTHAST and ANDRÉ STOLL (eds), *La creatividad femenina en el mundo barroco: María de Zayas — Isabel Rebeca Correa — Sor Juana Inés de la Cruz*, 2 vols (Kassel: Reichenberger, 1999)

BOUZA, FERNANDO, *Communication, Knowledge, and Memory in Early Modern Spain*, trans. by Sonia López and Michael Agnew (Philadelphia: University of Pennsylvania Press, 1999)

BOYER, PATSY, 'The "Other" Woman in Cervantes's *Persiles* and Zayas's *Novelas*', *Cervantes*, 10.1 (1990), 59–68

—— 'Toward a Baroque Reading of "El verdugo de su esposa"', in *María de Zayas: The Dynamics of Discourse*, ed. by Amy Williamsen and Judith Whitenack (London: Associated University Presses, 1995), pp. 52–71

BRIGGS, ROBIN, 'The Experience of Bewitchment', in *The Witchcraft Reader*, ed. by Darren Oldridge, 2nd edn (London: Routledge, 2008), pp. 53–63; first pub. in *Witches and Neighbours*, 2nd edn (Oxford: Blackwell, 2002)

BRONTË, CHARLOTTE, *Jane Eyre* (Toronto: Bantam Books, 1981)

BROWN, DAN, *The Da Vinci Code* (London: Transworld Publishers, 2003)

BROWN, KENNETH, 'María de Zayas y Sotomayor: escribiendo poesía en Barcelona en época de guerra (1643)', *Dicenda. Cuadernos de filología hispánica*, 11 (1993), 355–60

BROWNLEE, MARINA, *The Cultural Labyrinth of María de Zayas* (Philadelphia: University of Pennsylvania Press, 2000)

—— 'Genealogies in Crisis: María de Zayas in Seventeenth-Century Spain', in *Generation and Degeneration: Tropes of Reproduction in Literature and History from Antiquity through Early Modern Europe*, ed. by Valeria Finucci and Kevin Brownlee (Durham, NC: Duke University Press, 2001), pp. 189–208

—— 'Postmodernism and the Baroque in María de Zayas', in *Cultural Authority in Golden Age Spain*, ed. by Marina Brownlee and Hans Gumbrecht (Baltimore, MD: Johns Hopkins University Press, 1995), pp. 107–30

BUTLER, JUDITH, *Gender Trouble* (London: Routledge, 1990)

CALDERÓN DE LA BARCA, PEDRO, *Las cadenas del demonio* (Madrid: La viuda de Blas de Villanueva, 1726) <http://www.cervantesvirtual.com/obra/la-gran-comedia-las-cadenas-del-demonio/> [accessed 28 August 2016]

—— *La dama duende*, ed. by Fausta Antonucci (Barcelona: Crítica, 2005)

—— *La devoción de la cruz*, ed. by M. Delgado (Madrid: Cátedra, 2000)

—— *The Fake Astrologer (El astrólogo fingido)*, dual-language edition, trans. by Max Oppenheimer (Lawrence, KS: Coronado Press, 1976)

—— *El galán fantasma* (Charleston, SC: Bibliobazaar, 2007)
—— *El jardín de Falerina*, (Charleston, SC: Bibliobazaar, n.d.)
—— *El mágico prodigioso*, ed. by Bruce Wardropper (Madrid: Cátedra, 1985)
—— *El médico de su honra* (Barcelona: Linkgua, 2005)
—— *La vida es sueño*, ed. by Ciriaco Morón (Madrid: Cátedra, 2005)
CALVI, GIULIA, *La mujer barroca* (Madrid: Alianza, 1992)
CAMERON, EUAN, *Enchanted Europe: Superstition, Reason & Religion, 1250–1750* (Oxford: Oxford University Press, 2010)
CAMPAGNE, FABIÁN ALEJANDRO, 'Witchcraft and the Sense-of-the-Impossible in Early Modern Spain: Some Reflections Based on the Literature of Superstition (ca. 1500–1800)', *Harvard Theological Review*, 96.1 (2003), 25–62
CAMPBELL, GWYN, and JUDITH WHITENACK (eds), *Zayas and Her Sisters*, II: *Essays on Novelas by 17th-Century Spanish Women* (New York: Global Publications Binghamton University, 2001)
CANAVAGGIO, JEAN, *Cervantes*, trans. by J. R. Jones (New York: Norton, 1990)
CARDAILLAC HERMOSILLA, YVETTE, 'La magia en las novelas de María de Zayas', in *La creatividad femenina en el mundo barroco hispánico: María de Zayas — Isabel Rebeca Correa — Sor Juana Inés de la Cruz*, ed. by Monika Bosse, Barbara Potthast and André Stoll, 2 vols (Kassel: Reichenberger, 1999), I, 351–77
CÁRDENAS ROTUNNO, ANTHONY, 'Rojas's "Celestina and Claudina": In Search of a Witch', *Hispanic Review*, 69.3 (2001), 277–97
CARMONA SÁNCHEZ, JOSÉ IGNACIO, *La España mágica: mitos, leyendas y curiosidades pintorescas* (Madrid: Nowtilus, 2012)
CARO BAROJA, JULIO, *Brujería vasca* (San Sebastián: Txertoa, 1985)
—— *El Señor Inquisidor y otras vidas por oficio* (Madrid: Alianza, 1968)
—— 'Witchcraft and Catholic Theology', in *Early Modern Witchcraft: Centres and Peripheries*, ed. by Bengt Ankarloo and Gustav Henningsen (Oxford: Clarendon Press, 1990), pp. 19–45
—— *The World of the Witches* (London: Phoenix, 2001)
CARO MALLÉN DE SOTO, ANA, *El conde Partinuplés* (Barcelona: Linkgua, 2007)
—— *Valor, agravio y mujer* (Barcelona: Linkgua, 2008)
CARVAJAL Y SAAVEDRA, MARIANA, *Navidades de Madrid y noches entretenidas*, ed. by Dámaso Chicharro (Jaén: Instituto de Estudios Giennenses, 2005)
CASO, ADOPLHO, *Romeo and Juliet. Original Text of: Masuccio Salernitano, Luigi da Porto, Matteo Bandello, William Shakespeare* (Boston, MA: Dante University of America Press, 1992), Kindle ebook
CASTAÑEGA, MARTÍN DE, *Tratado de las supersticiones y hechicerías* (Madrid: De la luna, 2001)
CASTILLO SOLÓRZANO, ALONSO DE, 'La fantasma de Valencia', in *Novelas amorosas de diversos ingenios del siglo XVII* (Madrid: Castalia, 1986), pp. 169–200
—— *La Garduña de Sevilla y anzuelo de las bolsas*, ed. by Federico Ruiz Morcuende (Madrid: Ediciones de La Lectura, 1922) <http://www.cervantesvirtual.com/obra/la-garduna-de-sevilla-y-anzuelo-de-las-bolasas-0> [accessed 20 May 2019]
—— *Tardes entretenidas*, 9 (Madrid: Librería de los bibliófilos españoles, 1908) <https://archive.org/details/tardesentretenid09castuoft> [accessed 30 March 2017]
CASTILLO, DAVID, *(A)wry Views* (West Lafayette, IN: Purdue University Press, 2001)
—— *Baroque Horrors. Roots of the Fantastic in the Age of Curiosities* (Ann Arbor: University of Michigan Press, 2010)
—— 'Exemplarity Gone Awry in Baroque Fantasy: The Case of Cervantes', *Revista Canadiense de Estudios Hispánicos*, 33.1 (2008), 105–20
CERTEAU, MICHEL DE, *The Possession at Loudun* (Chicago, IL: University of Chicago Press, 1970)

CERVANTES SAAVEDRA, MIGUEL DE, *Don Quijote de la Mancha*, ed. by Fransciso Rico (Barcelona: Galaxia Gutenberg, 2004)
—— *Don Quixote*, trans. by John Rutherford (London: Penguin, 2000)
—— *Novelas ejemplares I & II*, ed. by Harry Sieber (Madrid: Cátedra, 1980)
CHARNON-DEUTSCH, LOU, 'The Sexual Economy in the Narratives of María de Zayas', in *María de Zayas: The Dynamics of Discourse*, ed. by Amy Williamsen and Judith Whitenack (London: Associated University Presses, 1995), pp. 117–32
CHARTIER, ROGER, *Forms and Meanings: Texts, Performances, and Audiences from Codex to Computer* (Philadelphia: University of Pennsylvania Press, 1995)
—— *Inscription and Erasure: Literature and Written Culture from the Eleventh to the Eighteenth Century* (Philadelphia: University of Pennsylvania Press, 2005)
CHRISTIAN, WILLIAM, *Apparitions in Late Medieval and Renaissance Spain* (Princeton, NJ: Princeton University Press, 1981)
CIRUELO, PEDRO, 'Tratado por el cual se reprueban las supersticiones y supercherías', in *Brujería y exorcismos en España: textos fundamentales*, ed. by Servando Gotor (Zaragoza: Lecturas Hispánicas, 2014), pp. 71–247
CIXOUS, HÉLÈNE, 'The Laugh of the Medusa', *Signs*, 1.4 (Summer 1976), 875–93
CLAMURRO, WILLIAM, 'Ideological Contradiction and Imperial Decline: Toward a Reading of Zayas's "Desengaños amorosos"', *South Central Review*, 5.2 (1988), 43–50
—— 'Madness and Narrative Form in "Estragos que causa el vicio"', in *María de Zayas: The Dynamics of Discourse*, ed. by Amy Williamsen and Judith Whitenack (London: Associated University Presses, 1995), pp. 219–33
CLARK, STUART, *Thinking with Demons: The Idea of Witchcraft in Early Modern Europe* (Oxford: Oxford University Press, 1997)
COCOZZELLA, PETER, 'María de Zayas: Writer of the "novela ejemplar"', in *Woman Writers of the Seventeenth Century*, ed. by Katharina Wilson and Frank Warnke (Athens: University of Georgia Press, 1989), pp. 189–227
COHEN, HENRY, 'The Reworking and Incorporation of Two of Marguerite de Navarre's "Heptaméron" *Nouvelles* by María de Zayas y Sotomayor in Her *Novela* "Tarde llega el desengaño"', *Comparative Literature Studies*, 56.1 (2019)
COHN, NORMAN, *Europe's Inner Demons: The Demonisation of Christians in Medieval Christendom* (London: Pimlico, 1975)
COLÓN, ISABEL, 'María de Zayas y Sotomayor: algo más que una pesimista en el siglo XVII', *Estafeta literaria*, 633 (March 1978), 17–18
CORTÉS TIMONER, MARÍA MAR, 'María de Zayas y el derecho a ser de las mujeres', *Cahiers d'Études des Cultures Ibériques et Latino-américaines*, 2 (2016), 143–58
COSTA PASCAL, ANNE-GAËLLE, *María de Zayas, une écriture féminine dans l'Espagne du Siècle d'Or: une poétique de la séduction* (Paris: L'Harmattan, 2007)
COVARRUBIAS HOROZCO, SEBASTIÁN DE, *Tesoro de la lengua castellana o española* (Navarra: Universidad de Navarra; Madrid: Iberoamericana-Vervuert, 2006)
COX-DAVIES, NINA, 'Re-Framing Discourse: Women before their Public in María de Zayas', *Hispanic Review*, 71.3 (2003), 325–44
CRUICKSHANK, DON W., 'Literature and the Book Trade in Golden Age Spain', *The Modern Language Review*, 73.3 (1978), 799–824
CRUZ, ANNE, 'The Walled-In Woman in Medieval and Early Modern Spain', *Gender Matters: Discourses of Violence in Early Modern Literature and the Arts*, ed. by Mara R. Wade (Leiden: Brill, 2014), pp. 349–66
—— 'Violence Repeated: Zayas, the Pleasure Principle, and beyond', *Studi Ispanici*, 40 (2015), 11–22
CRUZ, ANNE, and MARY PERRY (eds), *Culture and Control in Counter-Reformation Spain* (Minneapolis: University of Minnesota Press, 1992)

CRUZ, SOR JUANA INÉS DE LA, *Los empeños de una casa*, ed. by García Valdés (Madrid: Cátedra, 2010)
CUTTING, GARY, *Michel Foucault's Archaeology of Scientific Reason* (Cambridge: Cambridge University Press, 1989)
DAVIDSON, JANE, *Early Modern Supernatural: The Dark Side of European Culture, 1400–1700* (Santa Barbara, CA: Praeger, 2012)
DAVIES, OWEN, *Cunning-Folk: Popular Magic in English History* (London: Hambledon Continuum, 2003)
—— *Magic: A Very Short Introduction* (Oxford: Oxford University Press, 2012)
—— 'Urbanisation and the Decline of Witchcraft: An Examination of London', in *The Witchcraft Reader*, ed. by Darren Oldridge, 2nd edn (London: Routledge, 2008), pp. 353–66; first pub. in *Journal of Social History*, 30 (1997), 597–617
DELGADO BERLANGA, MARÍA JOSÉ, 'Danzando en un hilo mitológico: formación e inversión del "yo mujer" en la novela de María de Zayas, "Mal presagio casar lejos"', in *Zayas and Her Sisters*, II: *Essays on Novelas by 17th-Century Spanish Women*, ed. by Gwyn Campbell and Judith Whitenack (New York: Global Publications Binghamton University, 2001), pp. 111–20
DÍEZ BORQUE, JOSÉ MARÍA, 'El feminismo de doña María de Zayas', in *La mujer en el teatro y la novela del siglo XVII: Actas del II° Coloquio del Grupo de Estudios sobre Teatro Español* (Toulouse: Université de Toulouse II–Le Mirail, 1978), pp. 63–88
DONOVAN, JOSEPHINE, 'From Avenger to Victim: Genealogy of a Renaissance Novella', *Tulsa Studies in Women's Literature*, 15.2 (1996), 269–88
—— 'Women and the Framed Novella: A Tradition of Their Own', *Signs*, 22.4 (1997), 947–80
DOPICO BLACK, GEORGINA, *Perfect Wives, Other Women: Adultery and Inquisition in Early Modern Spain* (Durham, NC: Duke University Press, 2001)
DWORKIN, ANDREA, *Our Blood* (New York: Perigree Books, 1976)
EISENSTEIN, ELIZABETH, *The Printing Revolution in Early Modern Europe* (Cambridge: Cambridge University Press, 1983)
EL SAFFAR, RUTH, 'Ana/Lysis and Zayas: Reflections on Courtships in Literary Women in the "Novelas amorosas y ejemplares"', in *Maria de Zayas: The Dynamics of Discourse*, ed. by Amy Williamsen and Judith Whitenack (London: Associated University Presses, 1992), pp. 192–216
ELLIOTT, JOHN H., 'The Decline of Spain', *Past and Present*, 20 (1961), 52–75
—— *Imperial Spain, 1469–1716* (London: Penguin, 1963; repr. 1990)
—— 'Revolution and Continuity in Early Modern Europe', *Past and Present*, 42 (1969), 35–56
—— 'Self-Perception and Decline in Early Seventeenth-Century Spain', *Past and Present*, 74 (1977), 41–61
—— *Spain and its World, 1500–1700* (New Haven, CT: Yale University Press, 1989)
ENRÍQUEZ DE SALAMANCA, CRISTINA, 'Irony, Parody and the Grotesque in a Baroque Novella: "Tarde llega el desengaño"', in *Maria de Zayas: The Dynamics of Discourse*, ed. by Amy Williamsen and Judith Whitenack (London: Associated University Presses, 1995), pp. 234–53
ETTINGHAUSEN, HENRY, 'The Illustrated Spanish News: Text and Image in the Seventeenth-Century Press', in *Art and Literature in Spain, 1600–1800: Studies in Honour of Nigel Glendinning*, ed. by Charles Davies and Paul Julian Smith (London: Tamesis, 1993), pp. 117–33
—— 'The News in Spain: *Relaciones de sucesos* in the Reigns of Philip III and IV', *European History Quarterly*, 14 (1984), 1–20

―― 'Sexo y violencia: noticias sensacionalistas en la prensa española del siglo XVII', *Edad de Oro*, 12 (1993), 95–107
EVANGELISTI, SILVIA, *Nuns: A History of Convent Life* (Oxford: Oxford University Press, 2007)
EVANS-PRITCHARD, EDWARD E., *Witchcraft, Oracles, and Magic among the Azande*, abridged and with an intro. by Eva Gillies (Oxford: Clarendon Press, 1976)
FARIÑA BUSTO, MARÍA JESÚS, and BEATRIZ SUÁREZ BRIONES, 'Desde/hacia la Otra: Ginoafectividad y homoerotismo femenino en la narrativa de María de Zayas', in *Zayas and Her Sisters*, II: *Essays on Novelas by 17th-Century Spanish Women*, ed. by Gwyn Campbell and Judith Whitenack (New York: Global Publications Binghamton University, 2001), pp. 121–38
FARMER, JULIA, 'Inscribing Victory: Rivalry and Mise en Abyme in María de Zayas's Novella Collections', *MLN*, 126.2 (2011), 245–58
FAYE, DJIDIACK, *La narrativa de María de Zayas y Sotomayor* (unpublished doctoral dissertation, Universidad de León, 2009)
FELTEN, HANS, *María de Zayas y Sotomayor: Zum Zusammenhang zwischen moralistischen Texten und Novellenliteratur* (Frankfurt: Klostermann, 1978)
FELTEN, UTA, 'En torno a la escoptofilia femenina en María de Zayas', in *Escenas de transgresión: María de Zayas en su contexto literario-cultural*, ed. by Irene Albers and Uta Felten (Madrid: Iberoamericana, 2009), pp. 65–73
FERNÁNDEZ ÁLVAREZ, MANUEL, *Casadas, monjas, rameras y brujas: la olvidada historia de la mujer española en el Renacimiento* (Madrid: Espasa, 2010)
FLORES ARROYUELO, FRANCISCO, *El diablo en España* (Madrid: Alianza, 1985)
FOA, SANDRA, *Feminismo y forma narrativa: estudio del tema y las técnicas de María de Zayas y Sotomayor* (Valencia: Albatros, 1979)
―― 'Humor and Suicide in Zayas and Cervantes', *Anales cervantinos*, 16 (1977), 71–83
FORD, JOHN, *'Tis Pity She's a Whore*, in *Elizabethan and Jacobean Tragedies* (Tonbridge: Ernest Benn, 1984), pp. 637–731
FOUCAULT, MICHEL, *The Order of Things* (London: Routledge, 1989); first pub. in English by Tavistock, 1970
FOX-LOCKERT, LUCÍA, *Women Novelists in Spain and Spanish America* (Metuchen, NJ: Scarecrow Press, 1979)
FRAZER, JAMES GEORGE, *The Golden Bough: A New Abridgement* (Oxford: Oxford University Press, 1994)
FREUD, SIGMUND, *The Uncanny*, trans. by D. McLintock (London: Penguin, 2003)
FRIEDMAN, EDWARD, 'Avenging the Intertext: The Narrative Rhetoric of María de Zayas's "La más infame venganza"', *Cincinnati Romance Review*, 17 (1998), 27–34
―― 'Constructing Romance: The Deceptive Idealism of María de Zayas's "El jardín engañoso"', in *Zayas and Her Sisters*, II: *Essays on Novelas by 17th-Century Spanish Women*, ed. by Gwyn Campbell and Judith Whitenack (New York: Global Publications Binghamton University, 2001), pp. 45–61
―― 'Enemy Territory: The Frontiers of Gender in María de Zayas's "El traidor contra su sangre" and "Mal presagio casar lejos"', in *Ingeniosa invención: Essays on Golden Age Spanish Literature for Geoffrey L. Stagg in Honor of his Eighty-fifth Birthday*, ed. by Ellen Anderson and Amy Williamson (Newark, DE: Juan de la Cuesta, 1999)
―― 'Innocents Punished: The Narrative Models of María de Zayas', *Confluencia*, 20.1 (2004), 9–16
GABRIELE, JOHN, 'El mundo al revés: la construcción de una narrativa femenina en "La traición en la amistad" de María de Zayas y Sotomayor', *Actas del XIV Congreso de la Asociación de Hispanistas* (Newark: Juan de la Cuesta, 2004)

GALIANI, FERDINANDO, *Vocabulario delle parole del dialetto napoletano, che piu' si scostano dal dialetto toscano* (Naples: Giuseppe-Maria Porcelli, 1789); online at <https://archive.org/details/vocabolariodel100toscgoog/page/n5> [accessed 20 May 2019]

GAMBOA, YOLANDA, 'Architectural Cartography: Social and Gender Mapping in María de Zaya's Seventeenth-Century Spain', *Hispanic Review*, 71.2 (Spring 2003), 189–203

—— *Cartografía social en la narrativa de María de Zayas* (Madrid: Biblioteca Nueva, 2009)

—— 'Gender Coding in the Narratives of María de Zayas', in *Women, Society and Constraints: A Collection of Contemporary South African Gender Studies*, ed. by Jeanette Malherbe, Marc Kleijwegt and Elize Koen (Pretoria: Unisa Press, 2000), pp. 197–209

GASKILL, MALCOLM, *Witchcraft: A Very Short Introduction* (Oxford: Oxford University Press, 2010)

GILBERT, SANDRA, and SUSAN GUBAR, 'Inflection in the Sentence: The Woman Writer and the Anxiety of Authorship', in *Feminisms: An Anthology of Literary Theory and Criticism*, ed. by Robyn Warhol and Diane Price Herndl (London: Macmillan, 1997), pp. 21–31

GILI GAYA, SAMUEL, 'Apogeo y desintegración de la novela picaresca', in *Historia general de las literaturas hispánicas*, III (Barcelona: Barna, 1953), pp. iii–xxv

GINZBURG, CARLO, *The Cheese and the Worms: The Cosmos of a Sixteenth-Century Miller*, trans. by John Tedeschi and Anne Tedeschi (Baltimore, MD: Johns Hopkins University Press, 1976)

—— *The Night Battles: Witchcraft and Agrarian Cults in the Sixteenth and Seventeenth Centuries*, trans. by John Tedeschi and Anne Tedeschi (Baltimore, MD: Johns Hopkins University Press, 1966)

GLENDINNING, NIGEL, 'New Light on the Text and Ideas of Cadalso's "Noches Lúgubres"', *The Modern Language Review*, 55.4 (1960), 537–42

—— 'The Traditional Story of "La difunta pleiteada", Cadalso's "Noches lúgubres", and the Romantics', *Bulletin of Hispanic Studies*, 38.3 (1961), 206–15

GORFKLE, LAURA, 'Seduction and Hysteria in María de Zayas's "Desengaños amorosos"', *Hispanófila*, 115 (1995), 11–28

GOTOR, SERVANDO (ed.), *Brujería y exorcismos en España: textos fundamentales* (Zaragoza: Lecturas Hispánicas, 2014)

GOYRI DE MENÉNDEZ PIDAL, MARÍA, *La difunta pleiteada: estudio de literatura comparativa* (Madrid: Librería General de Victoriano Suárez, 1909) <https://archive.org/stream/ladifuntapleitea00goyr/ladifuntapleitea00goyr_djvu.txt> [accessed 26 December 2018]

GOYTISOLO, JUAN, 'El mundo erótico de María de Zayas', in *Disidencias* (Barcelona: Seix Barral, 1977), pp. 63–115

GRACIÁN, BALTASAR, *Arte de ingenio. Tratado de la agudeza*, ed. by Arturo del Hoyo (Madrid: Aguilar, 1960) <http://www.cervantesvirtual.com/obra/arte-de-ingenio-tratado-de-la-agudeza--0/> [accessed 30 August 2016]

GREEN, TOBY, *Inquisition* (London: Pan Books, 2007)

GREENBLATT, STEPHEN, 'The Meaning of Mutilation', in *The Body in Parts: Fantasies of Corporeality in Early Modern Europe*, ed. by Hillman and Mazzio (London: Routledge, 1997), pp. 221–42

GREER, MARGARET, 'María de Zayas and the Female Eunuch', *Journal of Spanish Cultural Studies*, 2.1 (2001), 41–53

—— *María de Zayas Tells Baroque Tales of Love and the Cruelty of Men* (University Park: Pennsylvania State University Press, 2000)

—— 'The (M)Other plot: house of God, Man and Mother in María de Zayas', in *María de Zayas: The Dynamics of Discourse*, ed. by Amy Williamsen and Judith Whitenack (London: Associated University Presses, 1995), pp. 90–116

GREER, MARGARET, and ANDREA JUNGUITO, 'Economies of the Early Modern Stage', *Revista Canadiense de Estudios Hispánicos*, 29.1 (2004), 31–46

GRIEVE, PATRICIA, 'Embroidering with Saintly Threads: María de Zayas Challenges Cervantes and the Church', *Renaissance Quarterly*, 44.1 (1991), 86–106

GRISWOLD, SUSAN, 'Topoi and Rhetorical Distance: The "Feminism" of María de Zayas', *Revista de Estudios Hispánicos*, 14.2 (1980), 97–116

GROOM, NICK, *The Gothic: A Very Short Introduction* (Oxford: Oxford University Press, 2012)

GUILLÉN, FELISA, 'El marco narrativo como espacio utópico en los "Desengaños amorosos" de María de Zayas', *Revista de literatura*, 60 (1998), 527–35

GUMBRECHT, HANS, 'Cosmological Time and the Impossibility of Closure', in *Cultural Authority in Golden Age Spain*, ed. by Marina Brownlee and Hans Gumbrecht (Baltimore, MD: Johns Hopkins University Press, 1995), pp. 304–22

GÓMEZ, JESÚS, 'Boccaccio y Otálora en los orígenes de la novela corta en España', *Nueva Revista de Filología Hispánica*, 46.1 (1998), 23–46

HALICZER, STEPHEN, *Between Exaltation and Infamy: Female Mystics in the Golden Age of Spain* (Oxford: Oxford University Press, 2002)

—— 'The Jew as Witch: Displaced Aggression and the Myth of the Santo Niño de la Guardia', in *Cultural Encounters: The Impact of the Inquisition in Spain and the New World*, ed. by Mary Elizabeth Perry and Anne Cruz (Berkeley: University of California Press, 1991), pp. 146–56

HEGSTROM, VALERIE, 'The Fallacy of False Dichotomy in María de Zayas's "La Traición en la amistad"', *Bulletin of the Comediantes*, 46.1 (Summer 1994), 59–70

HENNINGSEN, GUSTAV, *El abogado de las brujas: brujería vasca e Inquisición* (Madrid: Alianza, 1980)

—— *The Salazar Documents: Inquisitor Alonso de Salazar Frías and Others on the Basque Witch Persecution* (Leiden: Brill, 2004)

HERNÁNDEZ PECORARO, ROSILIE, '"La fuerza del amor" or The Power of Self-Love: Zayas' Response to Cervantes' "La fuerza de la sangre"', *Hispanic Review*, 70.1 (Winter 2002), 39–57

HOGLE, JERROLD, *The Cambridge Companion to Gothic Fiction* (Cambridge: Cambridge University Press, 2002)

HUARTE DE SAN JUAN, JUAN, *Examen de ingenios*, in *Electroneurobiología* 3.2 (1996), 1–322 <http://electroneubio.secyt.gov.ar/Juan_Huarte_de_San_Juan_Examen_de_ingenios.pdf> [accessed 8 December 2018]

HUPPERT, GEORGE, '*Divinatio et Eruditio*: Thoughts on Foucault', *History and Theory*, 13.3 (1974), 191–207

HUXLEY, ALDOUS, *The Devils of Loudun* (London: Vintage, 1952; repr. 2005)

IFE, BARRY, *Reading and Fiction in Golden-Age Spain: A Platonist Critique and Some Picaresque Replies* (Cambridge: Cambridge University Press, 1985)

JAMES I, *Demonology* (Edinburgh: Robert Waldegrave, 1597; facsimile repr. San Diego: The Book Tree, 2002)

JEHENSON, YVONNE, and MARCIA WELLES, 'María de Zayas's Wounded Women: A Semiotics of Violence', in *Gender, Identity, and Representation in Spain's Golden Age*, ed. by Anita Stoll and Dawn Smith (Lewisburg, PA: Bucknell Press, 2000), pp. 178–202

JEHENSON, YVONNE, 'Playing Out Desiring Fantasies in María de Zayas's "Amar sólo por vencer"', in *Zayas and Her Sisters*, II: *Essays on Novelas by 17th-Century Spanish Women*, ed. by Gwyn Campbell and Judith Whitenack (New York: Global Publications Binghamton University, 2001), pp. 97–110

JOHNSON, CARROLL, 'Of Witches and Bitches: Gender, Marginality and Discourse in "El casamiento engañoso" y "Coloquio de los perros"', *Cervantes: Bulletin of the Cervantes Society of America*, 11.2 (1991), 7–25

JONES, ANN ROSALIND, 'Writing the Body: Toward an Understanding of "L'Écriture féminine"', in *Feminisms: An Anthology of Literary Theory and Criticism*, ed. by Robyn Warhol and Diane Price Herndl (London: Macmillan, 1997), pp. 370–82
JORDAN, CONSTANCE, *Renaissance Feminism: Literary Texts and Political Models* (Ithaca, NY: Cornell University Press, 1990)
JUNG, URSULA, 'Autoras barrocas de la Península Ibérica: producción literaria femenina entre clausura, certamen poético y "mercado"', *Notas: Reseñas iberoamericanas. Literatura, sociedad, historia*, 7.2 (2000), 2–16
—— 'La honra manchada? La reescritura de "El médico de su honra" en los "Desengaños amorosos" de María de Zayas', in *Escenas de transgresión: María de Zayas en su contexto literario-cultural*, ed. by Irene Albers and Uta Felten (Madrid: Iberoamericana, 2009), pp. 159–76
KAGAN, RICHARD, 'Lucrecia de León, la profetisa', in *La mujer barroca*, ed. by Giulia Calvi (Madrid: Alianza, 1992), pp. 29–50
—— *Lucrecia's Dreams: Politics and Prophecy in Sixteenth-Century Spain* (Berkeley: University of California Press, 1992)
KAHILUOTO RUDAT, EVA, 'Ilusión y desengaño: el feminismo barroco de María de Zayas y Sotomayor', *Letras femeninas*, 1.1 (1975), 27–43
KALLENDORF, HILAIRE, 'The Diabolical Adventures of Don Quixote, or Self-Exorcism of the Novel', *Renaissance Quarterly*, 55.1 (Spring 2002), 192–223
KAMEN, HENRY, 'The Decline of Spain: A Historical Myth?', *Past and Present*, 81 (1978), 24–50
—— *Early Modern European Society* (London: Routledge, 2000)
—— *The Spanish Inquisition: An Historical Revision* (London: Phoenix, 1997)
—— 'Tolerance and Dissent in Sixteenth-Century Spain: The Alternative Tradition', *The Sixteenth Century Journal*, 19 (1988), 3–23
KAMINSKY, AMY, 'Dress and Redress: Clothing in the "Desengaños amorosos" of María de Zayas y Sotomayor', *Romantic Review*, 79.2 (1988), 377–91
—— 'María de Zayas and the Invention of a Women's Writing Community', *Revista de Estudios Hispánicos*, 35 (2001), 487–509
KARTCHNER, ERIC, 'Fictional Realities of "El prevenido, engañado"', in *Zayas and Her Sisters, II: Essays on Novelas by 17th-Century Spanish Women*, ed. by Gwyn Campbell and Judith Whitenack (New York: Global Publications Binghamton University, 2001), pp. 21–32
KEITT, ANDREW, *Inventing the Sacred: Imposture, Inquisition, and the Boundaries of the Supernatural in Golden Age Spain* (Leiden: Brill, 2005)
—— 'The Miraculous Body of Evidence: Visionary Experience, Medical Discourse, and the Inquisition in Seventeenth-Century Spain', *The Sixteenth Century Journal*, 36.1 (2005), 77–96
KELLY, JOAN, 'Early Feminist Theory and the "Querelle des femmes", 1400–1789', *Signs*, 8.1 (1982), 4–28
KIECKHEFER, RICHARD, *Magic in the Middle Ages* (Cambridge: Cambridge University Press, 1989)
KING, MARGARET, *Women of the Renaissance* (Chicago, IL: University of Chicago Press, 1991)
KOHN, MARY ELLEN, *Violence against Women in the Novels of María de Zayas y Sotomayor* (Ann Arbor, MI: UMI Dissertation Services, 1994)
KORS, ALAN CHARLES, and EDWARD PETERS (eds), *Witchcraft in Europe, 400–1700: A Documentary History* (Philadelphia: University of Pennsylvania Press, 2001)
KRABBENHOFT, KENNETH, *Neoestoicismo y género popular* (Salamanca: Universidad de Salamanca, 2001)

KRAMER, HEINRICH, *The Hammer of Witches: A Complete Translation of the 'Malleus Maleficarum'*, trans. by Christopher S. Mackay (Cambridge: Cambridge University Press, 2006)

—— *The Malleus Maleficarum*, trans. by Montague Summers (New York: Dover Publications, 1928) <http://www.malleusmaleficarum.org/downloads/MalleusAcrobat.pdf> [accessed 7 February 2017]

KUHN, THOMAS, *The Structure of Scientific Revolutions* (Chicago, IL: University of Chicago Press, 1962)

LAGRECA, NANCY, 'Evil Women and Feminist Sentiment: Baroque Contradictions in María de Zayas's "El prevenido engañado" and "Estragos que causa el vicio"', *Revista Canadiense de Estudios Hispánicos*, 28.3 (Spring 2004), 565–82

LANGLE DE PAZ, TERESA, 'Beyond the Canon: New Documents on the Feminist Debate in Early Modern Spain', *Hispanic Review*, 70.3 (2002), 393–420

—— 'En busca del paraíso ausente: "Mujer varonil" y "Autor feminil" en una utopía feminista inédita del siglo XVII español', *Hispania*, 86 (2003), 463–73

LAQUEUR, THOMAS, *Making Sex: Body and Gender from the Greeks to Freud* (Cambridge, MA: Harvard University Press, 1990)

LARA MARTÍNEZ, MARÍA, *Brujas, magos e incrédulos en la España del siglo de oro: microhistoria cultural de ciudades encantadas* (Cuenca: Alderabán, 2013)

LARNER, CHRISTINA, 'Was Witch-Hunting Woman-Hunting?', in *The Witchcraft Reader*, ed. by Darren Oldridge, 2nd edn (London: Routledge, 2008), pp. 253–56; first pub. in *Witchcraft and Religion: The Politics of Popular Belief* (Oxford: Blackwell, 1984), pp. 79–91

LARSON, CATHERINE, 'Gender, Reading, and Intertextuality: Don Juan's Legacy in María de Zayas's "La traición en la amistad"', *INTI: Revista de Literatura Hispánica*, 40–41 (1994), 129–38

LASPÉRAS, JEAN-MICHEL, 'Personnage et récit dans les "Novelas amorosas y ejemplares" de María de Zayas y Sotomayor', *Mélanges de la Casa de Velázquez*, 15 (1979), 365–84

LAUTMAN, FRANÇOISE, and SIMONE LOSSIGNOL, 'Entre la sainteté et la légende. Entre l'art urbain et l'imagerie populaire: Geneviève de Brabant', *Ethnologie française*, 11.3 (1981), 247–50

LEA, HENRY CHARLES, *The Inquisition in the Spanish Dependencies* (London: Macmillan, 1908) <https://archive.org/details/inquisitioninspaooleahrich> [accessed 30 August 2016]

LEBÈGUE, RAYMOND, 'Les Sources de l'*Heptaméron* et la pensée de Marguerite de Navarre', *Comptes rendus des séances de l'Académie des Inscriptions et Belles-Lettres*, 100 (1956), 466–73 <http://www.persee.fr/doc/crai_0065-0536_1956_num_100_4_10671> [accessed 26 February 2017]

LENA, SYLVANIA, 'Doña María de Zayas y Sotomayor: A Contribution to the Study of her Works', *Romantic Review*, 14 (1922), 199–232

LEONI, MONICA, 'María de Zayas's "La traición en la amistad": Female Friendship Politicized?', *South Atlantic Review*, 68.4 (2003), 62–84

LERNER, GERDA, *The Creation of Feminist Consciousness from the Middle Ages to Eighteen-seventy* (Oxford: Oxford University Press, 1993)

LEVACK, BRIAN, 'The Decline of Witchcraft Prosecutions', in *The Witchcraft Reader*, ed. by Darren Oldridge, 2nd edn (London: Routledge, 2008), pp. 341–48; first pub. in *The Athlone History of Witchcraft and Magic in Europe*, 5 (The Athlone Press, 1999)

—— *The Witchcraft Sourcebook* (London: Routledge, 2004)

LEWIS, MATTHEW, *The Monk* (London: Penguin, 1998)

LEWIS-SMITH, PAUL, *Calderón de la Barca: La vida es sueño* (London: Grant & Cutler, 1998)

LOPE DE VEGA, FÉLIX, *El caballero de Olmedo*, ed. by Francisco Rico (Madrid: Cátedra, 2008)

—— *Los comendadores de Córdoba* (Madrid: Alonso Martín, 1610) <http://www.cervantesvirtual.com/obra-visor/los-comendadores-de-cordoba--0/html/ff88edce-82b1-11df-acc7-002185ce6064_1.htm> [accessed 23 February 2017]

—— *Lo fingido verdadero*, in *Comedias*, 1 (Barcelona: Iberia, 1967)
—— *El laurel de Apolo* (London: Leclere y Compañía, 1824) <https://babel.hathitrust.org/cgi/pt?id=hvd.32044025050386;view=1up;seq=9> [accessed 30 August 2016]
—— *Novelas a Marcia Leonarda* (Madrid: Alianza, 1968)
—— *La prueba de los ingenios*, in *Obras de Lope de Vega, 30. Comedias Novelescas*, ed. by Marcelino Menéndez-Pelayo (Madrid: Atlas, 1971)
—— *San Nicolás de Tolentino*, in *Obras de Lope de Vega 10. Comedias de Vidas de Santos*, ed. by Marcelino Menéndez-Pelayo (Madrid: Atlas, 1965)
—— *La vengadora de las mujeres* (Charleston, SC: BiblioBazaar, 2010)
LOPE DE RUEDA, *Eufemia — Armelina — El deleitoso* (Madrid: Espasa-Calpe, 1963)
LÓPEZ-DÍAZ, MARÍA DOLORES, 'Un novelista poco conocido: José Camerino y sus "Novelas amorosas"', *Revista de filología*, 8 (1992), 291–98
LURKER, MANFRED, *The Routledge Dictionary of Gods and Goddesses, Devils and Demons* (London: Routledge, 2004)
MAALOUF, AMIN, *On Identity* (London: Harvill Press, 2000)
MABILLARD, AMANDA, 'Sources for Romeo and Juliet', *Shakespeare Online* (21 Nov 2009) <http://www.shakespeare-online.com/sources/romeosources.html> [accessed 29 March 2017]
MACFARLANE, ALAN, *Witchcraft in Tudor and Stuart England* (London: Routledge, 1970)
MAESTRO, JESÚS, 'Metafísica de la literatura. La magia o el poder sobrenatural de la palabra: Rojas, Cervantes, Calderón', in *Der Prozess der Imagination, Magie und Emipirie in der spanischen Literatur der frühen Neuzeit*, ed. by Gerhard Penzkofer and Wolfgang Matzat (Tübingen: Niemeyer, 2005)
MAILLARD, MARÍA LUISA, *Vida de María de Zayas* (Madrid: Eila, 2015)
MALDONADO, FELIPE, 'Otra María de Zayas... y van cuatro', *Estafeta literaria*, 501 (Oct 1972), 10–13
MALINOWSKI, BRONISLAW, *Magic, Science and Religion and Other Essays* (London: Souvenir Press, 1948)
MARAVALL, JOSÉ ANTONIO, *La cultura del Barroco* (Barcelona: Ariel, 1975)
MARISCAL, GEORGE, *Contradictory Subjects: Quevedo, Cervantes and Seventeenth-Century Spanish Culture* (Ithaca, NY: Cornell University Press, 1991)
MAROTO CAMINO, MERCEDES, 'María de Zayas and Ana Caro: The Space of Woman's Solidarity in the Spanish Golden Age', *Hispanic Review*, 67 (1999), 1–16
—— 'Negotiating Woman: Ana Caro's *El Conde Partinuplés* and Pedro Calderón de la Barca's *La vida es sueño*', *Tulsa Studies in Women's Literature*, 26.2 (Fall 2007), 199–216
—— 'Spindles for Swords: The Re/Dis-Covery of María de Zayas' Presence', *Hispanic Review*, 62.4 (Autumn 1994), 519–36
MARTÍN SOTO, RAFAEL, *Magia e Inquisición en el antiguo reino de Granada* (Málaga: Arguval, 2000)
MASUCCIO SALERNITANO, *Il Novellino*, ed. by Alfredo Mauro (Bari: Laterza, 1940) <http://www.letteraturaitaliana.net/pdf/Volume_3/t56.pdf> [accessed 14 December 2018]
—— *The Novellino*, trans. by W. G. Waters (London: Lawrence and Bullen, 1895) <https://archive.org/details/novellinoofmasuco1masu/page/n5> [accessed 14 December 2018]
MATOS-NIN, INGRID, 'Lo medieval en una novela renacentista de María de Zayas', *Grafemas: Boletín electrónico de la AILCFH* (2007) <http://people.wku.edu/inma.pertusa/encuentros/grafemas/diciembre_07/matos_nin.html> [accessed 11 February 2017]
—— 'El concepto del demonio en dos novelas de María de Zayas y Sotomayor', *Tropos*, 29 (Spring 2003), 6–18
—— 'La importancia de la verosimilitud en "El desengaño amando y premio de la virtud" de María de Zayas y Sotomayor', *Confluencia*, 22.1 (Fall 2006), 58–66

—— *Las novelas de María de Zayas, 1590–1650: lo sobrenatural y lo oculto en la literatura femenina española del siglo XVII* (Lewiston, NY: Edwin Mellen, 2010)
—— 'Lisis o la remisión de la enfermedad del amor en las novelas de María de Zayas y Sotomayor', *Letras femeninas*, 32.2 (2006), 100–16
—— 'Lisis: The Semantics of Love and Healing in María de Zayas and Sor Juana Inés de la Cruz', *Rondas literarias de Pittsburgh, 2009* (Pittsburgh, PA: Duquesne University, 2010), 173–80
MAURICI FRADES, MAGDALENA, 'Genoveva de Brabante: génesis del personaje y su lugar en la historia de la edición', *Bulletin Hispanique*, 110.2 (2008), 573–600
MAUSS, MARCEL, *A General Theory of Magic*, trans. by Robert Brain (London: Routledge, 1950)
McGRADY, DONALD, 'Were Sercambi's Novelle Known from the Middle Ages on? (Notes on Chaucer, Sacchetti, *Cent Nouvelles nouvelles*, Pauli, Timoneda, Zayas)', *Italica*, 57.1 (Spring 1980), 3–18
McKENDRICK, MELVEENA, 'The "mujer esquiva": A Measure of the Feminist Sympathies of the Seventeenth-Century Spanish Dramatists', *Hispanic Review*, 40.2 (Spring 1972), 162–97
—— *Theatre in Spain, 1490–1700* (Cambridge: Cambridge University Press, 1989)
—— *Woman and Society in the Spanish Drama of the Golden Age: A Study of the 'Mujer Varonil'* (Cambridge: Cambridge University Press, 1974)
—— 'Women Against Wedlock: The Reluctant Brides of Golden Age Drama', in *Women in Hispanic Literature: Icon and Fallen Idols*, ed. by Beth Miller (Berkeley: University of California Press, 1983), pp. 115–46
McNERNEY, KATHLEEN, 'Recovering Their Voices: Early Peninsular Women Writers', in *Multicultural Iberia: Language, Literature, and Music*, ed. by Dru Dougherty and Milton Azevedo (Berkeley: University of California Press, 1999), pp. 68–80
MEDINA, ALBERTO, 'María de Zayas o la imposibilidad del amor: causalidad y amor cortés en "Mal presagio casar lejos"', *Bulletin of Hispanic Studies*, 75.4 (1998), 411–24
MELLONI, ALESSANDRA, *Il sistema narrativo di María de Zayas* (Turin: Quaderni Ibero-Americani, 1976)
MENÉNDEZ PELAYO, MARCELINO, 'Artes mágicas, hechicerías y supersticiones en los siglos XVI y VII', in *Brujería y exorcismos en España: textos fundamentales*, ed. by Servando Gotor (Zaragoza: Lecturas Hispánicas, 2014), pp. 23–70
MENESES, LEONOR DE, 'El desdeñado más firme', in *Entre la rueca y la pluma: novela de mujeres en el Barroco*, ed. by Evangelina Rodríguez Cuadros and Marta Haro Cortés (Madrid: Biblioteca Nueva, 1999)
MERRIM, STEPHANIE, *Early Modern Women's Writing and Sor Inés de la Cruz* (Nashville, TN: Vanderbilt University Press, 1999)
MESSINGER CYPRES, SANDRA, 'Los géneros re/velados en "Los empeños de una casa" de Sor Juana Inés de la Cruz', *Hispamérica*, 22 (1993), 177–85
MIDELFORT, ERIK, 'Heartland of the Witchcraze', in *The Witchcraft Reader*, ed. by Darren Oldridge, 2nd edn (London: Routledge, 2008), pp. 99–106; first pub. in *History Today*, 31 (Feb 1981), pp. 27–31
MIHALY, DEANNA, 'Socially Constructed/Essentially Other: Servants and Slaves in María de Zayas' *Desengaños amorosos*', *Romance Languages Annual*, 10.2 (1999), 719–25
MILTON, JOHN, *Paradise Lost* (London: Penguin, 1996)
MOLL, JAIME, 'La primera edición de las "Novelas amorosas y exemplares" de María de Zayas y Sotomayor', *Dicenda*, 1 (1982), 177–79
MONTAIGNE, MICHEL DE, *Les Essais* (Paris: Livre de Poche, 2001)
MONTER, WILLIAM, 'Witchcraft, Confessionalism and Authority', in *The Witchcraft Reader*,

ed. by Darren Oldridge, 2nd edn (London: Routledge, 2008), pp. 198–204; first pub. in *The Athlone History of Witchcraft and Magic*, 4 (The Athlone Press, 2002), pp. 9–12, 22–25

Montesa Peydro, Salvador, 'Significado de la estructura barroca de la novelas de Doña María de Zayas y Sotomayor', *Analecta malacitana*, 3.2 (1980), 261–76

—— *Texto y contexto en la narrativa de María de Zayas* (Madrid: Dirección General de la Juventud y Promoción Sociocultural, 1979)

Morby, Edwin, 'The *Difunta pleiteada* Theme in María de Zayas', *Hispanic Review*, 16 (1948), 238–42

Muchembled, Robert, *A History of the Devil from the Middle Ages to the Present*, trans. by Jean Birell (Cambridge: Polity Press, 2003)

Nagasawa, Yujin, *Miracles: A Very Short Introduction* (Oxford: Oxford University Press, 2017)

Nalle, Sara T., 'Literacy and Culture in Early Modern Castile', *Past and Present*, 125 (1989), 65–96

Navarre, Marguerite de, *The Heptameron*, trans. by P. A. Chilton (London: Penguin, 2004)

Navarro Durán, Rosa, 'La "rara belleza" de las damas en las novelas de María de Zayas y Mariana de Carvajal', in *Belleza escrita en femenino*, ed. by Àngels Carabí and Marta Segarra (Barcelona: Universidad de Barcelona, 1998), pp. 79–86

Nelken, Margarita, 'La novela, el teatro y la licencia de la pluma', in *Las escritoras españolas* (Barcelona: Labor, 1930; repr. Madrid: horas y HORAS, 2011), pp. 151–65

Nieremberg, Juan Eusebio, *Oculta Filosofía de la Sympatia y Antipatia de las Cosas, Artificio de la Naturaleza, y Noticia Natural del Mundo* (Madrid: La Imprenta del Reyno, 1633; facsimile repr. Whitefish, MO: Kessinger, 2010)

O'Brien, Eavan, 'Female Friendship Extolled: Exploring the Enduring Appeal of María de Zayas's Novellas', *Romance Studies*, 26.1 (2008), 43–59

—— 'Games in "The Garden of Deceit": A Seventeenth-Century Novella by María de Zayas y Sotomayor', *The Modern Language Review*, 104.4 (2009), 955–65

—— 'Locating the Diary of Persecuted Innocence: María de Zayas's Adaptation of Hagiographic *Historias*', *Bulletin of Spanish Studies*, 87.3 (2010), 295–314

—— 'Personalizing the Political: The Habsburg Empire of María de Zayas's *Desengaños amorosos*', *Bulletin of Hispanic Studies*, 88.3 (2011), 289–305

—— 'Verbalizing the Visual: María de Zayas, Mariana de Carvajal, and the Frame-Narrative Device', *Journal of Early Modern Cultural Studies*, 12.3 (2012), 116–41

—— *Women in the Prose of María de Zayas* (Woodbridge: Tamesis, 2010)

Oldridge, Darren, *The Devil in Tudor and Stuart England* (Stroud: History Press, 2000)

—— *The Devil: A Very Short Introduction* (Oxford: Oxford University Press, 2012)

Oldridge, Darren (ed.), *The Witchcraft Reader*, 2nd edn (London: Routledge, 2008)

Oltra, José Miguel, 'Zelima o el arte narrativo de María de Zayas', in *Formas breves del relato (Coloquio Casa de Velázquez-Departamento de Literatura Española de la Universidad de Zaragoza. Madrid, 1985)* (Zaragoza: Secretariado de Publicaciones de la Universidad de Zaragoza, 1986), pp. 177–90

Ordóñez, Elizabeth, 'Woman and Her Text in the Works of María de Zayas and Ana Caro', *Revista de estudios hispánicos*, 19.1 (1985), 3–15

Ortiz, Alberto, *El aquelarre: mito, literatura y maravilla* (Sitges: Editores del Desastre, 2015)

Parker, Geoffrey, 'Some Recent Work on the Inquisition in Spain and Italy', *The Journal of Modern History*, 54.3 (September 1982), 519–32

Parker-Aronson, Stacey, 'Cognitive Dissonance in María de Zayas's "La esclava de su amante"', *Letras femeninas*, 29.2 (2003), 141–65

—— 'Monstrous Metamorphoses and Rape in María de Zayas', *Revista Canadiense de Estudios Hispánicos*, 29.3 (2005), 525–47

Paun de García, Susan, 'La burlada Aminta: From Object/Desire to Subject/Vengeance', in *Zayas and Her Sisters*, II: *Essays of Novelas by 17th-Century Spanish Women*, ed. by Gwyn Campbell and Judith Whitenack (New York: Global Publications Binghamton University, 2001), pp. 3–19
—— 'Magia y poder en María de Zayas', *Cuadernos de ALDEUU*, 8 (1992), 43–54
—— 'Zayas as Writer: Hell hath no fury', in *María de Zayas: The Dynamics of Discourse*, ed. by Amy Williamsen and Judith Whitenack (London: Associated University Presses, 1995), pp. 40–51
Peel, Ellen, 'Psychoanalysis and the Uncanny', *Comparative Literature Studies*, 17.4 (1980), 410–17
Pellicer, José de, *Avisos históricos* (Madrid: Taurus, 1965)
Peña, Manuel, 'Caro Baroja y la religiosidad de la España del Siglo de Oro', *Historia Social*, 55 (2006), 25–44
Pérez de Montalbán, Juan, *La mayor confusión* (Madrid: Juan Gonçalez, 1624) <http://www.cervantesvirtual.com/obra-visor/la-mayor-confusion--0/html/fee71404–82b1–11df-acc7–002185ce6064_2.html#I_0_> [accessed 23 February 2017]
—— *Para todos. Exemplos morales, humanos y divinos* (Madrid: La Imprenta del Reyno, 1632) <http://www.cervantesvirtual.com/obra-visor/para-todos-exemplos-morales-humanos-y-divinos--0/html/> [accessed 27 August 2016]
Pérez-Abadín Barro, Soledad, 'La "Arcadia" y otros modelos literarios del "Coloquio de los perros": apuntes sobre magia', *Nueva Revista de Filología Hispánica*, 54.1 (2006), 57–102
Pérez-Erdélyi, Mireya, *La pícara y la dama: la imagen de las mujeres en las novelas picaresco-cortesanas de María de Zayas y Sotomayor y Alonso de Castillo Solórzano* (Miami: Universal, 1979)
Perry, Mary Elizabeth, *Crime and Society in Early Modern Seville* (Hanover, NH: University Press of New England, 1980)
—— 'Crisis and Disorder in the World of María de Zayas y Sotomayor', in *María de Zayas: The Dynamics of Discourse*, ed. by Amy Williamsen and Judith Whitenack (London: Associated University Presses, 1995), pp. 23–39
—— *Gender and Disorder in Early Modern Seville* (Princeton, NJ: Princeton University Press, 1990)
Pfandl, Ludwig, *Historia de la literatura nacional española en la edad de oro*, trans. by Jorge Rubió Balaguer (Barcelona: Sucesores de Juan Gili, 1933)
Place, Edwin, *María de Zayas: An Outstanding Woman Short-Story Writer of Seventeenth-Century Spain*, University of Colorado Studies, 13 (Boulder: University of Colorado Press, 1923)
Polo García, Victorino, 'El romanticismo literario de Doña María de Zayas y Sotomayor', in *Murcia. Anales de la Universidad* (1967), pp. 557–66
Praag, J. A. van, 'Sobre las novelas de María de Zayas', *Clavileño*, 15 (1952), 42–43
Prieto, Char, 'María de Zayas o la forja de la novela de autora en los albores del nuevo milenio', *Memorias de la palabra: Actas del VI Congreso Iberoamericano* (Madrid: Iberoamericana, 2004), pp. 1477–83
Quevedo, Francisco de, *La vida del buscón*, ed. by Edmond Cros (Madrid: Ollero y Ramos, 2002)
Rabell, Carmen, 'Notes Toward a Forensic Reading of the Spanish Novellas of the Golden Age', *Revista Canadiense de Estudios Hispánicos*, 22.1 (1997), 65–86
Redondo Goicoechea, Alicia, 'La retórica del yo-mujer en tres escritoras españolas: Teresa de Cartagena, Teresa de Jesús y María de Zayas', *Compás de letras. Monografías de literatura española. En torno al yo*, 1 (1992), 49–63
Rhodes, Elizabeth, *Dressed to Kill: Death and Meaning in Zayas's 'Desengaños'* (Toronto: University of Toronto Press, 2011)

——'Gender and the Monstruous in *El burlador de Sevilla*', *MLN*, 117.2 (2002), 267–85
RIBADENEYRA, PEDRO DE, *Vidas de santos: antología del Flos sanctorum*, ed. by Javier Azpeitia (Madrid: Lengua de Trapo, 2000)
RIERA, CARME and LUISA COTONER, 'Los personajes femeninos de doña María de Zayas, una aproximación', *Literatura y vida cotidiana, Seminario de estudios de la mujer* (Zaragoza: Universidad Autónoma de Madrid (1987), 149–62
——'Zayas o la ficción al servicio de la educación femenina', in *Breve historia feminista de la literatura española*, IV (San Juan: Anthropos Editorial de la Universidad de Puerto Rico, 1997), pp. 281–303
RÍO, MARTÍN DEL, *Investigations into Magic*, trans. by P. G. Maxwell-Stuart (Manchester: Manchester University Press, 2000)
RIVERS, ELÍAS, 'María de Zayas como poeta de celos', in *La creatividad femenina en el mundo barroco hispánico: María de Zayas — Isabel Rebeca Correa — Sor Juana Inés de la Cruz*, ed. by Monika Bosse, Barbara Potthast and André Stoll, 2 vols (Kassel: Reichenberger, 1999), I, 323–33
ROBBINS, ROSSELL HOPE, *The Encyclopedia of Witchcraft and Demonology* (London: Hamlyn, 1959)
ROBERTS, ARTHUR J., 'The Sources of Romeo and Juliet', *Modern Language Notes*, 17.2 (1902), 41–44
ROCA FRANQUESA, JOSÉ MARÍA, 'Aventurarse perdiendo (Novela de Doña María de Zayas y Sotomayor)', in *Homenaje al Excmo. Sr. Dr. D. Emilio Alarcos García*, II (Valladolid: Sever-Cuesta, 1965), pp. 401–10
——'Ideología feminista en doña María de Zayas', *Revista de la Facultad de Filología*, 26 (1976), 293–311
RODRÍGUEZ CUADROS, EVANGELINA, and MARTA HARO CORTÉS (eds), *Entre la rueca y la pluma: novela de mujeres en el Barroco* (Madrid: Biblioteca Nueva, 1999)
RODRÍGUEZ GARRIDO, JOSÉ ANTONIO, 'El ingenio en la mujer: *La traición en la amistad* de María de Zayas entre Lope de Vega y Huarte de San Juan', *Bulletin of the Comediantes*, 49.2 (1997), 357–73
ROIG, JAUME, *Spill or the Book of Women* (n.d.) <http://www.spanport.ucla.edu/santiago/roigsant.html> [accessed 23 August 2016]
ROJAS, FERNANDO DE, *La Celestina*, ed. by Dorothy Severin (Madrid: Cátedra, 1987)
ROJAS ZORRILLA, FRANCISCO DE, *Los bandos de Verona* (n.d.) Kindle ebook
ROMERO DÍAZ, NIEVES, 'En los límites de la representación: la traición de María de Zayas', *Revista Canadiense de Estudios Hispánicos*, 26.3 (Spring 2002), 475–92
——'Ha nacido una estrella', *Laberinto*, 3 (2000–01)
——*Nueva nobleza, nueva novela: reescribiendo la cultura urbana del barroco* (Newark, DE: Juan de la Cuesta, 2002)
ROPER, LYNDAL, *Witch Craze: Terror and Fantasy in Baroque Germany* (New Haven, CT: Yale University Press, 2004)
ROSS, ERIC, 'Syphilis, Misogyny, and Witchcraft in 16th-Century Europe', *Current Anthropology*, 36.2 (April 1995), 333–37
ROUSSET, JEAN, *La Littérature de l'âge baroque en France: Circé et le paon* (Paris: Librairie José Conti, 1983)
ROYLE, NICHOLAS, *The Uncanny* (Manchester: Manchester University Press, 2003)
RUBIERA MATA, MARÍA JESÚS, 'La narrativa de origen árabe en la literatura de Siglo de Oro: el caso de María de Zayas', in *La creatividad femina en el mundo barroco hispánico: María de Zayas — Isabel Rebeca Correa — Sor Juan Inés de la Cruz*, ed. by Monika Bosse, Barbara Potthast and André Stoll, 2 vols (Kassel: Reichenberger, 1999), I, 335–49
RUGGIERO, GUIDO, *Binding Passions: Tales of Magic, Marriage, and Power at the End of the Renaissance* (Oxford: Oxford University Press, 1993)

RUSSELL, JEFFREY BURTON, *Satan: The Early Christian Tradition* (Ithaca, NY: Cornell University Press, 1981)
—— *Lucifer: The Devil in the Middle Ages* (Ithaca, NY: Cornell University Press, 1984)
—— *Mephistopheles: The Devil in the Modern World* (Ithaca, NY: Cornell University Press, 1986)
SALSTAD, LOUISE, 'The Influence of Sacred Oratory on Maria de Zayas: A Case in Point, "La fuerza del amor"', *MLN*, 113 (1998), 426–32
SAMSON, ALEX, 'Distinct Dramatists? Female Dramatists in Golden Age Spain', in *A Companion to Spanish Women's Studies*, ed. by Xon de Ros and Geraldine Hazbun (Woodbridge: Tamesis, 2011), pp. 157–72
SÁNCHEZ ORTEGA, MARÍA HELENA, 'Sorcery and Eroticism in Love Magic', in *Cultural Encounters: The Impact of the Inquisition in Spain and the New World*, ed. by Mary Elizabeth Perry and Anne Cruz (Berkeley: University of California Press, 1991)
SÁNCHEZ, ELIZABETH, 'Magic in *La Celestina*', *Hispanic Review*, 46.4 (Autumn 1978), 481–94
SANTOLARIA SOLANO, CRISTINA, 'Teatro y mujer en el Siglo de Oro: *La traición en la amistad* de Dª María de Zayas y Sotomayor', in *Actas. Asociación Internacional Siglo de Oro* (1996), pp. 1479–89
SARDUY, SEVERO, *Barroco* (Paris: Gallimard-Folio, 1975)
SCARRE, GEOFFREY, and JOHN CALLOW, *Witchcraft and Magic in Sixteenth- and Seventeenth-Century Europe* (Basingstoke: Palgrave, 1987)
SCHARDONG, ROSANGELA, '"El celoso extremeño": fuente para una novela feminista de Doña María de Zayas y Sotomayor', *Anales del 2. Congresso Brasileiro de Hispanistas* (São Paulo: Associação Brasileira de Hispanistas, 2002) <http://www.proceedings.scielo.br/scielo.php?script=sci_arttext&pid=MSC0000000012002000200038&lng=en&nrm=iso> [accessed 11 February 2017]
SCHOLZ WILLIAMS, GERHILD, 'Pierre de Lancre and the Basque Witch-Hunt', in *The Witchcraft Reader*, ed. by Darren Oldridge, 2nd edn (London: Routledge, 2008), pp. 180–84; first pub. in *Defining Dominion: The Discourse of Magic and Witchcraft in Early Modern France* (Ann Arbor: University of Michigan Press, 1999), pp. 89, 90–93, 95–96, 119
SCHWARTZ, LÍA, 'Discursos dominantes y discursos dominados en textos satíricos de María de Zayas', in *La creatividad femenina en el mundo barroco hispánico: María de Zayas — Isabel Rebeca Correa — Sor Juana Inés de la Cruz*, ed. by Monika Bosse, Barbara Potthast and André Stoll, 2 vols (Kassel: Reichenberger, 1999), I, 301–21
SCOT, REGINALD, *The Discoverie of Witchcraft* (London: John Rodker, 1930; facsimile repr. New York: Dover, 1970)
SENABRE SEMPERE, RICARDO, 'La fuente de una novela de Doña María de Zayas', *Revista de filología española*, 46 (1963), 163–72
SERCAMBI, GIOVANNI, *Il Novelliere. Testo restaurato*, ed. by Edoardo Mori (Bolzano, 2017) <https://www.mori.bz.it/Rinascimento/Sercambi.pdf> [accessed 5 January 2019]
SERRANO PONCELA, SEGUNDO, 'Casamientos engañosos (Doña María de Zayas, Scarron y un proceso de creación literaria)', *Bulletin Hispanique*, 64 (1962), 248–59
SERRANO Y SANZ, MANUEL, *Apuntes para una biblioteca de escritoras españolas* (Madrid: Sucesores de Rivadeneyra, 1903) <https://archive.org/details/apuntesparaunabio1serruoft> [accessed 30 August 2016]
SHAHEEN, NASEEB, 'Shakespeare's Knowledge of Italian', *Shakespeare Survey*, 47 (1994), 161–69
SHAKESPEARE, WILLIAM, *Antony and Cleopatra*, in *Tragedies by William Shakespeare* (London: J. M. Dent & Sons, 1906; repr. 1950)
SHERIDAN, ALAN, *Michel Foucault: The Will to Truth* (London: Tavistock, 1980)
SIMERKA, BARBARA, 'Feminist Epistemology and Premodern Patriarchy, East and West: "The Kagero Diary" by Michitsuna's Mother and the Novellas of María de Zayas', *Letras Femeninas*, 35.1 (Summer 2009), 149–67

SIMPSON, JACQUELINE, 'Margaret Murray's Witch Cult', in *The Witchcraft Reader*, ed. by Darren Oldridge, 2nd edn (London: Routledge, 2008), pp. 93–98; first pub. in *Folklore*, 105 (London: Routledge, 1994), pp. 89–94, 96

SLUHOVSKY, MOSHE, 'The Devil in the Convent', *The American Historical Review*, 107.5 (2002), 1379–1411

SMITH, ANDREW, and DIANA WALLACE, 'The Female Gothic: Then and Now', *Gothic Studies*, 6.1 (2004), 1–7

SMITH, NIGEL, 'Gautier, Freud, and the Fantastic: Psychoanalysis *avant la lettre*?', in *Functions of the Fantastic: Selected Essays from the Thirteenth International Conference on the Fantastic in the Arts*, ed. by Joseph Sanders (Santa Barbara, CA: Greenwood Publishing Group, 1995), pp. 67–75

SMITH, PAUL JULIAN, *The Body Hispanic: Gender and Sexuality in Spanish and Spanish American Literature* (Oxford: Clarendon Press, 1989)

—— *Writing in the Margin: Spanish Literature of the Golden Age* (Oxford: Clarendon Press, 1988)

—— 'Writing Women in Golden Age Spain: Saint Teresa and María de Zayas', *MLN*, 102.2 (1987), 220–40

SOLANA SEGURA, CARMEN, 'Las heroínas de las "Novelas amorosas y ejemplares" de María de Zayas frente al modelo femenino humanista', *Lemir*, 14 (2010), 27–33

SOONS, ALAN, *Alonso de Castillo Solórzano* (Boston: Twayne, 1978)

SOUFAS, TERESA, *Dramas of Distinction: A Study of Plays by Golden Age Women* (Lexington: University Press of Kentucky, 1997)

—— 'María de Zayas's (Un)Conventional Play "La traición en la amistad"', in *The Golden Age Comedia: Text, Theory, and Performance*, ed. by Charles Ganelin and Howard Mancing (West Lafayette: Purdue University Press, 1994), 148–64

—— *Women's Acts: Plays by Women Dramatists of Spain's Golden Age* (Lexington: The University Press of Kentucky, 1997)

STACKHOUSE, KENNETH, 'Verisimilitude, Magic, and the Supernatural in the *Novelas* of María de Zayas y Sotomayor', *Hispanófila*, 62 (1978), 65–76

STALLYBRASS, PETER, 'Patriarchal Territories: The Body Enclosed', in *Rewriting the Renaissance: The Discourses of Sexual Difference in Early Modern Europe*, ed. by Margaret W. Ferguson, Maureen Quilligan and Nancy J. Vickers (Chicago, IL: University of Chicago Press, 1986), pp. 123–42

STEADMAN, JOHN, 'Milton and Wolleb Again (Paradise Lost, I, 54–56, 777)', *The Harvard Theological Review*, 53.2 (April 1960), 155–56

STOLL, ANITA, and DAWN SMITH (eds), *Gender, Identity, and Representation in Spain's Golden Age* (London: Associated University Presses, 2000)

STROUD, MATTHEW, 'Artistry and Irony in María de Zayas's "La inocencia castigada"', in *Zayas and Her Sisters, II: Essays on Novelas by 17th-Century Spanish Women*, ed. by Gwyn Campbell and Judith Whitenack (New York: Global Publications Binghamton University, 2001), pp. 79–95

—— 'The Demand for Love and the Mediation of Desire in "La traición en la amistad"', in *María de Zayas: The Dynamics of Discourse*, ed. by Amy Williamsen and Judith Whitenack (London: Associated University Presses, 1995), pp. 155–69

SULLIVAN, HENRY W., *Tirso de Molina & The Drama of the Counter Reformation* (Amsterdam: Rodopi, 1976)

SYLVANIA, LENA, *Doña María de Zayas Sotomayor: A Contribution to the Study of Her Works* (New York: Columbia University Press, 1922)

TAMBIAH, STANLEY J., *Magic, Science, Religion, and the Scope of Rationality* (Cambridge: Cambridge University Press, 1990)

TAPIÉ, VICTOR-LUCIEN, *Le Baroque. Que sais-je?* (Paris: Presses universitaires de France, 1961)
TATAR, MARIA, 'The Houses of Fiction: Towards a Definition of the Uncanny', *Comparative Literature Studies*, 33.2 (Spring 1981), 167–82
TAUSIET, MARÍA, 'Healing Virtue: *Saludadores* versus Witches in Early Modern Spain', *Medical History Supplement*, 29 (2009), 40–63
—— *Ponzoña en los ojos: brujería y superstición en Aragón en el siglo XVI* (Madrid: Turner, 2000)
—— *Urban Magic in Early Modern Spain: Abracadabra Omnipotens* (Basingstoke: Palgrave Macmillan, 2014)
TEDESCHI, JOHN, 'Inquisitorial Law and the Witch', in *Early Modern Witchcraft: Centres and Peripheries*, ed. by Bengt Ankarloo and Gustav Henningsen (Oxford: Clarendon Press, 1990), pp. 83–120
—— 'The Question of Magic and Witchcraft in Two Unpublished Inquisitorial Manuals of the Seventeenth Century', *Proceedings of the American Philosophical Society*, 131.1 (1987), 92–111
THOMAS, KEITH, *Religion and the Decline of Magic* (London: Penguin, 1971)
TICKNOR, GEORGE, *History of Spanish Literature*, III (Boston, MA: Houghton, Mifflin and Company, 1863; fourth enlarged edition) <https://archive.org/details/historyofspanish008446mbp> [accessed 7 January 2017]
TIMONEDA, JUAN DE, *El patrañuelo*, ed. by Rafael de Ferreres (Madrid: Castalia, 1971)
—— *El patrañuelo* (Biblioteca Virtual Universal) <http://www.biblioteca.org.ar/libros/131110.pdf> [accessed 5 January 2019]
TIRSO DE MOLINA, *El burlador de Sevilla o El convidado de piedra*, ed. by Alfredo Rodríguez López-Vázquez (Madrid: Cátedra, 1989)
—— *El condenado por desconfiado* (Barcelona: Linkgua, 2007)
TODOROV, TZVETAN, *The Fantastic: A Structural Approach to a Literary Genre* (Ithaca, NY: Cornell University Press, 1970)
TREVOR DAVIES, REGINALD, *Four Centuries of Witch Beliefs* (London: Methuen & Co., 1947)
—— *Spain in Decline, 1621–1700* (London: Macmillan, 1957)
—— *The Golden Century of Spain, 1501–1621* (London: Macmillan, 1964)
VAL, JOAQUIN DEL, 'La novela española en el siglo XVII', in *Historia general de las literaturas hispánicas*, III (Barcelona: Barna, 1953), pp. xlv–lxxx
VALBUENA PRAT, ÁNGEL, 'La cuentista Doña María de Zayas y el "Castigo de la miseria"', in *La novela picaresca española*, II (Madrid: Aguilar, 1978)
—— 'La evolución de la picaresca y otras formas de novela: los atisbos psicológicos de doña María de Zayas', in *Historia de la literatura española*, III (Barcelona: Gustavo Gili, 1981), pp. 173–206
VALBUENA, OLGA LUCÍA, 'Sorceresses, Love Magic, and the Inquisition of Linguistic Sorcery in *Celestina*', *PMLA*, 109.2 (1994), 207–24
VALENCIA, PEDRO DE, *Discurso acerca de los cuentos de las brujas*, Obras completas, 7 (León: Universidad de León, 1997)
VASILESKI, IRMA, *María de Zayas y Sotomayor: su época y su obra* (New York: Plaza Mayor, 1972)
VÉLEZ DE GUEVARA, LUIS, *El diablo cojuelo* (Barcelona: Crítica, 1999)
VILLALÓN, CRISTÓBAL, *El Crotalón* (Biblioteca Virtual Universal, 2003) <http://www.biblioteca.org.ar/libros/89158.pdf> [accessed 8 January 2017]
VITAR, BEATRIZ, 'El mundo mágico en el Madrid de los Austrias a través de las cartas, avisos y relaciones de sucesos', *Revista Dialectología Tradiciones Populares*, 56.1 (2001), 97–128

VITORIA, FRANCISCO DE, *Sobre la magia*, ed. by Luis Frayle Delgado (Salamanca: San Esteban, 2006)

VOLLENDORF, LISA, 'Fleshing out Feminism in Early Modern Spain: María de Zayas's Corporeal Politics', *Revista Canadiense de Estudios Hispánicos*, 22.1 (Fall 1997), 87–108

—— 'The Future of Early Modern Women's Studies: The Case of Same-Sex Friendship and Desire in Zayas and Carvajal', *Arizona Journal of Hispanic Cultural Studies*, 4 (2000), 265–84

—— 'Good Sex, Bad Sex: Women and Intimacy in Early Modern Spain', *Hispania*, 87.1 (2004), 1–12

—— 'Our Bodies, Our Selves: Vengeance in the Novellas of María de Zayas', *Cincinnati Romance Review*, 16 (1997), 93–100

—— 'Reading the Body Imperiled: Violence against Women in María de Zayas', *Hispania*, 78.2 (1995), 272–82

—— *Reclaiming the Body: María de Zayas's Early Modern Feminism*, North Carolina Studies in the Romance Languages and Literatures (Chapel Hill: University of North Carolina Press, 2001)

VOROS, SHARON, 'Fashioning Feminine Wit in María de Zayas, Ana Caro, and Leonor de la Cueva', in *Gender, Identity, and Representation in Spain's Golden Age*, ed. by Anita Stoll and Dawn Smith (London: Associated University Presses, 2000)

WALPOLE, HORACE, *The Castle of Otranto: A Gothic Story* (Oxford: Oxford University Press, 1996)

WALTERS, MARGARET, *Feminism: A Very Short Introduction* (Oxford: Oxford University Press, 2005)

WARNER, MARINA, *Alone of All Her Sex: The Myth and the Cult of the Virgin Mary* (New York: Vintage, 1976)

WELLEK, RENÉ, 'The Concept of Baroque in Literary Scholarship', *Journal of Aesthetics and Art Criticism*, 5.2 (1946), 77–109

WELLES, MARCIA, 'María de Zayas and her *novella cortesana*: A Re-Evaluation', *Bulletin of Hispanic Studies*, 55 (1978), 301–10

WELLES, MARCIA, and HELEN BROWN LEVINE, 'The Alchemy of Perversion in María de Zayas's "Tarde llega el desengaño"', in *Zayas and Her Sisters, II: Essays on Novelas by 17th-Century Spanish Women*, ed. by Gwyn Campbell and Judith Whitenack (New York: Global Publications Binghamton University, 2001), pp. 63–78

WHINNOM, KEITH, 'The Problem of the "Best-seller" in Spanish Golden Age Literature', *Bulletin of Hispanic Studies*, 57.3 (1980), 189–98

WHITENACK, JUDITH, '"Lo que ha menester": Erotic Enchantment in "La inocencia castigada"', in *María de Zayas: The Dynamics of Discourse*, ed. by Amy Williamsen and Judith Whitenack (London: Associated University Presses, 1995), pp. 170–91

WILLIAMS, CHARLES, *Witchcraft* (New York: Meridian, 1959)

WILLIAMSEN, AMY, 'Challenging the Code: Honour in María de Zayas', in *María de Zayas: The Dynamics of Discourse*, ed. by Amy Williamsen and Judith Whitenack (London: Associated University Presses, 1995), pp. 133–51

—— 'Engendering Early Modern Discourse: Subjectivity and Syntactic Empathy in "Al fin se paga todo"', in *Zayas and Her Sisters, II: Essays on Novelas by 17th-Century Spanish Women*, ed. by Gwyn Campbell and Judith Whitenack (New York: Global Publications Binghamton University, 2001), pp. 33–43

WILLIAMSEN, AMY, and JUDITH WHITENACK (eds), *María de Zayas: The Dynamics of Discourse* (London: Associated University Presses, 1995)

WILLIS, ANGELA, 'Fleeing the Model Home: María de Zayas Rewrites the Rules of Feminine Sensuality and "Honra" in the Boccaccesca "Novela Cortesana"', *Letras Femeninas*, 35.2 (Winter 2009), 65–89

Wilson, Katharina, and Frank Warnke (eds), *Women Writers of the Seventeenth Century* (Athens: University of Georgia Press, 1989)

Ximénez de Sandoval, Felipe, 'Doña María de Zayas y Sotomayor, una escritora fantasma', *Varia historia de ilustres mujeres*, ed. by Felipe Ximénez de Sandoval (Madrid: Epesa, 1949), pp. 207–15

Yates, Frances, *The Occult Philosophy in the Elizabethan Age* (London: Routledge, 1979)

Yllera, Alicia, 'Las dos versiones del "Castigo de la miseria" de María de Zayas', in *Actas del XIII Congreso de la Asociación Internacional de Hispanistas*, ed. by Francisco Sevilla and Carlos Alvar (Madrid: Castalia, 1998), pp. 827–36

—— 'Las novelas de María de Zayas: ¿una novela de ruptura? Su concepción de la escritura novelesca', in *La creatividad femenina en el mundo barroco hispánico: María de Zayas — Isabel Rebeca Correa — Sor Juana Inés de la Cruz*, ed. by Monika Bosse, Barbara Potthast and André Stoll, 2 vols (Kassel: Reichenberger, 1999), I, 221–38

Zamora Calvo, María Jesús, *Ensueños de razón: el cuento inserto en tratados de magia (siglos XVI y XVII)* (Madrid: Iberoamericana, 2005)

Zayas y Sotomayor, María de, *A shameful revenge and other stories*, trans. by John Sturrock (London: The Folio Society, 1963)

——*Desengaños amorosos*, ed. by Alicia Yllera (Madrid: Cátedra, 1983)

——*The Disenchantments of Love*, trans. by Patsy Boyer (Albany: State University of New York Press, 1997)

——*The Enchantments of Love*, trans. by Patsy Boyer (Berkeley: University of California Press, 1990)

——*Erotische Novellen: exemplarische Liebesnovellen* (Frankfurt: Insel Verlag, 1991)

——*Exemplary Tales of Love and Tales of Disillusion*, trans. by Elizabeth Rhodes and Margaret Greer (Chicago, IL: University of Chicago Press, 2009)

——*Honesto y entretenido sarao (primera y segunda parte)*, ed. by Julián Olivares, 2 vols (Zaragoza: Universidad de Zaragoza, 2017)

——*Nouvelles amoureuses et exemplaires* (Belval: Circé, 2013)

——*Novelas (La burlada Aminta y venganza del honor; El prevenido engañado)*, ed. by José Hesse (Madrid: Taurus, 1965)

——*Novelas amorosas y ejemplares*, ed. by Agustín Amezúa (Madrid: Aldus, 1948)

——*Novelas amorosas y ejemplares*, ed. by Julián Olivares (Madrid: Cátedra, 2000)

——*Novelas completas*, ed. by María Martínez del Portal (Barcelona: Bruguera, 1973)

——*Novelas de Doña María de Zayas y Sotomayor*, Biblioteca Universal Económica, 2 (Madrid: G. Juste, 1877)

——*Novelas ejemplares y amorosas o Decameron español*, ed. by Eduardo Rincón (Madrid: Alianza, 1968)

——*Novelle amorose ed esemplari* (Turin: Einaudi, 1995)

——*La traición en la amistad*, ed. by Michael McGrath (Newark, DE: European Masterpieces, 2007)

INDEX

Adorno, Theodor 34, 83, 137
Alarcón, Juan Ruiz de 49, 60
Albers, Irene 3, 31
Alemán, Mateo 5, 27, 28
Alfonso X 'el Sabio' (*Cantigas*) 101, 109 n. 20
'Amar sólo por vencer' 19, 94, 116
Amezúa, Agustín de 1, 13, 17, 21, 23, 24, 28, 29, 31, 134
aquelarre, see also witches' sabbath 62
Aquinas, St Thomas 43, 92
astrology 7, 34, 48, 60, 144–45
 Zayas and astrology 134–37
'Aventurarse perdiendo' 127, 131, 132
Avisos (Barrionuevo, Pellicer) 6, 112, 113, 149

Bandello, Matteo 15, 87, 139 n. 9, 142, 146, 149–51
 possible source of 'La burlada Aminta' 118, 152 n. 5
 possible source of 'El imposible vencido' 16, 117
 possible source of 'Tarde llega el desengaño' 16, 93
Barbeito Carneiro, Isabel 15, 17, 22, 100
Barcelona 21, 24–25, 71, 97, 98, 128
Barrionuevo, *see Avisos*
baroque 43, 44, 60, 81, 93, 106, 141, 151
baroque, the 60, 151
Basque country (region) 48, 51, 53, 54, 55
beatos and *beatas* 3, 111
bewitched 33, 48, 52, 56, 79
Boccaccio, Giovanni 15, 87, 109 n. 7, 110 n. 22, 142, 146, 149
 possible source of 'El imposible vencido' 16
 possible source of 'El jardín engañoso' 104, 105, 118, 151
 possible source of 'El juez de su causa' 150
Boyer, Patsy 7, 9 n. 2, 32, 39 n. 64, 82, 104
Brown, Kenneth 24, 25
Brownlee, Marina 3, 4, 19, 21, 27, 30, 31, 34, 35, 79, 84, 87, 89, 106, 122, 138 n. 5, 148, 149
bruja, see also witch 5, 48, 51, 65, 76
 'bruja' versus 'hechicera' 52–55
'La burlada Aminta y venganza de honor' 15, 19, 118, 133, 150

Calderón de la Barca, Pedro 3, 6, 49, 60, 65, 87, 101, 123, 135, 140 n. 24
 El médico de su honra 91 n. 19, 120, 131, 140 n. 24
Camus, Jean-Pierre (*histoires tragiques*) 143, 146, 148
Cardaillac Hermosilla, Yvette 4, 33

Caro Mallén de Soto, Ana 16–19, 49
Carvajal y Saavedra, Mariana de 28, 142, 146
Castañega, Martín de 6, 43, 48, 51, 54, 57, 59, 63
'El castigo de la miseria' 15, 17, 28, 47, 71–73, 87, 88, 97–99, 119
 Masuccio as possible source 15, 71
Castillo Solórzano, Alonso de 17, 18, 28, 37 n. 21, 49, 69 n. 49, 93, 119, 142, 146
Cervantes Saavedra, Miguel de 2, 5, 6, 11, 13, 24, 27, 28, 34, 60, 71, 86, 87, 119, 134, 142
 'El coloquio de los perros' 5, 51–54, 64
 on enchantment and free will 134, 140 n. 26
 influence of 'El casamiento engañoso' on 'El castigo de la miseria' 72
 influence of 'El curioso impertinente' on 'El verdugo de su esposa' 120
Church, the 3, 4, 14, 26, 33, 54, 57, 58, 64, 73, 76, 85, 114, 116, 123, 127
 diabolical anti-church 48, 54, 57
Ciruelo, Pedro 6, 43, 48, 57, 63, 78
 on astrology 137
 on dreams 126–29
Clark, Stuart 54, 57, 64
convent, the 1, 5, 12, 16, 26, 57, 73, 75, 76, 78, 81, 84, 101, 102, 115, 120, 126, 128, 130
Covarrubias, Sebastián 6, 44, 63, 79, 95
Cruz, Sor Juana Inés de la 19, 20
culto, see also vulgo 35, 66, 87, 145, 146 n. 5
cunning-folk, *see* folk healers

'El desegaño amando y premio de la virtud' 12, 32, 35, 46, 77–81, 85–87, 98, 133
Devil, the (*demonio, diablo*) 3, 4, 6, 33, 42, 48, 50, 53, 61, 64, 66, 71, 73, 78, 82, 83, 85, 88, 92–108, 111–14, 124, 127, 129, 143–45, 150, 151
 devils 55, 62, 66
 as epitome of ugliness 93–94
 and free will 135, 140 n. 25
 as inspiration for evil 63, 94–98, 131
 pact or deal with 49, 51, 80, 90, 101, 102, 106, 124–25, 151
 as preternatural agent 42–45, 62
 purported magnanimity in 'El jardín engañoso' 35, 98, 99, 103–08, 125
disembodied voices 4–6, 42, 111, 114, 124–26, 138, 141, 145
duendes (hobgoblins, imps, sprites) 65, 78, 92

eerie 6, 49, 74, 114, 125, 131
  eerie miracle 119–23
enchanted 33, 124
  enchanted (spring) garden 103, 141
enchantment 4, 33, 81, 84, 87, 134
  and free will 83
episteme 3, 70, 137, 140 n. 21, 146
  Renaissance episteme, see also Neoplatonic world-view 58–61, 66, 111
epistemology (epistemic shift) 3–5, 34, 140 n. 21, 144
'La esclava de su amante' 19, 28, 95, 115
Esquer (Escuer) 13, 24, 38 n. 50
'Estragos que causa el vicio' 28, 95, 98, 105, 116, 125, 132
Ettinghausen, Henry 148, 149

fantastic, the 4–6, 35, 74, 108, 114, 138, 141, 145, 146
  in Zayas 123–32
fatalism (Zayas's fatalistic outlook) 4, 6, 47, 136, 145, 146
feminism (feminist consciousness) 2, 68 n. 31, 94
  Zayas as a feminist, see Zayas
'Al fin se paga todo' 28, 72, 140 n. 25
Foa, Sandra 72, 86, 97, 101, 118
folk healers (folk magic, cunning-folk) 3, 47, 48, 57, 66
Fontanella, Francesc 22, 24, 25
Foucault, Michel 3, 25, 58–60
Frazer, James George 45
free will 63
  and astrology 7, 35, 47, 111, 135–38
  De auxiliis controversy 134
  and enchantment 33, 83, 134
Freud, Sigmund 124, 126, 127, 129, 140 n. 21
'La fuerza del amor' 12, 13, 16, 73–77, 87, 94

Gamboa, Yolanda 13, 25, 30
ghost(s) 12, 34, 50, 65, 70, 78, 117, 119, 120, 142
  Octavio's ghost 77, 78, 88, 119
Góngora y Argote, Luis de 3, 13, 60
Gothic, the 6, 30, 32, 39 n. 69, 125, 126, 138
Goytisolo, Juan 1, 29, 30, 32, 126
Greer, Margaret 4, 7, 20, 27, 28, 30, 34, 75, 84, 98, 102, 104, 105, 119, 122, 129
Grieve, Patricia 31, 109 n. 20, 114, 116, 138 n. 5
Griswold, Susan 3, 12, 31

hagiography 5, 35, 114–23, 125, 132, 138 n. 5
hanged man, see also undead 41, 73, 74, 111, 119–26, 131, 141, 145
hechicera, see also sorceress 3, 5, 51–55, 57, 58, 65, 73, 76, 79, 80, 113
hechicería, see also sorcery 48, 52, 53, 82
Hernández Pecoraro, Rosilie 75, 138 n. 5
hex, see also bewitch and spell 41, 45, 80
Holy Office, see Inquisition
homosexuality (homoeroticism, sodomy) 98, 143, 145, 148
  Zayas's portrayal of homoerotic relationships 19–21

Huarte de San Juan, Juan 22, 112

'El imposible vencido' 15, 16, 78, 103, 114, 117–19, 123
  Bandello as possible source 118
incorrupt (pristine) cadavers (corpses) 34, 42, 111, 124, 129–32, 141, 145
'La inocencia castigada' 15, 24, 28, 33, 35, 47, 81–88, 96, 98, 105, 116, 132, 134
Inquisition, the 32, 64, 75, 76, 82, 113, 126, 127
  attitude towards magic and witchcraft 3, 5, 33, 42, 54, 55, 57, 58, 62, 66, 144
Italy, see Zayas in Italy

'El jardín engañoso' 35, 98, 99, 103–08, 118, 132, 151
  Boccaccio as probable source 15, 104, 105
'El juez de su causa' 37 n. 30, 151

Lagreca, Nancy 11, 31
Langle de Paz, Teresa 30, 100
Lemos, Conde de 13–18
lesbian relations, see Zayas's sexuality
Logroño 3, 48, 54, 56, 57, 63, 148
Lope de Rueda (Armelina) 49
Lope de Vega Carpio 16–20, 50, 52, 60, 95, 117, 146, 150
Lucrecia de León 127

maga, see also witch 52, 53
magician 47, 49, 59, 66, 71, 72, 78, 80, 81, 97–99, 100, 102, 104, 105, 141, 151
magus, see also magician 47, 59, 72, 97, 111
magic 3–6, 11, 31–35, 40–61, 64, 66, 70–87, 90, 100, 102, 108, 111, 119, 138, 144, 145
  amatory or love magic 5, 46, 49, 50, 53, 57, 58, 72, 73, 85
  black magic or goetia 47, 49, 50, 55, 64, 70, 73, 74, 80, 87, 90, 102
  in Golden Age literature 49–51
  and the Inquisition 55–58
  magical practices and attitudes to magic 45–49
  natural magic 47, 59
Malleus maleficarum 52
Maravall, José Antonio 3, 35
Martín Soto, Rafael 57, 86, 144
marvellous 4, 6, 31, 33, 41, 42, 66, 70, 111, 114, 124, 134, 146
  the fantastic-marvellous 124, 145
  marvellous order, see preternatural order
'Mal presagio casar lejos' 19, 21, 94, 98, 115, 116, 119, 131, 132, 136
'La más infame venganza' 14, 95, 115, 116, 120, 125, 126
Masuccio Salternitano 15, 16, 87, 142, 146, 149
  possible source of 'El castigo de la miseria' 71
  possible source of 'El prevenido engañado' 93
Matos-Nin, Ingrid 78, 79, 82, 101, 106
Merrim, Stephanie 27, 28, 30, 148, 149

miracle 3, 4, 6, 20, 42, 64, 66, 101, 108, 111–14, 117, 119–25, 135, 138 n. 1, 141, 144, 145, 148
'mira' versus 'miracula' 43, 44
miraculous 4–6, 34, 41, 43, 66, 101, 103, 108, 112, 114, 122, 123, 125, 131, 138, 145
miraculous, the 4–6, 35, 64, 112, 114, 119, 123, 124, 144–46
the fantastic-miraculous 124, 125, 131, 145
miraculous order, the 6, 43
Moll, Jaime 23
Montesa Peydro, Salvador 3, 25, 32, 86, 95, 134, 139 n. 21
mujer varonil 22, 23

Naples 13–17, 21, 22, 48, 73, 75, 76, 100, 118, 131, 143
Neapolitan dialect 14
Navarre, Marguerite de (*Heptámeron*) 15, 142, 146
purported source of 'Tarde llega el desengaño' 16, 150
purported source of 'El prevenido engañado' 16, 93
necromancer 32, 41, 47, 61, 66, 71, 78, 81, 82, 105, 124, 142
Neoplatonic world-view 47, 48, 58, 137, 145
Nieremberg, Juan Eusebio (*Oculta Filosofia*) 59
novella craze, the 141–43

O'Brien, Eavan 2, 25, 30, 84, 100, 104, 106, 114, 132, 138 n. 5
Olivares, Julián 13, 15, 24–26, 29, 30, 98

Paun de García, Susan 4, 30, 33, 106, 140 n. 21
Pellicer, *see Avisos*
Pérez de Montalbán, Juan 17–19, 23, 24, 28, 118, 126, 142, 146
perfidious sisterhood (women) 6, 84, 105, 120, 132, 133

'La perseguida triunfante' 15, 35, 80, 99–102, 105, 107, 108, 111, 114, 115, 123, 132
possible sources 101

Pfandl, Ludwig 1, 29
premonitory dreams 5, 70, 111, 114, 124, 126–29, 131, 138, 145
preternatural 4, 42, 43, 45, 50, 61, 62, 72, 80, 87, 112, 124, 145
preternatural, the 42, 44, 45, 49, 55, 61, 64, 66, 70, 87, 111–14, 144
preternatural (marvellous) order, the 4, 42
'El prevenido engañado' 28, 29, 30, 72, 93, 98
Masuccio as possible source 16, 93
'pulp fiction' 5, 27, 138, 145, 148, 151

Quevedo, Francisco de 2, 14, 27, 28, 67 n. 21

relaciones de sucesos 148–51
Rhodes, Elizabeth 7, 28, 31, 116, 122, 126, 132

Ribadeneyra (*Flos sanctorum*) 101, 114–16, 132, 138 n. 6
Río, Martín del 6, 44, 45, 47, 59, 61, 64, 66, 78, 80, 91 n. 10, 126
Rojas, Fernando de (*La Celestina*) 5, 50, 52, 55, 66
Romero Díaz, Nieves 31, 141, 146 n. 1
Rosset, François de (*histoires tragiques*) 143, 146, 148
Ruggiero, Guido 46, 64, 73, 85, 86, 144

Salamanca 13, 43, 58, 118, 128, 137
Salazar y Frías, Alonso 6, 48, 56–58, 60, 62, 67, 76, 112
saludadores (*santiguadores*) 3, 48, 57, 64
Sánchez Ortega, María Helena 46, 73, 85, 86, 144
Sappho 20
Scarron, Paul 28, 29, 72, 93, 98
sceptical (attitude, stance) 4, 6, 42, 58, 61, 66, 74, 113
scepticism with regards to magic and witchcraft 58, 66, 70
Sercambi, Giovanni 109 n. 6, 142, 146
Serrano y Sanz, Manuel 13, 21
Shakespeare, William 11, 60, 117, 139 n. 9, 146
Smith, Paul Julian 2, 30
sorceress, *see also hechicera* 3, 5, 41, 48, 50–53, 58, 61, 66, 73, 75, 79–81, 145
sorcery, *see also hechicería* 4, 6, 33, 35, 42, 49, 52, 55, 70, 73, 76, 82, 87, 111, 112, 114, 144
sortílega 58
spell 33, 35, 41, 45, 46, 49, 50, 53, 58, 64, 70, 71, 73, 74, 77–85, 87, 88, 90, 99, 102, 113, 116, 123, 124, 134
spellbound 79, 102, 123
Stackhouse, Kenneth 32
Sullivan, Henry 134, 135
supernatural, the 3–6, 31–35, 42–44, 58, 64, 65, 66, 70, 83, 86, 108, 111–14, 124, 126, 127, 129, 132, 134, 138, 141, 143–46, 148
sensu lato 42, 66, 70, 90, 108, 124, 138, 145
sensu stricto 42, 61, 66, 112, 113, 144

'Tarde llega el desengaño' 15–17, 93, 118, 132
Bandello as possible source 15, 16
thaumaturgical order, the 3, 41, 44
Ticknor, George 29, 30, 143
Timoneda, Juan de (*El patrañuelo*) 15
possible source of 'La perseguida triunfante' 101
Tirso de Molina 95, 107, 134, 135
Todorov, Tzvetan 123, 124, 129, 145
'La traición en la amistad' 19
'El traidor contra su sangre' 12, 17, 28, 95, 116, 129, 132, 136
Trent, the Council of 57, 85, 118, 119

uncanny 34, 74
uncanny, the 124, 145
undead, the 34, 120, 132, 141, 145

Valencia, Pedro de 6, 56, 61, 62, 66, 112

Vélez Guevara, Luis de (*El diablo cojuelo*) 51
'El verdugo de su esposa' 35, 114, 116, 119–23, 126, 132
Villalón, Cristóbal de (*El Crótalon*) 51, 52
Virgin Mary, the 33, 34, 64, 100, 102, 113, 120, 121, 123, 144
  of the Immaculate Conception 12, 117
  Marian cult 121
  miracles 4, 113, 117, 120, 141
  Mother of God 100, 111, 117, 120, 121, 130
Vitoria, Francisco de 43, 44, 48, 64, 78
Vollendorf, Lisa 20, 26, 30, 84, 116
vulgo, see also culto 35, 66, 87, 112, 145

Walpole, Horace 126, 143
Warner, Marina 116, 121
Welles, Marcia 31, 126
Whitenack, Judith 4, 30, 33, 83, 84, 134
Williamsen, Amy 106, 140 n. 24
witch 3, 5, 33, 41, 46, 48, 51–53, 55, 56, 58, 61–66, 76, 82, 85, 113, 133, 141, 144, 145

witchcraft 5, 32, 33, 42, 43, 48, 49, 51, 52, 54–58, 60–62, 64, 70, 76, 112, 142–44, 148
witches' sabbath (*aquelarre*) 51, 53, 55, 148
witch-hunt (witchcraft persecutions, 'witch-craze') 3, 32–34, 42, 54–56, 66, 137
  number of victims 68 n. 31
wonder (*mira*) 3, 42–44, 47, 114, 121

xorguiña (*jorguiña*), *see also* witch 53

Zayas y Sotomayor, María de:
  as a best-selling author 11, 27, 28
  as a (proto-) feminist 5, 27, 28, 29, 30–32, 104, 105, 118, 145
  in Italy 5, 13–15, 101
  knowledge of French 15, 16, 150
  sexuality 19–21